COCONUT PRINCE

Memoir of a  BLACK SHEEP

Antony Aris-Osula

RITE TONE

COCONUT PRINCE: MEMOIR OF A BLACK SHEEP

ISBN: 978-1-9993793-1-5 (paperback)

ISBN: 978-1-9993793-0-8 (eBook)

This book is a memoir. It reflects the author's present recollections of experiences over time. Some names and characteristics have been changed, some events have been compressed, and some dialogue has been recreated.

Front Cover image and book design by RiteArtz

First edition 2021

www.coconutprince.com

Dedicated To
Priscilla, Wynne and Albert

CONTENTS

FOREWORD

Angie Le Mar

Multi-award-winning comedienne, writer and director

There are some people you will bump into and know for sure, just by their spirit, that they will be in your life for ever. A quick hello at a radio station turned into 'we must meet again'. That's where the journey started with my dear friend Antony. If you ever have the pleasure of meeting him, you will be mesmerised by his life; it is a whole film.

I once read a book called Tuesdays with Morrie, about a man who met up with a dear old friend who was filled with wisdom and passed down his knowledge weekly. My experience with Antony was similar, but our regular meets were at the glamorous Costa Coffee shop in Catford, and each meeting ran for hours. If you saw two black people praying over coffee, it was us. He has a unique way of making you feel in the moment, and you care nothing about who is watching while he prays over you and speaks into your life. At the time, as a new born-again Christian, I had so many questions. Being able to sit and speak and really find answers about my journey meant I would walk away from our meetings feeling incredibly inspired.

We spoke in detail about this book, and I had the privilege of reading through pages of it and talking through Antony's life. I would enjoy listening to him share his stories – stories that left me feeling many emotions: laughter, then sadness, then joy again. It really was a roller coaster of emotions. It's about time someone shared in great detail about how a black child navigates life having been adopted by white parents and living near Eltham (a predominantly white area). It is so fascinating. I'm sure Antony felt I was being Oprah with all my questions...I guess I was preparing him for her.

His life story just blew me away and he's not even old. The story of his childhood really felt like a deep upheaval; that maybe he should have been left with some scarring issues in life, or at best an identity crisis. But no, his loving memory of this difficult time - a time many would fight against in today's society – is quite something. It's important to read how he has become an amazing person for it. A spiritual, gifted man, too.

During many of our Costa meets, I shared with Antony what God had given me to write. He sat there as I spoke through the story, then he would pray and prophesy over the project and show me what was on his heart. The fact that I accepted this shows that I had built up huge trust in Antony. After my stage production, Take Me Back, was a huge success, that I could look back on his prophecy and say, "You said that in Costa."

The reason I share that story? It's important to know just how far we have come as friends. I am so proud to write this foreword, because I waited patiently for you all to get an insight into what I have been hearing about for a few years; an insight into a life you will be inspired by. We are here for life and to encounter many people and different experiences. It's important that even in hard times we do not let life ruin us; we do not let life leave us warped and angry. Reading Antony's story will make you understand the phrase: "When life gives you lemons, make lemonade".

I am grateful for our friendship, and I pray that my friend – who is also a talented actor and presenter, and a preacher who takes you to a new place – will be able to show the world why we should keep on moving towards our light. I am praying for success for this book; that it will touch people the way Antony has touched and blessed my life.

Angie Le Mar
Managing Director, Straight To Audience Productions

PROLOGUE

The Void

'I want my mummy...I want my *mummy*!' I cried from the pit of my soul, from the very core of my being. Was I being over-dramatic? Well, although this was coming from a trained actor, it was the truth. Was I a scared little toddler lost in the shopping centre, throwing a tantrum? No, I was a thirty-year-old man, a husband and a father of two with responsibilities and generally good mental health. Why, then, was I kneeling on this hard wooden floor with tears streaming down my cheeks, feeling this overwhelming sense of vulnerability mixed with sorrow and pain?

I closed my eyes and tried to visualise a face looking back at me, but I drew a blank. I always drew a blank, no matter how hard I tried. If I just closed my eyes tighter, scrunched my face hard enough, maybe, just maybe, a picture would emerge. Maybe a face that looked vaguely familiar, with eyes that connected with mine, would make an undeniable primal connection with my soul. I could then gaze up at this face for hours, scrutinising and memorising every crease, every wrinkle, every detail, to satisfy a lifetime of curiosity and a void filled with rich with unanswered questions.

But that face never came. No memories flooded my mind, and the void didn't speak back to me; it remained dark and empty. My mind was used to drawing a blank when I tried to visualise this face shrouded in mystery. I never imagined a day when the shadows of my mind would retreat and give way to the form of a soft ebony face. My heart had been ready for such a day, for such an overwhelming experience for many years, but my head had long accepted in a fatalistic way that this might never happen. That it only happened in Hollywood and weepy made-for-TV movies. Not in real life certainly, not in *my* life. My adult mind couldn't help but wonder, though, if on the other side of the void a woman was on her knees, swaying from side to side and saying through tear-filled eyes, 'I want my son!' How could she possibly recognise my face? It had matured and evolved, shaped by a life she had never witnessed. I would be just as much a stranger to her as she would to me.

I resolved that if she couldn't come to me, then I would go to her. I would track her down wherever she might be. We would be reunited. Our much older faces and eyes would connect, and our dreams of each other would materialise in time and space. Daydreams and fantasies would transform into lived experiences and memories. I promised myself on that cold wooden floor, that I would do everything possible to put a face to that dark void. I would see those eyes at least one more time before I left this earth.

'God, if You can hear my prayer, grant the impossible.' If He could just nudge me in the right direction, connect me with the right people and condense time and space, I would be set. If I could have spoken into the void, I actually would have yelled. No anger or malice, but a fiercely urgent cry that demanded an answer. I tried yelling 'I want my mummy', but the darkness remained silent. If she was there in the deep, she gave no indication of it. How could she recognise the broken voice of a random man coming out of a foreign face, anyway? No, I would have to cry out her given name. Maybe then she would answer...

CHAPTER ONE

Alone

Death is sudden and unapologetic. It isn't shy and timid, or polite and considerate. It does what it wants and occupies its own space without regard for anyone or anything. You can't negotiate with death or plead your case. It separates loved ones and equalises rich and poor, weak and strong. It is the one true certainty of existence. I guess you're wondering whether you made the right choice picking up this book with all this talk of death compared with the happy front cover, right? Sorry, folks. I have to start with the heavy rain fall to get to the end of the rainbow.

My first date with death was on 18th March 1993, when my mother died. I was thirteen years old. It was as painful as you would expect, and her presence lingered everywhere in our house, intensifying the sense of absence and loss like surround sound. Returning to the house on the day of her funeral, I could smell her lavender-scented potpourri baskets everywhere as soon as I went into the bathroom. As the dam of my flood gates burst, I was overwhelmed with a feeling of emptiness. It's funny how even a previously annoying scent or piece of music can encapsulate a person when they're gone.

To say I missed her would be stating the obvious. The deeper pain I felt that day, and for years, to come was in witnessing my dad slowly breaking down as he grieved for his wife of more than forty years. It was beyond heart-wrenching to watch Dad, who had dedicated his life to his spouse and the whole family, struggle to come to terms with this massive hole in his heart. I had always been close to him, and to see him in such pain was difficult – more so as I knew there was nothing I or any of my five siblings could do to ease his pain and fill that void.

There were six of us children: my eldest sister Anne, my brothers Lindsay, Martin and Terry, my second sister Claire and me coming in last. There was a twelve-year gap between me and Claire, so in some ways I might as well have been an only child. After my mother's death, my father tried to live on through his grown-up children and five grandchildren, taking an even greater interest in their lives and directing all his energy in to making them happy. It was all a futile attempt to distract his grief-filled mind from the loss of the most important treasure in his life. I had loved Mum dearly, and I missed her immensely, but as time went on, I learned to deal with her death. I also had my brand-new Christian faith to give my life a sense of meaning and hope for the future. Dad, however, was at the other end of the spectrum. He was advanced in age, and his faith was agnostic at best. His life was increasingly behind him and he struggled to find any meaning or new sense of purpose.

My next taste of death was even more bitter than the first. My mother's death was sudden and caught us relatively by surprise. Though she had been ill for a few weeks, her illness should not have been terminal. It was her refusal to be hospitalised that contributed to the doctors being unable to save her poisoned kidneys in time. We had always thought Dad would die first, as morbid as that sounds. He was frail in body and plagued with ill health throughout his life, but on the flip side he was mentally very strong and resilient. Against the odds, he coped a lot better with being widowed than my mother would have. Being a very traditional couple, Mum relied on Dad for practical matters and would have admitted herself that he was the stronger of the pair. As devastated as he was, my father was a natural survivor, so he somehow lived with the pain in his soul in the same way he would the pain in his body.

Christmas 1999, the year I turned twenty, was the last one of the twentieth century, of the decade, and the last one where I would see my dad alive. Everyone was worrying about Y2K and the possible end of the world at the stroke of midnight, while something much more personal plagued my mind. It seems fitting that Dad's life would fade out like a broken Christmas tree light.

In my family, as with most, Christmas Day was a major event full of decorations, bags of presents, a large overdressed tree and my father staying up all night on Christmas Eve cooking two oversized turkeys for the next day. Long before the modern metrosexual or Jamie Oliver, my father was often the cook and cleaner, and didn't need any fanfare either. I never liked turkey that much, even though I traditionally ate two large turkey legs at the dinner table. It was an established fact in my home that I would eat anything that moved, and it became a competition between myself and my sister Anne's husband Dave how much we could eat. I always appreciated the great effort my dad made to get these supersize birds from the supermarket to our home without a car, dragging them and several shopping bags on to the bus, then preparing them with military precision.

Some of my earliest memories are of Dad and me going to East Street market, an outdoor market in London, to get some toys that would make up my Christmas gift quota. We would then race to Lewisham Shopping Centre, leaving with an abundance of shopping bags after only God knows how much cash had exchanged hands. I can still smell the crisp wad of notes unfolded by Dad. It was as if his coat pockets were a 'pocket dimension', where this endless surplus of cash came from. We weren't rich by any stretch, but Dad walked around with vast amounts of cash on him. For years I was the only child in the family before the grandchildren arrived, so I was the biggest recipient of all this festive effort for some time.

Our relationship as father and son was like any other healthy, normal one, except for outward appearance. We couldn't have looked more different if we had tried. As with my mother,I had long suspected that he wasn't my biological father, and I wouldn't have been alone in my suspicions, which grew from childhood. I was dark-skinned, he was pale; my hair was afro, his was lank straight. The constant stares were an early indication, especially as we walked through Lewisham Shopping Centre. In fact, any and everywhere we were seen together provoked the same reaction. This pretty much applied to myself and the rest of the family, but I spent the most time with Dad. When I raised the observation with my mum that she and I looked nothing alike, she simply smiled and changed the subject. The truth could be a dirty word in our household at times and such language was best avoided.

The inconvenient truth to be avoided that Christmas was the inevitability of enduring another major family loss. I believe my father always went to such great lengths to make Christmas magical because he was an only child from a struggling working-class household and wanted to give us what he had never really had. He wasn't overly religious, though he believed in 'the man upstairs'. The madness and stress of the season always triggered his delicate temper, making me wonder why he bothered so much each year. Step on a Christmas light and you wouldn't hear the end of it as you waited for the dust to settle. I was never scared, as Dad wouldn't hurt a fly, but my ears would ache! As a relatively large family it was always bustling at our house over the festive season, even after Mum's death – though it was never the same. That empty seat at the table would be impossible to ignore. As certain as there would be Christmas *Top of the Pops*, arguments over watching *EastEnders* and laughter watching *Only Fools and Horses*, there would be too much food, too much noise and people coming in and out of our house throughout the day.

Dad was diagnosed with cancer, or 'the big C' as he often called it, around the spring of 1999. The news hit him like a freight train and I could tell that he was terrified. This would be the fight of his life, and the question of whether he still had the fight left in him after his years of grief loomed large. We all, including Dad, knew that the real task was about making the cancer process as pain-free as possible rather than defeating it, though we would try our best all the same. He always quoted the Bible passage from Psalm 90 about living 'three score years and ten', and he just so happened to be seventy years old. Dad had always been a very slim man, with weathered, wrinkled skin and a wisp of straight grey hair that never left him during his unpleasant bouts of chemotherapy. We were all in a state of denial in spite of the fact that Dad was a minimum forty-a-day smoker. I'm actually amazed that he lived so long with the combination of his having just one healthy lung after losing the other to tuberculosis many years previously, his brutal work regime and of course the endless smoking. Early memories are tinged with the smell of Benson & Hedges. Like a sensory soundtrack of my early years, the smell still immediately reminds me of him.

Unlike when Mum died, I had time to deal with the inevitability of my father's passing. That also meant a long-drawn-out process that consisted of harrowing chemotherapy sessions, emotional pain and going through the motions of life, counting down the days till the inevitable occurred. Dad had always been there for and supported me, while encouraging me to accept myself. I struggled a lot with negative thinking, seeing the glass as half empty, which used to drive him crazy. He would always lovingly and patiently correct me. I understand clearly now that he was preparing me for a future without him; one that he wasn't going to see but knew he had to secure before the end came. Much of my future rested on the clarity of my worldview and how I would navigate the waters of being a black man with an unusual start in life, and holding to a belief system that was at odds with the mainstream world. With that slate, my mind couldn't afford to harbour a pessimistic outlook.

One year into my Theology degree at the London School of Theology, then known as London Bible College (LBC), I was contemplating the big questions of God and the universe while my dad's world was ending. It seems poignant that as I was growing in understanding of my heavenly Father I was gradually losing my human father, who was ebbing away like a candle wick. I never doubted God was real, even in the face of my pain but at times I was upset with Him and wondered why He kept taking away the people I loved and who loved me. I had long accepted that death was a natural part of life and had always had the fear of my elderly parents dying and leaving me alone. However, my fear had grown more sophisticated to a concern about whether or not my dad had made peace with his Maker yet; whether he was spiritually ready for the great crossing over. I would have to trust my heavenly Father to take care of the situation with my earthly father, who meant the world to me.

It was from this elderly, frail human father that I had learned how to be a man, how to treat people equally and how the world really worked. As a little boy my growing skills triggered a beaming smile across his face. I remember his amazed, proud face when I drew a cartoon figure on a scrap of paper within minutes and when he showed me how to make a trophy cup out of left-over cigarette foil or a human figure using dead matches as arms and legs on the plasticine body I had just made. I wondered what life would be like without him.

I was living on campus when Dad moved in with my big sister Claire and her boyfriend Joe, so I missed a lot of the worst parts of his deteriorating condition. It brought my sister to tears just watching him, and I didn't envy her that. She was in her early thirties and I don't know where she drew the strength from to take care of him on a daily basis.

That summer I experienced an empty home for the first time in my life. This was the only house I remembered living in. It hurt when they subsequently knocked down the entire council estate, including my old house that I grew up in, to make way for luxury houses and a brand-new landscape. My first home, 8 Ebdon Way, the terrace house next to the power station and across the road from the local train station, was gone for ever. It now exists only in memories and a few salvaged photographs.

It wasn't very comfortable staying at the house back in 1999, as the soul of the place was absent and campus increasingly felt more like home by then. I was grasping at anything that would give me solace and comfort through this emotional time, and this led me in a brief relationship with a close friend over the summer. Jane (not her real name) was a warm, easy going and fun-loving woman who happened to be almost a decade my senior. She was of a chocolate complexion like myself, and womanly, with the most winning smile ever, looked as young as me. I may have been mature for my age, but I was still only twenty and a bit superficial. We both attended church, and after clashing at first like faux enemies we became close friends as I confided in her about everything I was going through. The relationship shocked me just as much as it did her, even though I pushed for it. Initially it was purely platonic, with constant teasing and banter, almost like little brother/bigger sister... until it wasn't any more.

At the same time, I had hardly recovered from an unrequited love for another woman, Deirdre (also not her real name), for more than two years. She was the complete opposite: fair-complexioned, slender, very reserved and cerebral. A mere two years my senior, she acted as though I were her younger brother. That particular friendship ended the moment I revealed my inner feelings, and though I hoped things would change, she felt it was better to cut me out of her life for good, which broke my heart. Maybe it was the loss of my mother that caused me to constantly reach out for relationships with women, making me very intense at times. I scared women away with my earnest confessions of wanting a serious relationship at such a young age. My male peers were all about kicking it and having some fun, while I was picking out a wedding tuxedo and thinking about baby names.

It was at a wedding of mutual friends that I saw my unrequited love Deirdre again after many months. Her cold indifference towards me triggered my vulnerability and insecurities. I'm sure this was further enhanced by what was happening with my father and it wasn't the best time in my life. I had talked to Dad about her and how I felt a connection I couldn't describe. He would smile and tell me that the world wouldn't end if she refused to be my girlfriend, which I found impossible to believe at the time. I was deeply in love; it went way beyond physical attraction. This was a woman I respected, admired and was even inspired by. But to her I was simply invisible. I was wondering if anyone would love and accept me for who I was, intense and sensitive, or whether I was destined to be alone and misunderstood.

Of course, I did the most logical thing I could while feeling this way...I spoke with Jane. As always, she was happy to hear from me given that as our conversations were usually light-hearted and fun, though I wasn't in that kind of mood this time. She could tell that I was agitated and deflated. After the wedding that evening we spoke for hours on the phone about anything and everything. My heart was broken over Deirdre, but I wasn't about to tell Jane that. Was it because I was harbouring some latent feelings for her, too? Can you even have feelings for two people at the same time? Maybe it was the vulnerability taking over, but the conversation took an unexpected shift towards the romantic possibilities that we by conversation's end, began to 'consummate'. This was the only form of consummation in the relationship that ever took place, as we both believed in abstinence and were drawn to the tenderness in each other. She was a great friend and for a very brief time my first proper girlfriend.

Subconsciously, though, I could feel that I was latching on to a replacement. A person who could fill the soon-to-be void in my life. I hadn't realised that it was impossible to fill a void by replacing someone with someone else. The hole will always be there and is unfillable. You just have to keep going, and love and treasure those who still remain in your life and those who are yet to arrive. Jane was great, but we both started to doubt the long-term future of our 'undercover' relationship. Keeping it under wraps was necessary due to the fact that I was training to be a minister and was expected to be focused, and deep down I knew this relationship probably wasn't going to go the distance. It feels wrong to say it, but the relationship was fulfilling a temporary need in my life, so it wasn't fair to become more attached. After some soul-searching, we decided to end the relationship. I missed Jane but knew that it was for the best, as I was too needy at the time to be the man she deserved and I realised that I still had more growing up to do. We agreed to remain friends.

Ever on the move, I'd lined up another distraction to occupy my mind for later that year: my first trip to the motherland, Africa. I was travelling to Ghana to stay with a missionary couple I had become friends with years before in my church. I had finally accepted their invitation to go out and share my preaching/teaching ministry with them. Pastors Robert and Valerie Kwami were much older than me and were role models in many ways. They would accommodate me at their home, where they preached and served within our denomination, the Church of God International, across the region. Robert was an experienced church planter and a native Ghanaian. Valerie, whom I nicknamed 'Madam', imitating the members of the church and staff she led, was a British-born Jamaican. She had moved to Ghana as a missionary and to oversee the national Bible school. This was real girl power in action.

I was initially torn about travelling during Dad's illness and almost cancelled the trip, but he was adamant that I went and experienced these people's lives. He was already in hospital, about to undergo his initial treatment, during what the doctors called a 'honeymoon period'. This is where the patient feels better and more like his or her old self before the gruelling treatment begins. I had a golden hour with him and he backed me 100 per cent of the way, as he always did, and assured me that he wasn't going anywhere before I got back. I never would have forgiven myself if anything had happened to him in my absence. For a moment he was his old self, the way I always knew him, with a twinkle in his eye and an effortless dose of wisdom. I had no idea this would be the last time I ever saw my Dad as the man he was, so this exchange holds a special place in my heart. I'm glad I left with his blessing. After all, I was doing the Lord's work, which Dad respected even without being a fully signed-up member of the 'God Squad'. After making a pact with the Almighty, I trusted that He would look after my dad until I returned.

* * *

My first introduction to Africa was a fever-filled, ten-hour, delayed flight with the now defunct Ghana Airways. Arriving at Accra airport at one in the morning – a strange foreign environment that felt a million miles from home – was beyond overwhelming. It was very different from my first ever flight abroad a couple of years earlier, to Orlando, Florida. Disney World this wasn't! I practically stumbled off the plane like a zombie from *Shaun of the Dead*, my body wracked with pain, likely a reaction to the compulsory cocktail of yellow fever injections and malaria tablets I had taken a few days previously. I had never felt so rotten in my life, and was no longer in the mood for this adventure. At least I would see some familiar smiling faces any minute now, I thought, as I shuffled through the customs queue.

An abrupt immigration officer asked for my passport and began to scan through it, but then his eyes suddenly seemed to stop and widen. 'Where is your visa, please?'

I vaguely heard the officer's phrase and I answered him, puzzled, 'Excuse me?'

He replied frostily, 'You are supposed to have a visa to enter this country. Where is it?'

Oops! A massive surge of panic raced up my spine and into my head, sharpening my senses and waking me up with a jolt. What visa? I obviously I hadn't done my homework properly. How could I have not known something as important as this? This was only my second international trip with my two-year-old passport, and I had naively thought that was all I needed. The immigration officers were not so naive and because of my Nigerian middle name, Ekundayo, they were convinced I was trying to slip into their country illegally with a fake passport. I was subsequently and unceremoniously marched off to the interrogation room. My protestations made no difference; I had entered Ghana illegally and they had a zero-tolerance policy...though, this being pre-9/11, things were not as bad as they could have been. It was no fun being shouted at in a language I couldn't understand, in a dark room, feeling like death warmed up. The effects of the jabs were incredibly strong on my body, but the fear and adrenalin kept me alert. I didn't know what was going to happen to me, and I was scared. I had never messed up like this before, and these guys at the airport carried guns and meant business. For the first time in my life, Dad was nowhere to be found to bail me out.

After what felt like for ever, but was actually more like a couple of hours, I was led out of the interrogation room by an official airport liaison officer. He spoke fluent English and was reasonably friendly, under the circumstances. It was a breath of fresh air to be spoken to rather than shouted at and intimidated. He didn't read me my rights, but instead gently asked me questions and proceeded to offer me a way out of this mess. He took me to the arrivals hall to see if I could find my friend Pastor Robert. No Robert there? Maybe he was outside the airport with a car, wondering what had taken me so long. 'Can you see your friend here?' the liaison officer asked me. I scanned the sea of African faces hustling outside at such a ridiculously early time of the morning, until the realisation sank in: there was nobody there for me inside or outside the airport. This was not good, and it clearly didn't help my credibility with the officer, who seemed to be growing increasingly impatient by the minute. I was looking less like a Christian missionary coming to serve the souls of Ghana and more like a potential drug smuggler or someone trying to 'disappear'. What was I going to do now? I had no idea. The first moment I was alone I closed my eyes and, then desperately and earnestly prayed.

The Ghanaian authorities were within their rights to put me on the first flight back to England at best or lock me up for further questioning at worst. Where on earth was Robert Kwami? I had sent the Kwamis a letter confirming my arrival details more than two weeks before I travelled. I had no contact number for them, as they did not have a landline and they lived more than five hours outside Accra in a town called Kumasi. As the officer began to show signs of impatience I suddenly remembered, or rather I was inspired to recall, a phone call I had made while waiting for hours at Heathrow Airport. There had been plenty of time due to the delay with the Ghana Airways flight.

Mother Letts, as she was affectionately called, was the elderly but sharp mother of Valerie Kwami, and was one of those beloved church mothers who had practically built her local church back in London from the ground up by holding services in her home until the growing congregation could afford to rent a building. I had informed her of my trip to visit her daughter and family, and for some reason she had insisted that I call her when I got to the airport in England before I flew. I had plenty of time on my hands, so I gave her a call. She told me that she felt the urge to give me the phone number of one of our denomination's most prominent ministers, Bishop Grey, who lived in Accra. I had never met Bishop Grey, but was well acquainted with his dynamic minister son, the late John Grey, who was something of a legend in revivalist circles as a powerful preacher and healer. I wrote the number down diligently, not considering the importance that such a random contact would have for me in the very near future. Mother Letts was a very spiritual woman, prophetic even, and always on point. Bishop Grey held massive sway in this region of Africa and was very well known in the area as a man of influence. I had taken his number out of politeness, not giving it any thought.

I rummaged through my pocket, looking for this piece of paper that could be my salvation; like Charlie Bucket from *Charlie and the Chocolate Factory* searching for a golden ticket, praying I hadn't lost it in transit. My immediate fate rested on this little piece of scrap paper with a telephone number written on it. Eureka! I had found it. If I hadn't believed before that Mother Letts was hearing from God, she made me a true believer that morning, as the officer permitted me to go and make a phone call.

The next challenge was how to make a phone call without any Ghanaian currency or a phone card. A porter caught my eye in the airport lobby area and swiftly came over to see how he could be of assistance. Unfortunately, he had a lot of friends who were falling over themselves to help me as I unwisely followed him in to the porters' hang-out area of the airport. I gave the first porter a £5 note to get me a phone card, and his friend, also a porter, wanted money, for keeping him company. Before long, an argument ensued among the group of around ten men, and I didn't need to speak their language to know that it was over who would take a slice of this foreign boy's money. This night had gone from bad to worse, as I found myself at the mercy of a group of men who were probably underpaid and knew that I had foreign currency on me. Who could blame them for being opportunistic when I'd only been in the country five minutes before noticing the level of poverty its people seemed to endure and that hustling was a way of life for them. Then I saw the liaison officer looking miffed with the porters keeping me company as he raced over and sharply took my arm to lead me towards the phone area of the lobby. *Saved by the bell*, I thought, as I quickly thanked God under my breath.

I made one simple phone call and then the nightmare ended. Bishop Grey was at the airport immigration office within an hour, and as we awkwardly met for the first time I apologised for waking him up and thanked him for saving my bacon. Bishop Grey was an older giant, tan-skinned black man with gravitas, reminding me of James Earl Jones in *Coming to America* and Uncle Phil from the *Fresh Prince of Bel Air* rolled into one. Bishop Grey really did have influence at the airport, as they all knew him and seemed to relax towards me as he negotiated my release into his care. They allowed me to stay in the country, but I had to surrender my passport until I left to return to the UK. I wasn't happy about this, but my only other choice was to return home that morning, and that way I would have wasted all the money I had saved and not completed my mission.

So where were the Kwamis? Well, like a comedy punchline, the letter I had sent to them arrived two weeks after I did, during my month-long stay in Ghana. So, the Kwamis had no idea that I was even in the country!

Bishop Grey managed to get hold of Robert at the church office, and after a rushed breakfast I was on an exhausting solo five-hour coach trip to Kumasi to meet with the family. The trip was back on track. I was still feeling rubbish, but was more determined than ever to make the most of this experience. If Dad could go through his permanent challenges with dignity, then I could go through my temporary ones now. After a road trip that would best be described as a bad night at sea, so regular were the pot holes in the road, I was finally met by Pastor Robert at the coach stop, and the rest of the trip was relatively plain sailing.

There was something spiritual and life-affirming about standing on African soil. It felt alien, yet strangely familiar to me. Ghana is a beautiful country filled with beautiful people, and was the nearest I had been to where my roots lay. Nigeria and Ghana are in close proximity to each other in West Africa, with just two small countries between them. If it hadn't been for my visa incident, I could have ventured into Nigeria for an expedition with Robert. For the first time in my life it felt as if I was connecting to my alienated African heritage, which had previously seemed so distant and foreign but was now tangible. I had never seen so many black faces in my entire life, or walked the streets being in the majority race, seeing billboards advertising products with smiling black faces or enjoying the novelty of playing spot the white man amid the crowds. I was used to the opposite scenario after being programmed to see myself as a minority, and the odd black face amid a sea of white, which was the default position in England. I was overwhelmed and uncomfortable. This was hard to take, as it was the first time I had been outside the West, and the culture shock jolted as if I had put my wet finger into a plug socket.

Even in this sea of black faces, however, I was constantly singled out and called *obruni*, meaning 'white man' in the native Twi dialect. Even in Africa I couldn't escape this perception of not being black enough. To be fair, any black person who came from the West would be called *obruni*, especially by the locals, who were not used to seeing people who looked like them but acted more like the other white-faced foreigners they had come into contact with. It wasn't meant as an offensive slur like it was back home, but as a tongue-in-cheek observation. In England I was black and in Ghana I was white. It was as straightforward as that.

I felt at times like a white tourist, absorbing the sights and experiences of the poor village locals of Kumasi living in sub-par conditions. Sometime later, Robert would show me other parts of Ghana that were truly extravagant and luxurious beyond imagination, but I had to see the reality of the majority first. Seeing too much of the good life would not have inspired me to share the plight of the people once back home, and that was the point of my being there; to serve the bigger picture. It did cause me to reflect, however, on why the only Africa I had ever seen on British television news cycles and documentaries was the one gripped by extreme poverty, with flies landing on potbellied, malnourished infants, or the ravages of war. I had no idea of the diverse nature of Africa – that the continent was made up of the extremes of poverty and great wealth. Western conspiracy theories aside, nothing had prepared me for the trip to Cape Coast and the famous castle there which held a multitude of haunting, destiny-changing memories.

It was while standing in this museum of a castle that it really hit me how black, or African, I was, and how connected I felt to the traumatic history of the transatlantic slave trade that permeated every area of this nightmarish building. Seeing the horrors of the slave trade on the soil where most of the atrocities took place is much harder to swallow than simply reading about it in the history books. When I saw the tiny cells where black men, women and children were kept like trapped rats before being bundled onto ships, I felt my skin get heated with rage and my fists clench. The auction signs signified the cost of a human being, and the point of no return at the castle's exit to the docking area brought home the reality that these people were being sent to their death. The lucky ones would die on the ships through being trampled or through sickness. A worse fate awaited the less fortunate in America, the Caribbean and throughout the British Empire.

Watching the 1970s TV series *Roots*, (based on the novel written by Alex Haley) on an old VHS tape while staying at the Kwamis' home just before we made the trip to Cape Coast Castle possibly didn't help matters. It was impossible to process the experience on an objective level, fully immersed as I was in my emotions. The irony was not lost on me that I had been nurtured by a nation that had been directly involved in the trade that had enslaved my ancestors hundreds of years earlier. My heart and mind were racing violently as I tried to process all this information. Surely I had no right to carry hostility and anger towards *all* white people because of what *some* white people did hundreds of years ago. That would be as stupid and malignant as when white people demonise all black people because they were once mugged or assaulted by a black person.

It reminded me of the early 1990s, when many black teenagers first saw the movies *Boyz n the Hood* and *Menace II Society*, and witnessed the systematised prejudice that was deliberately created to suppress the potential of the black community; to show that the future of the black community was bleak and filled with the misty haze of death, drugs and incarceration throughout America and the Western world. In England many of my friends, were affected by this depiction of reality growing up. It disturbed and angered them as they saw themselves fighting against an oppressive system that labelled them public enemy number one.

Entering adolescence, I started to become conscious of racial politics. Regardless of my upbringing, when I walked out of my house, I was a black male and in the wrong part of town at the wrong time and could be perceived as a threat. Serious questions flooded my mind as I suddenly saw the world in colour. How does it even feel to be a black man when you are not in the minority and don't have to blend in?

Perhaps I would always have to navigate this tension of embracing my blackness and being aware of the unequal treatment and exploitation of black people historically and in the present, alongside the truth that I have personally benefited by growing up in the comfortable West, in a white society. Equally true is the fact that I didn't choose the reality I was born into, and I have had to live with this duality of inheriting both the blessings and the curses, the liabilities and the privileges. I was no longer the same person after arriving in Africa. Though not a militant Afrocentric by any means, I had made peace with a part of my identity that I had previously been estranged from and gradually began to see myself as a legitimate part of the story of global black history.

Meanwhile, after preaching and teaching at open-air meetings across Kumasi, my soul was nourished by giving hope and spiritual encouragement to the villagers, who were intrigued by this young black-looking white man from a far-off land. The mission was accomplished, and I had received much more from the trip than I had given out. Ghana had embraced me, and it left an indelible mark on my life.

The next challenge was getting back my confiscated passport from the customs office before my flight took off, and this time my flight was with British Airways, so I didn't anticipate a delay. It did prove to be a race against time, however. The clock was ticking and I was sent from one location to another, with the person holding my passport nowhere to be found and the prospect of making Ghana my new home a growing possibility. As myself and Pastor Robert, who was seeing me off, rushed around Accra airport with the boarding time fast approaching, we finished my time there as I had begun it four weeks earlier. We prayed with urgency, in desperate need of divine intervention. Heavenly Father had a way of answering my desperate prayers of need, but was this cutting it too fine?

Touching down on British soil at London's Heathrow airport, full of achievement, a sense of self-discovery filled me. I had an interesting story to tell after only just getting my passport back an hour before my flight was to take off!

Pretty soon I was drawn back into the world I had left a month before. While I was being reborn in Africa, Dad had been languishing in a London hospital, having the worst experience of his life, thanks to the chemotherapy, which literally stripped that very life out of him. My world had changed, its scope broadened, just as things had grown darker for my family.

It was officially confirmed that the treatment had not been successful, and it was then a matter of making my father comfortable. I had missed the worst of the treatments and was secretly grateful to have been thousands of miles away. It may sound selfish, but this was how I felt. I didn't want to see the only man I loved, my hero, stripped hollow by medication and in constant pain. He refused to see most of us, myself included, over the next couple of months. With time running out, my brothers, sisters, in-laws and I set out to make his last Christmas the best one ever and make him proud.

The plan was to have it at the house in Ebdon Way, where I was staying alone at the time. We would cook the infamous turkeys and make the effort for Dad that he had always made for us. My sisters and sisters-in-law agreed to sort out the food and other arrangements, and my brothers and I agreed to eat the food and bring in the drinks. I'm kidding! We all agreed to play our part and were each assigned a task.

As Christmas Day approached, Dad went into a rapid decline and refused to see any of the family. He was confined to the spare room in my sister's flat and rejected any one of us who went to see him. I had a feeling our Christmas plans were going to be cancelled, and as the day grew closer my suspicions were confirmed. I remember waking up to deafening silence in the family home on Christmas Eve 1999. This had become the norm over the last few months, but never at such a festive time of the year. The telephone rang. It was Claire informing me that the family Christmas was off and I should make alternative arrangements for myself. I wasn't surprised, and not happy that my intuition had been correct, but I had wondered how we were going to pretend to be having the best Christmas ever when the life and soul of the season was withering away before our eyes. At least we had been spared the uncomfortable situation of a strained Christmas lunch and the look in each other's eyes, silently communicating that none of us wanted to be there.

It was Dad who held our family together. As siblings, few of us were very close to each other, and we rarely spent time together apart from in Dad's company. My siblings were of a different generation entirely. Claire, who was the next one up from me at twelve years my senior, and our eldest brother Lindsay, aged forty, were the ones I was closest to and had most in common with. My sister Anne, the eldest of all of us, and my brothers Martin and Terry, had their own immediate families and lives to live. I knew that once my father had gone, the family unit as we knew it would likely pass with him. I think deep down he knew it too, and it broke his heart.

Home alone on Christmas Day after coming back from a church service that had momentarily lifted my spirits, I thought about the goodness of God. God was good, but Christmas was rubbish. That one was, at least, as I was stuck on my own without a single invite from anyone. To be fair, nobody was in the festive mood and each was probably spending the time in their own way. Everyone bar me had other families they belonged to while I only had myself. But however bad the day was for me it would have been even worse for Dad (and Claire and Joe in the same flat).

I went to bed that night with a heavy heart and a lonely feeling that I just couldn't shake. Something was hovering over me, and whatever it was it didn't feel right. Boxing Day arrived. This day had always been an emotional climb-down in our family after the high of Christmas Day, as it was our beloved mum's birthday. We traditionally went to the crematorium to pay our respects to her so Dad went from the enjoyment of being with his family one day to being bombarded with grief the very next. We had to witness this ritual for six years straight. Dad had not celebrated his birthday since then due to the unfortunate timing of his wife dying on the same day, which doubly ensured that the date was engraved in his heart and mind. We used to joke that Mum had done it on purpose so we would never forget her.

It was the day after Boxing Day that I received a phone call to get to Claire's flat as soon as possible. This was déjà vu. I vividly remembered receiving a call like this when my mum was in hospital the last time. This time around I jumped on the 321 bus towards New Eltham and saw that Anne had arrived just before me and was consoling Claire who was beyond hysterical. By the expression on their faces, it was clear that this was the end of the road for Dad, and so began the frantic phone calls to my other siblings, trying to get them there urgently.

I was numb with fear, knowing it was the day I had been dreading for months, even years before cancer arrived on the scene, and frankly I still wasn't prepared for it. What was I going to do? Dad had been the constant thread throughout my young life. Who would I talk to about all my adventures? Who would share the milestones yet to be reached? Who would be proud of me? I wanted him to meet my future wife and kids, and before that see me graduate from university. I would have settled for at least one more year with him; but as the man he was, not the hollow shell he had become.

He was already unconscious, with the deep, gasping sound of his breathing filling the atmosphere, like air being violently sucked through an airbag. It would stop for a minute and then restart. Each breath could've been the last but then the noise would restart. Claire had popped out for a minute to get something before this countdown of breath began, leaving just me and Anne with Dad while we waited for the others to get there. We were the eldest and youngest of six children, kneeling by Dad's bedside, neither of us wanting to be witnesses to this moment but equally unable to leave him. He had been there for every one of us, and we were not going to let him down when he needed us the most. Dad's breathing started to slow down once Claire had left, as if he knew he could slip away while she wasn't in the building. They were extremely close, so it made perfect sense. Everyone else was fairly settled with their families and support systems, but Dad always concerned about Claire's well-being. She was the caretaker in the family. I'm sure he would have wanted to have walked her down the aisle and see her have a family of her own. He loved her boyfriend Joe like a son that was for sure. I think he knew I would be OK, as he knew the strength of my deep-rooted faith and the prospects I had before me. I just hoped he knew how much I was going to miss him and perhaps even realised that I was beside him as he lay there. Who knows how conscious a person is when they are dying and what their level of sensory awareness is?

All of a sudden, a deep, loud breath pierced the room, ending the steady rhythm that had gradually slowed down in shortened intervals. I looked across at Anne as we recognised in each other's tear-filled eyes that this was it. We waited for another breath, but it never came. It was the end. We cried, then Claire returned moments later, hit by the news as if by a speeding lorry, feeling total disbelief that he had left without her being there. Dad had seemingly refused to return the favour to Mum of dying on her birthday, thus sparing us all the double mourning yet again. But whatever day he died it would not have mattered; it was a dark day that would feel like a knife to the heart for as long as we lived.

My other siblings arrived shortly afterwards and the rest of the day became a blur. I was seated on the wooden floor crying uncontrollably, to the surprise of my siblings, who thought that, being the God-fearing person I was, I would be the most serene and composed. I didn't care about any of that, or what they rightly or wrongly assumed. What we, or specifically I, had just lost could never be replaced and as happy for him as I was that he was no longer in pain, it tore me up that I would never see him again. The day I had dreaded from as far back as I could remember had arrived, and it was all over.

Preparations began for Dad's final send-off. The council house we had lived in at one time or another over a thirty-year period would be returned to Greenwich Council. The children he had raised would come together one final time to honour him. I never got to say anything at his funeral. I will always regret that and wish I had pushed harder to say my final words to him.

This funeral was nothing like the countless black funerals I had at-tended over the years in a predominantly black church. For a start, it wasn't remotely religious and our father was cremated, so there was no graveside ritual. We did have the beautiful song 'You're the Best Thing That Ever Happened to Me', sung by Gladys Knight & The Pips, during the service, which struck an emotional chord. But what was rendered to ashes was not just the man but all our history and memories; the strong consistent pillar that had supported our family. At the beginning of a new century, January 2000, we said goodbye to the man who had selflessly ushered us all through life in the previous century. The closest he came to seeing the twenty-first century was at the Odeon Leicester Square cin-ema, watching *Back to the Future Part II* with me, with its hoverboards and flying cars, sharing a large bag of Butterkist popcorn. He missed it by just a few days. It seemed really symbolic that his passing coincided with the closing of an era. A fitting end for a priceless, old-fashioned gentleman.

New Year's Eve 1999 was not only the end of the decade in which I came of age, but the final day of an entire century. As the musical prophet Prince once sang, the time had finally and suddenly arrived, finally making what had been a futuristic, almost apocalyptic, song perfect for the mo-ment we were living in right there and then. Except there was no party. Rather than hanging out at a nightclub or on Trafalgar Square watching fireworks, I was at a church in Wood Green with my college room-mate Wayne Angelo Nicholas Brown. His father, Bishop Eric Brown, was the senior pastor of the church, and I occasionally attended with Wayne dur-ing term time. Rather than screaming with elation, hugging random strangers and singing 'Auld Lang Syne', I was sombre; in deep contem-plation of not only what I would gain in this new year and century, but also what I had lost in the one I had just left behind. There was no 'End of the World' or 'Millennium Bug' computer crisis that would plunge us back into the Stone Age as ominously predicted. Rather, I spent my last night of the twentieth century at a Pentecostal church in Wood Green, north London, looking out the window of the back hall, seeing the display of fireworks and hearing the shouts of 'Happy New Year' from the street.

People wondered what this new millennium would bring. Whatever it brought for the rest of the world, I knew it would mark the rest of my life without a father. Somehow, I had to become the man Dad had believed I was destined to be, without him there to encourage me. This thought made me determined to honour his memory by being the best man I could be. He was no longer there to guide me, but I would look to God to show me the path and trust that I had the right foundations laid within me to stand on my own two feet. They say that there is a light at the end of every tunnel. Well, the tunnel I was passing through was the darkest I had ever experienced, and was as bleak and pitch-black as I could imagine. It would take a giant floodlight of epic proportions, capable of illuminating several football pitches, to put an end to this dark spot.

The start of 2000 brought a faint hope that things couldn't get any worse. There really wasn't anyone else for me to lose, although I did have a decent relationship with Claire and Joe. I even stayed at their flat for a short spell before I wearing out my welcome. Little brothers, after all, are best served in small doses and at big intervals. There was love for my family, but I had never felt that they were heavily invested in my life, or that they would be moving forward. There was no malice or falling out – just the sober realisation that the glue which had held this delicate family unit together was gone.

There was no more Ebdon Way, either, as I lost the only home I had ever known, while I was away at seminary. This absence of several months meant I was not eligible for the local government to provide either the existing home for me or a new one, regardless of my being technically homeless. It was a legal loophole, as I was not registered on the council's list. I would be living on campus at London Bible College (LBC), which had become 'home' for me in the months that followed. What I would do during the holidays I had no idea, but I tried to take my mind off such real-world problems.

My campus room-mate, the honourable Wayne Brown, tried his hardest to be there for me and raise my spirits. Wayne was determined to get me out of my funk, trying every trick under the sun and playing his favourite role: the mischievous clown. We shared a lot together; not only as room-mates, but as two black students at this majority-white seminary. It felt like the episode of *The Fresh Prince of Bel Air*, when Will Smith attends a posh white private school and everyone is fascinated by his 'otherness' and repeatedly mistake him for his cousin Carlton. This happened to us all the time. People would finish a conversation with me that they had previously started with Wayne and vice versa, although words cannot describe how dissimilar the two of us looked, besides both being black men. It was funny at first, but soon grew tiresome and then downright offensive. It didn't take much to set me off during this delicate season, to be honest.

Wayne was determined to get me out of my depression but each attempt failed. The one ace Wayne had up his sleeve was inviting me out to a gospel concert held in Walthamstow, East London, featuring the American gospel legend Vanessa Bell Armstrong. As much as I loved gospel music, what I truly loved was being on the scene, bumping into old friends and meeting new people in this exciting and vibrant fraternity. *Who knows? Maybe I'll meet someone interesting*, I thought to myself. After all, I was single and an eligible bachelor, with a wingman who had no issues in that department himself...and as he was in a relationship, he could deflect all the attention onto me.

As soon as the intermission arrived, I was out on the floor, prowling like a lion on the Serengeti, hugging friends, nodding across the room to acquaintances and shaking the hands of newly introduced people.

There were couples everywhere. I would have appreciated having a young lady to focus my attention on, enjoying her company rather than holding back the tidal wave of grief and sadness. Jane was still in my life, but not romantically. Deirdre had offered her condolences for my loss but made it very clear she had no romantic feelings for me whatsoever so everything was painfully quiet with regard to my love life. I loved meeting new people, more than actually reconnecting with known people, especially as word had travelled concerning my bereavement in this tight-knit ecosystem. I appreciated the condolences, but the idea was to take my mind off what I was dealing with rather than be constantly reminded of it.

As I walked around, I glimpsed a familiar face out of the corner of my eye. Part of one of my friendship groups, Darren was like the younger guy who ran with the older guys in the crew. The crew was absent that night and I could see that he was with a young lady and another couple, so my curiosity was piqued.

I found my way over to Darren with the shameless agenda of quizzing him on his company for the evening. She was beautiful: slender, with a light beige complexion, a pretty face and large eyes. I was beyond impressed. *How on earth had Darren got hold of a girl like the one on his arm?* I thought to myself bemusedly. It's not that there was anything wrong with him; in fact he was tall, dark and handsome, and a musician (much sought after in the black church world), but she was out of all our leagues. Besides, only a few days before he had been feeling elated that he had collected a couple of young girls' phone numbers at our national church convention, earning himself the nickname Nuff Numbers. Now he had seemingly graduated to having a sophisticated lady on his arm.

I said hello and greeted the other guy and his date, but I was really just feigning interest as I waited for Darren to introduce me to the girl he was with.

'This is Jahlene', he proudly announced, with the obvious subtext that he knew he had struck gold. I was genuinely chuffed for him, while at the same time feeling more than a bit hard done by. I gave him the shoulder hug, which was boys' code and subtext for 'Well played, sir,' and said that we would catch up later.

Having recently had an experience with an older woman, Jahlene seemed a little young for my taste, as she was wasn't out of her teens, but for some reason I couldn't get her out of my head all evening. Trying to dismiss these thoughts, as going after another man's date was not my style, I stood scanning the hall for a moment, wondering if the future Mrs Aris was somewhere in the crowd. How would I even know? *Not tonight*, I thought, as I shrugged and joined the long queue to get a hot Jamaican patty and soda.

Suddenly, I remembered telling Wayne I would only be a few minutes when I left him to go walkabouts. He should have known me by then; when I'm let loose at a social gathering I'm *never* just a few minutes. Too many people to see and too much schmoozing to be had! And I really needed it after the few weeks I'd just had.

When the night was over, Wayne and I travelled back across the city to our student digs. I thanked him for the fun night out and his efforts to take my mind off my situation. After saying goodnight, I lay in our darkened bedroom, silently reflecting. Without having to wear the smiling veneer of earlier, I could breathe and explore my true feelings. Before drifting out of consciousness, I wondered whether I would always feel so desperately and painfully alone.

CHAPTER TWO

'I Asked God for a Brown Baby'

'Why am I brown and you're white, Mummy?' I asked in the inquisitive voice of a three-year-old boy.

'Because I asked God for a brown baby,' I replied, this time in the voice of a reassuring woman.

I was standing on a stage, microphone in hand in the darkened room, facing a crowd of onlookers. I went on to finish the set right up to the punchline, though the truth is that this was not just a joke but my origin story. My origins as told to a rowdy crowd of drunk punters at a comedy club.

Rather than visiting a counsellor's office, I decided to share moments from my early years with a bunch of strangers. And now you're about to hear the story, so get your hot drink and hanky ready.

It was a chilly Thursday evening in January 2010. The stage I was standing on belonged to the infamous comedy club called Up the Creek, in London's Greenwich, and I was making my stand-up comedy debut. It was something that had been firmly on my bucket list, and I was finally doing what many people have dreamt of doing but never muster the courage to actually do. The thought of dying on stage had occurred to me, but

I tried to push it to the back of my mind. If I hadn't, I would never have got out of bed that morning for fear of failure. I vaguely heard my name being called out as my body launched itself onto the stage moments before my mind did. This was it – showtime.

As I stood shuffling about on that sticky, creaky wooden floor, microphone in hand, I was conscious of the long lead sprouting out of it like a snake and remembered to take firm hold of it. With the heat of the stage lights on my face, I took a deep breath and launched into my routine. I started with a joke about being stopped endlessly by people on the street and eventually by the police, and my mistakenly thinking it was because I looked like Brad Pitt. A couple of laughs in, I transitioned to the unusual situation of being a black child in a white family sometime in the early 1980s, probably watching *The A-Team*, while quizzing my white mother about this strange maternal situation. What she replied sounds like an incredulous set-up for a fictitious joke. The truly funny thing is that it was all true and it was my life! For years it felt like the joke was on me.

That night was my graduation from a comedy course run by Harry Denford. Denford was a middle-aged, rotund, bald-headed, white Jack-the-lad character whose catchphrase 'Bank it!' was a seal of approval when he heard a joke that worked. He taught us to use our lives as material for our routines. If you were fat, you would make your first joke about being overweight; if female you would joke about being a woman . . . you get the gist. The principle was to use anything an audience would observe about you within seconds to fuel your first joke and mess with their perceptions. Of course, there was no way any audience would be able to deduce that I had been adopted by white parents, but they could see that I was black. They may also have had presuppositions about this and as the audience was 95 per cent white, anything that would provide enough connection to get a laugh was fair game. In a way, I had been doing this my whole life – playing down any associations with my blackness to appear more palatable to within a white environment – so I might as well use it for my advantage this time and play with the stereotypes. I was surprised that I was even standing there, with all that was going on in my life, but I needed to do it. I had the sense that overcoming this fear and having this secretly longed-for experience would cleanse me and give me confidence. I just *had* to do it!

∗ ∗ ∗

I was born Antony Ekundayo Osula on 3rd June 1979 at the South London Hospital, Clapham. It was the year MP Margaret Thatcher became Britain's first female prime minister and the Conservative Party came to power. My biological mother, Priscilla Omosede Osula, was a student in her mid-twenties. She arrived in England from Nigeria a few months prior to my birth to undertake a secretarial course. She had never married, according to my birth certificate, where the section about my biological father is conspicuously blank, or more specifically a line had been put through it. My name, Ekundayo, is Yoruba and means 'something sorrowful that has turned into joy'. Nigerians and especially the Yoruba tribe, name their children with personal significance, so I guess I was a good thing that came out of a bad situation.

Priscilla was an independent woman at a time when it wasn't easy to be. She was determined to provide a good life for herself and her infant son in spite of the obstacles she faced as being a single mother in the late 1970s in this foreign land that was significantly colder than the one she had left. Priscilla searched for a registered childminder of good repute to take care of her infant son while she pursued her studies and worked.

She finally met one called Marion Smallwood, who lived in a south-eastern area of London called Kidbrooke. I had only been with her for a short while when, for a reason that remains unclear, she was no longer able to look after me. She did, however, recommend a good friend and fellow child called Wynne Aris. Mrs Aris had looked after children from various backgrounds and had plenty of recent experience with children from West Africa, and of course with their parents. A new arrangement was made and Mrs Aris began looking after me when I was a couple of months old. In the process, she and Priscilla struck up an unlikely friendship. This black twenty-five-year-old from Nigeria, who was an independent, single mother, and the white, fifty-something, socially conservative housewife from England, were united by their common interest in my well-being.

Priscilla often referred to Mrs Aris as 'Auntie', a common practice in Nigerian culture when addressing an older woman. Old enough to be Priscilla's mother, Mrs Aris had a natural maternal affection for her, too. However, this unlikely rapport was tested when an unfortunate and unpleasant event happened that would change the course of all our lives for ever.

Not much is known about my mother's time in England. What *is* known is that one evening in early 1980 she was held at an immigration office in Dover, from where she was suddenly and swiftly deported back to Lagos, minus her infant son. I was later told that Mrs Aris and her twelve-year-old daughter Claire travelled across the country to prevent her being flown home, but without success. They received an emotional request from a desperate Priscilla to look after Baby Tony until this awful misunderstanding could be sorted out and she could return to London. I still have no idea why she went from having legal immigration status in this country to being swiftly and aggressively kicked out. She wrote letters from Lagos and made determined plans to return to the UK. In spite of the small matter of somehow having violated her entitlement to stay she would nonetheless come back for her son.

That day never came. The last known contact Mrs Aris had from my mother was via a well-travelled blue-papered letter dated July 1980. This arrived one month after my first birthday, and in it she continuously and erratically repeated her intentions of coming back for me and resuming her studies. As the months went by, and I began to crawl, talk and relate to people, Mrs Wynne Aris was the first person I called Mum. A business arrangement became a promised fulfilled and I went from client status to family member.

No memories of my biological mother remained – neither her face nor her voice, though I must have missed her as I felt confused and unsettled as the weeks and months rolled into years. But any thoughts of her soon became a fading memory. The faces of my black mother and white Mrs Aris blended and merged until the only face I recognised as my mother's was that of Mrs Aris. It was white hands that changed my nappies and lifted me out of the playpen, comforted me when I was upset and fed me my bottle of milk when I was hungry. My new mother had swept-back, medium-length, silver-grey hair and thick-rimmed glasses. She smelled of Avon perfume and listened religiously to love-god soul singer Barry White. My earliest memories began with her.

Mrs Aris's faithful and hardworking husband Albert was in agreement with her decision that they would keepand raise me as their own son. Adoption back then was far from rare, or anything to bat an eyelid at, but this case was slightly different. Here was a white, working-class couple in their mid-fifties on a council estate raising a black baby in early 1980s London. They were not super-woke modern celebrities. I learned many years later that my experience was not as unique as I thought; that there was a trend in the late 1970s and early 1980s for Nigerian parents to leave their children in the UK to be raised by white families in the hope that they would have a better start in life. This was not my story exactly, but I was not alone in my transracial situation, even if it felt like it at the time. This was an unusual decision. It was far outside the norm, and I guess it displayed some courage and commitment on the part of my new parents to break from convention in such a way. I never knew any different, but they did, and I often wonder how they prepared themselves for the endless glares and probing questions; the pressure of frequent visits from the nice men and women in suits who came with their notes. I often had to leave the room while Mummy spoke with them over a plate of rich tea biscuits. I remember these social workers asking me questions, eyes squinted, hanging on my every word. Then one cup of tea later they were gone.

My parents fought a lengthy and expensive court case to keep me as their ward of court, to make them my legal guardians, thus preventing me from being wrenched from the only home I had ever known. I was never formally adopted. I only found this out aged eighteen, when I wanted to apply for my first passport. My birth certificate, which I had never seen, was somehow produced, and an appointment was made with Dad at a solicitor's office in Eltham, where I needed to legally denounce the name Osula and claim the name Aris. It wasn't hard for me, as I had only ever gone by that name, but it did feel weird, as the language was so firm and final. People have since asked me why I went along with it. It's simple: I was eighteen and this was the only obstacle standing between me and a once-in-a-lifetime trip to Florida.

I was oblivious to racial politics and the so-called wrongs or rights of my domestic situation, and frankly I didn't care. All I cared about was Mum making my dinner (after watching her favourite soaps, of course) and Dad buying me Star Wars action figures whenever possible. Growing up, love really was colour blind. I had a mum and a dad, three older brothers, two older sisters and two excitable Jack Russell terriers, one of which used to bite me unprovoked. Maybe he was racist! I was the only black (or 'coloured' one in pre-politically correct language) sibling and they were twenty years older than me on average, so I was the baby of the family.

With older than average parents and siblings, I grew up quickly and matured at an early age. Something wasn't quite right at home. I was an observant and smart cookie but I couldn't quite put my finger on it until I grew to understand how life worked outside my home. The Ferrier Estate had a really bad reputation for being rough and dangerous. I for one never had a single bad experience growing up there. It probably helped that my brother knew most of the 'persons of interest' on the estate (which looked as if it had been forged out of grey concrete Lego bricks) and none of them would mess with ''Arry's little brother'. My brother Martin wasn't called Harry or Harold, by the way; it was a nickname derived from our surname, Aris. I sometimes got the witty and inventive

'Anus' shouted out after the register in primary school, then some genius thought they had invented the joke in secondary school, too. What did make sense was that there were a lot of families from different ethnic backgrounds – Pakistani, Vietnamese, as well as African-Caribbean and English – and the unifying fact about these kids I played with on our estate was that they all resembled their parents. Of course, Mum and Dad *were* my parents, even though I looked nothing like them. After all, Mum did ask God for a brown baby, so case closed, right? At least, that was the story she told me. Why she was so specific with her request I have no idea.

There were a lot of tumultuous social changes under Thatcher's reign in 1980s London. Incidences like the Brixton riots between black protestors and the police were sparked by the inadequate investigation into the murders of young blacks in an arson attack on a house party in New Cross and the rise of far-right racist groups like the National Front. I was blissfully oblivious to most, if not all, of this at the time, as I was too busy growing up. London was becoming increasingly racially diverse and integrated. At least, it was in Kidbrooke, where I lived, and in neighbouring Lewisham, which had the nearest and best shopping centre for miles around, as well as a legendary outdoor market.

Maybe I'm romanticising my childhood memories, but it seemed a lot more socially acceptable to be in my transracial situation then than it would be now. If you walked around Lewisham Market and the shopping centre, you would see black people, white people and everyone in-between interacting with each other, laughing and bantering in cockney slang or Jamaican patois.

My earliest introduction to other black people was to two little girls called Elisabeth and Theresa. Mum looked after them as their childminder, the difference being that their parents actually came back for them at the weekend. I can't remember the last time I saw them, as I would only have been around five years old, but they were my playmates and I remember them fondly. Sometimes I wonder how they are and how

their lives turned out years after leaving Ebdon Way, or if they even remember it or me.

The next set of black faces belonged to my neighbours five doors
down, the Daley family. They originated from Jamaica and were a large
family like us, if not slightly larger, and their house was full of the rich
aroma of West Indian food, with the sounds of reggae and lover's rock
booming out of their open back window. They were completely different
from us but incredibly friendly. Mr and Mrs Daley would always say hello
and chat as we walked past their house. Mr Daley was a smooth, tall, fair-
skinned man, with an effortless, laid-back demeanor as if nothing trou-
bled him, and a walk like he owned every bit of ground underneath him.
Mrs Daley was slightly darker, with a loud, and infectious laugh which
came from a warm and embracing face. She was as talkative as her husband was of few words. I was always invited to their house for their granddaughter Taneka's birthday parties, surrounded by her countless cousins.
I felt as if I could blend in there, at least on a superficial level, as culturally
it was completely foreign, from everything from food to music and banter. I didn't realise at the time that the Daleys were providing a kind of
informal service to my parents by inviting me into an environment where
I could socialise with people who looked like me, thus making me a little
more comfortable around other black people. They were very good to me
and respected my parents, admiring them for the unconditional love they
gave me. As black people in a predominantly white society, they would
have known how tough it was for me as the only black person in my
household.

Curried goat, ackee and salt-fish, and spicy patties had a very different
taste and texture from Mum's tinned steak and kidney pie with instant
mashed potato. Such delicacies weren't very appetising until I was rein-
troduced to them many years later at the Pentecostal church down the
road. In every possible way, especially as far as things like diet were concerned, I was a little English boy. Mine was a typical but far from conventional white, working-class household that valued hard graft, generosity

and unpretentiousness. Mum was the exception to the rule regarding that last point. She imagined herself as classy, refined and a little bit above everyone in our area. She had been born into a lower middle-class family in another part of London and was a bit like the BBC character Hyacinth Bucket (pronounced 'bouquet', as the character always insisted). Star of the sitcom *Keeping Up Appearances*, Mrs Bucket was a suburban housewife who thought of herself as a long-lost member of the British Royal Family, much like Mum.

My mother was a housewife who split her time between looking after other people's babies and being an Avon representative. She didn't like to leave the house, as she was an undiagnosed agoraphobic. This was fine for looking after crawling infants, but problematic for a saleswoman. As far as Mum was concerned, her home was like Windsor Castle and she was most definitely the Queen. As an only child she was likely spoiled by her butcher father – she was the apple of his eye – until her doting husband took his place. She loved babies but tired of them a little when they grew up, much like she did with pets. She enjoyed meeting exotic people, but was a little close-minded and really cared about the appearance of things, a product of the era she grewhad grown up in. These kinds of contradictions sum my mother up perfectly. You couldn't define her easily. She was a bit of a fantasist, proud and old-fashioned, but she was open enough to 'adopt' a baby of African heritage. In spite of the curtain twitching she knew it would cause on our estate. I think deep down she probably enjoyed the attention and controversy it brought.

Dad worked practically every day of his life. In the latter years he owned a own cleaning business and believed religiously in an honest day's work. He did all he could to provide for his large family and uphold his responsibilities as a man. Born Albert Alfred Aris, he grew up in 1930s Islington, as the son of a seamstress mother and labourer father, who died during Albert's youth. From the beginning, all my father ever knew was hardship and grafting, with a strong sense of responsibility towards his hardworking mother as her only child. Witnessing her work herself into a literal early grave in her late forties, this work ethic passed down to him like a mantle, leading him to push himself even harder. His early years being defined by the harsh realities of making ends meet, he learned about sacrificing his own well-being in order to make sure everyone else in the family was OK. He transferred the sense of responsibility he had for his mother onto his future wife and family. No one dared call it martyrdom, but Dad didn't see it as abnormal to work eighteen-hour days, six days a week, as well as seven hours on a Sunday, hardly seeing the same family he was providing for.

The tragic thing is that my father had far more potential than opportunity. He was an extremely intelligent and worldly-wise man. Travelling to the Far East with the Royal Air Force, as he did aged eighteen, would have been an eye-opener for a young British lad from the working classes before foreign travel was available to all. Coming from the wrong side of the tracks, he wasn't able to go to university, nor was he born into money and privilege, so he was unable to escape the rigid class system of British society of the late 1940s. His need to work was likely born from an instinct to survive and make sure we all survived; to ensure that his family was not ripped apart by premature death and tragedy like his had been.

In spite of rarely seeing him through the week, I did have time with him at the weekend, bonding over trips to Lewisham or the cinema, which created a lifetime of great memories. We would talk about a lot of things and he always respected my opinion. Dad was always very open and honest with me about the reality of my being black and what that meant in the world around us. He often told me I needed to be better – at school, in life and as a person in society – than my white peers. This seemed strange, as he would talk about being colour blind in terms of not seeing me as the 'black one' in our family. Yet here he was instructing me to be conscious of this fact in the outside world. After talking to countless black friends raised in the UK over the years, he did exactly what their parents had done with them: tried to prepare me for the realities of race and life. Although he had never been black, he had been dealt a rough hand in the game of life. He had to fight for a quality of life that a privileged few had taken for granted in the more prosperous part of London he grew up in.

Maybe his time spent in the Far East as a young man shaped his thinking and taught him about the universal struggles of mankind, as it exposed him to slums and people desperately trying to make ends meet, just like his late mother back home. He taught me never to think that any person was beneath nor above me; that we are all equal and deserve dignity. This principle was ingrained in me before I found faith, and was one of the best lessons, if not *the* best, he ever taught me. Dad lived out what he taught. Ever the talker, he could carry a conversation with the CEOs of the global oil companies he used to work for as either the cleaner or as the front desk security man, as slight as he was. Then he would seamlessly switch gears, chatting with the other cleaners with the same generous and friendly spirit. I witnessed this first-hand countless times. To him people were people. He tried his best to love indiscriminately and was widely loved in return.

Mum and Dad were complete opposites in many ways; the dreamer and the realist, respectively. Somehow they made it work for an admirable forty years of marriage. He devoted his life to making her happy, then his children and always himself last. Happiness for him usually consisted of a packet of cigarettes and a cheeky bet on the horses. My parents fought like cat and dog during the years I was with them – and I assume long before that – but to be fair they never went to bed without making peace or calling a truce, because however heated things became, they loved and respected each other.

When people ask me what it was like growing up in a white household, as they always do when they discover my background, I have to take a deep breath before answering the question. It's not that skin colour did or didn't matter in my house; the issue was simply avoided. There was a lot of denial about my being black, the exception being Dad's reality checks, which produced a mixture of security and insecurity. I was secure in the fact that I had a family that loved and cared for me instead of being raised by the state or shipped from one foster home to another in an endless cycle. At the same time, I felt insecure as I feared that this family life could end at any time. Either my elderly parents were going to die and leave me all alone, or someone was going to knock on the door and take me away from them for ever. Both scenarios scared me and plagued my dreams throughout my childhood. One day I would be left all alone and who would take care of me then?

I wasn't an overly insecure child besides the issue of identity; rather I was very self-aware and observant. I have always been romantically involved with the mirror. It's like going through life voyeuristically looking at myself live, as if I am a film director narrating the Blu-Ray commentary of my life. It's easy to trace this back to looking in the bathroom mirror as a child. I was transfixed by this chubby brown face staring back at me with wild, 'picky', knotted hair, which would never stay in one place or be controlled by the hands of my out-of-depth mother. Claire later took on the challenge when Mum simply gave up. I have strong 4C hair, thick and resilient, and a Rubik's Cube challenge to any person not used to maintaining and styling a black person's hair on a daily basis.

My hair was one of the dead giveaways that I had a different family background from most black children. Hair is a big deal and a matter of pride in the black community, whether it be afro, locked, woven or straightened. For a child to show up at the school gate with uncombed, dry, brittle hair on a regular basiswas a talking point among the black parents. My family absolutely tried to master the art of looking after my different hair type but inevitably failed. Pre-Google, how could they know about black hair oils and only washing it once a week instead of daily like Caucasian hair, or only combing and styling when wet? It's not as if I came with a set of maintenance instructions like Gizmo the Mogwai from *Gremlins*. All my childhood memories of hair combing are associated with pain and the feeling of fear and dread, and I would sprint out of the bathroom like Usain Bolt on speed. This association of hair and pain was far too close and eventually they just gave up trying to coax me into submission, and my head continually looked like a pot scourer.

When I was about nine years old, Dad took me to an upmarket and exclusive black hair salon in Lewisham, called Stylistics Hair Studio. This was around 1988/89, a time when black people in the UK still looked to America for style and culture trends. The owner of the salon (I could tell he was by his alpha-male swagger and the reaction of the female stylists in the room) was a middle-aged, tall, portly but slick black man. He spoke with a smooth West Indian accent while giving Dad a live tour of all the hair products on the wall in a sales pitch that sounded as though he were selling him a car. I still recall the smell of strong chemicals used by the hair stylists as I stood there watching a number of black women of various shapes, sizes and skin tones.

I was deeply curious about black women, who were quite novel to me as I wasn't raised by one. I found them fascinating, though I wasn't sure how to relate to them outside of the occasional run-ins with our neighbours. I remember being smiled at sweetly by some of the ladies in the salon and blushing behind my chubby brown cheeks.

Pretending not to notice the other looks I got out of the corner of my eye - the curious stares at myself and Dad – was much harder. The strange sight of an elderly white man with a small young black boy was not something you encountered every day on the streets of Lewisham.

The owner of the salon went on to advise my father with words I will never forget. 'Sir, I have the solution to your son's hair problem. Here we have a product that will loosen his curls and make them more manageable.' He motioned to the shelf filled with bottles. Dad listened, taking in the sales spiel patiently, though he was not convinced. The salon owner had essentially suggested to my father that to solve the ongoing problem of my unmanageable hair I needed to have it chemically treated like Michael Jackson's, circa *Bad* album era. For those who don't get the reference, we are talking about a jherri curl – the big curled wet look of the 1980s. His suggestion was based on ease of maintenance and manageability as opposed to the obvious comedic value. How could I have gone to school with hair like that? I'd have been like an oil slick on legs, an accident waiting to happen. I was self-aware enough to think that he was being utterly ridiculous. It would have meant going from one extreme to the other. From an extra-dry head to a head swimming in oil and grease.

Thankfully, Dad did not take the man's advice, opting for a bottle of moisturiser instead. I like to think he saw the horror on my face at the owner's suggestion and spared my life. I loved Michael Jackson, but wasn't convinced about the idea of imitating his hairstyle of choice. In my childhood naivety I thought his skin tone change was what happened to all black people – that we gradually became lighter in tone as we got older. I genuinely believed this and didn't know about things like the skin condition vitiligo or skin bleaching, whichever you believe. I honestly remember looking forward to my dark brown skin getting lighter like his, or like that of my biracial best mate Lee Bossler. That would have been amazing.

I didn't want to be white, though at times it would have made life much easier; just light enough to not stand out so much or to be passable as at least one of my parents' natural children. I never hated my black skin, but I was at odds with it most of the time. It was an obstacle that constantly reminded me that I didn't fit in. I looked in the mirror, saw my hair, saw the family photos and observed my friends' families, and could see with my own eyes that all was not OK. There were a lot of questions but no real forum to ask them in. The world inside my home was normal, but everything was very different and so was I. It felt like I was living between two worlds sometimes: my mother's fantasy and resistance to the outside world and my father's, hard reality-driven world view. As much as Dad was a realist, he was always out working. Thus, his and Mum's worlds rarely collided and both were happy to live in the worlds they had constructed.

Perhaps Mum's fantastical answer to my three-year-old self's burning question was the best answer she could have given under the circumstances. It was certainly poignant, in retrospect. To burden a child's mind with the concept of race, in that I couldn't be their 'real son', or to introduce the idea of adoption, might have been overwhelming for me at that age. To my mind, I really was their child in the natural sense of the word. Unbelievable, maybe, but it's true. All I really knew was that the environment I was raised in didn't quite fit the way I looked. But I couldn't change anything, even if I wanted to. Like a mismatched pair of socks, I had to live with it, and it really wasn't the end of the world. I was repeatedly reassured by both parents that I was loved, and not only that but *chosen*. This 'brown baby' was lovingly requested and specially ordered like a kind of bespoke pizza or made-to-measure suit. I guess it sounded a lot better than 'Your mum left you with us and got deported, never to be seen or heard from again, so we kept you', or something like that.

I'm always reminded of an early conversation with Mum close to forty years ago, when I asked why she, unlike my black friends' mothers who had afro-texture hair and smooth ebony skin, had straight silver hair with a slight blue rinse, and pink, wrinkled skin. Mum was much more Mrs Slocombe of the 1970s UK sitcom *Are You Being Served?* than Clair Huxtable of the US sitcom *The Cosby Show*. At times I wished she was the latter, especially at the school gate, but she was my mum and I loved her very much. Every time I hear a Barry White song (her favourite was 'You're the First, the Last, My Everything'), it reminds me of her and I smile. She was the only mum I ever knew and I know she loved me as much as 'all the pennies in the world', which was one of her many poetic phrases. I thank God for answering my white mother's request and that she kept her promise to my brown mother, Priscilla, raising me as her own even though if it was for far longer than expected. I wish they were both still in my life and could have seen the many adventures I've had and the man I have become.

✳ ✳ ✳

As the night when I would be baring my comedic soul on stage in front of strangers arrived, I wondered what I had been thinking. I thought back to the exact moment I found out about the comedy course. I had excitedly told my work colleague and buddy Andrew Horton over lunch, executing my plan to get him signed up with me. We both worked at Premier Christian Radio, not far from Victoria, London. He was one of the funniest people in the office. Destined for comedy, he looked just like comedy acting legend Ronnie Barker: tall, white and portly, with an expressive face. Andrew, or 'Hortz' for short, was naturally funny in the dry, British, almost Monty Python-esque sort of way, which was very different from my one-liner, less cerebral kind of humour. I knew Hortz would be great on this course and doing stand-up. Regardless, I needed an accomplice for this new venture and I had excellent powers of persuasion, which worked a charm. We both found ourselves enlisted like army recruits, facing our fears and secret ambitions together.

The blinding light, the heat of the stage and the endlessly long microphone lead flapping at my feet conspired against me on the most nerve-wracking night of my life but they were thwarted in their efforts as I got through my five-minute set in reasonable triumph. I had lost my stand-up comedy virginity with a number of small laughs and at least a couple of big ones. The ground hadn't even nibbled at my feet, let alone swallowed me whole. *That's one big item ticked off the bucket list*, I thought to myself, breathing erratically from the adrenalin, wiping sweat off my face, and replaying the last few moments in my head as if I were looking over CCTV footage. *Did I just do that?*

Comedy life felt really good, and I went on to perform a few more gigs with a sense of growing confidence. Until I noticed all the gigs had one thing in common. Besides being in pubs, they were, almost without exception, made up of predominantly white audiences. This led to my questioning whether I had the ability to make people who looked like me laugh. Would I be able to cross over with my routine and appeal to a more diverse audience? Maybe I was getting carried away and ahead of myself, but much of my material was about struggles with racial identity. I could see that white audiences related to and found my routine funny, but lack of laughter from the few black people in the crowds caused me concern. It might have been that they were just miserable people or – gasp – that I just wasn't funny enough. But felt instinctively deeper than that. Either way, it didn't feel right, and neither did my material, which is the lifeblood of a performer. Paranoia started to creep in as I asked myself why the white punters were laughing so hard. Were they laughing at my dilemma or my blackness? Was it nervous laughter?

All this second-guessing became tiresome to the point of despondency. It never occurred to me just how important having an identity was for a comedian, and that was not remotely my experience at the time. I was whatever people or the environment needed me to be, which I had learned from my unique childhood circumstances and surroundings.

Back to the comedy drawing board I had to go. The question of whether I could be funny to black, white and any-colour-in-between audiences remained unsolved, much like the ones about my black mother's disappearance thirty years earlier.

CHAPTER THREE

Different Strokes

'Tony! *Diff'rent Strokes* is on!' I heard my mum shout out from the sitting room, causing me to drop whatever my three- or four-year-old self was doing at that moment to race towards the television set. *Diff'rent Strokes* was my favourite TV show, with the trademark catchphrase 'Whatch'u talkin' 'bout, Willis?' of its lead character, Arnold Jackson (who later became Drummond through adoption). Played by the late Gary Coleman, the phrase was used in almost every episode, even when it barely made sense, but it was funny and memorable.

It was 1983 and *Diff'rent Strokes*, already a hit in America, was one of the most popular TV programmes on air in the UK, thanks to its cute, lovable star, and its themes of family, race and love crossing boundaries. Arnold and his big brother Willis were two orphaned African-American brothers, taken in by the wealthy, white former employer of their late housemaid mother. The contrasting worlds of high-society Manhattan and lower-side, blue-collar Harlem often collided in comic fashion, but it was the theme of unconditional love between adoptive father Mr Drummond and his two sons across the taboo lines of colour and class that had viewers hooked. These kids saw him as their dad, and it was only the small-mindedness of outsiders that prevented them from getting it too. America was gradually changing, and the walls of racism and prejudice were coming down one brick at a time. Well, on television at least. When you consider that just fifteen years earlier the first interracial kiss between the handsome white Captain Kirk and the beautiful black Lieutenant Uhura on *Star Trek* had caused national outrage, this was progress.

I was the British Arnold Drummond in my young mind. I remember looking up at the TV screen in awe of this family in a situation just like mine. Well, just like mine minus the Manhattan penthouse, sassy maid and wealthy adoptive father. Oh, and importantly, there was no Willis. Only me. This was a family with not one but two black boys in white surroundings. They were accepted and loved, and were having the time of their lives with their adoptive older sister Kimberly, the biological daughter of Mr Drummond. It was amazing to see something like this on television, as it felt as though Gary Coleman had auditioned to play the part of me transplanted into a different setting. He was chubby-faced, I was chubby faced; he was talkative, I couldn't have stopped talking if you'd paid me. Though the one thing I wished we had in common was a Willis. Arnold had at least one person who was in the same boat as him, who he could relate to. I was all alone in that sense. The fact that this was a fictitional television show was lost on me as a child. I could finally relate to another family's set-up for at least thirty minutes a week and feel that I had a comrade-in-arms.

It wasn't until much later, as an adult, that I understood the show's title, *Diff'rent Strokes,* as a play on words, reflecting both the idea that people will do things differently according to what suits them and the literal difference in skin colour of the main characters, as in paint strokes. I wasn't aware at the time of the bold sociopolitical statement (or conceitedness, depending on your view) that was being made by the show, or that the situation of the comedy was its central premise. The thought that black people should stick exclusively with black people and white people with white people, was a completely foreign idea to me. I understand about cultural differences and even why it is easier and sometimes more comfortable to stick with your own, so to speak, but life just doesn't work like that. We will inevitably have to deal with people who are different from ourselves on a daily basis, especially in urban cities. I've always found the notion of apartheid or racial segregation abhorrent and a reality that shouldn't exist in an enlightened, multicultural, multiracial country or in a globalised world. For me, this classic forty-one-year-old prime-time sitcom represented a very serious breakthrough. For all its humour and sometimes preachy manner, it demonstrated that love could be colour blind, binding even the most unlikely people together as family. I just wish the show's young cast really had belonged to such a family so they could have avoided the harsh realities of their much-publicised tragic lives.

Another thing my life and *Diff'rent Strokes* had in common was that both situations were more idealistic than realistic to the outside world of the time. The love was certainly real, and the warmth of my home was genuine, but the general prevailing attitude of my household was that this scenario was normal. I gradually started to question this as I got older. My young mind thought that maybe it was just like the old cartoons, where a stork would be assigned the task of carrying a new baby from heaven to its parents waiting below on earth, or a puppy dog would be brought to a very shocked Mr and Mrs Cat. I remember hearing the whisperings about me, and one of the first muffled words I learned to decode was 'adoption' or 'adopted'. I asked Mum what it meant once and whether I was. She said, 'Of course not', with a straight face and no further clarification. Though I grew up in a world framed around avoiding an inconvenient truth, I did not have the knowledge or life experience to question it. When I did gain the maturity to analyse the situation, I realised a large part of my identity was false, and that it was filled with a great deal of confusion and isolation.

I wasn't a stupid child by any means, and I knew that my and my family's strokes were different. But I also knew that facing the reality of my origins would open up questions I wasn't ready to deal with, such as: if my parents are not my real parents, then who are? And what is there to stop them from coming to get me? The thought of a sudden knock at the door one day, resulting in me being taken away from home, often plagued my subconscious mind, in dreams. Or you could call them nightmares.

One Saturday evening in the summer of 1991, when I was twelve years old and Vanilla Ice was battling MC Hammer for street cred and musical supremacy, I had a reality-check encounter. I was attending St Joseph's Academy, a strict Roman Catholic school that had high expectations on the outside and a ghetto playground full of bullies on the inside. My time there also left a souvenir by way of a small circular scar on my cheek under my left eye. This came after standing up to one of the aforementioned bullies, a boy who at twelve years old was already built like Mike Tyson. He was harassing one of my white friends, whom I defended, only to be rewarded with a punch in the face by a fist wearing a large gold sovereign ring. My eye swelled up like a balloon and I instantly began to consider the direction of my future education.

A happier memory relates to one of my biggest schoolboy passions of 1991. I was a massive Teenage Mutant Ninja Turtles fan (though in the UK the 'Ninja' was swapped for the softer 'Hero'), as were most of the planet's children around 1989 to 1992, and I was verging on becoming obsessed. I remember watching a pirate VHS copy of the first TMNT film with my friends back in 1990. When it was finished, we put dressing-gown ties around our heads and grabbed snooker cues, belts and whatever we could lay our hands on and started ninja kicking each other out on the street. Thankfully, nobody died or got seriously injured, but boys will be boys — or in this case ninjas. More than anything I wanted to get my hands on the Ninja Turtles action figures, but there was one obstacle. They hadn't been widely imported from America at that point. One of my school friends, Leon Delvalley, told me there was a shop in Lewisham that had these hard-to-get-hold-of action figures. At first I didn't believe him, as he was prone to exaggeration, but to my gleeful surprise he was telling the truth. My heart started racing as I realised the search was over, but then the small matter of not having any money came up and I realised I couldn't walk away with half the shop! This was a major setback; a matter of life and death to this die-hard twelve-year-old Turtles fan. What I needed was a plan – one that had been executed a thousand times with expert precision: ask Dad to cough up the money for me. It had worked before, so why change a winning formula when I needed it most?

That following Saturday Dad and I were driven to Lewisham by Claire, who was the designated driver in the family, to find this obscure little off-road shop that housed the treasure trove of Turtle goodies. Everything was going well apart from one thing: I didn't have a clue how to find it. I didn't know the name of the road or remember where it was, and I have never had any navigation skills. I was never good at lying or bluffing either, while my father wasn't any good at holding his temper and wasn't known for being the most patient man. I knew I was going to get told off with every false step I took in the wrong direction as they waited in the car. Dad was a volcano about to erupt and Claire was rightly annoyed that she was spending her early Saturday evening standing around on the street instead of being out with her friends or getting on with her own affairs. Little brothers are the type of accessory big sisters have a love–hate relationship with, and you can guess which way the pendulum was swinging as five minutes turned to twenty. Under pressure, I began to crumble. It was fast becoming a lose–lose situation for me as I knew I was going to be grilled by Dad *and* go home without the Michelangelo with the ninja kick-leg action. *Things can't get any worse*, I thought, as I frantically paced up and down the road, sweat beads running down my chubby face.

'Excuse me, son. Are you lost?'

I turned around to see a small elderly black lady who had a gentle but firm Jamaican accent. 'No, I'm looking for a shop with my dad and my sister over there,' I said politely, still thinking about where the shop with the Ninja Turtles could be — so close yet so far.

She turned to me after glancing in the direction I had motioned, where Dad and Claire were standing by the car. 'No, son. Where are your parents?'

I was a young twelve-year-old, one of the youngest in my school year, and fairly naive. I repeated my previous answer and reminded her that I was looking for a particular toy shop on this road, but couldn't find it. It didn't help that my father was looking visibly frustrated and he and my sister were frantically beckoning me back towards the car. Unfortunately, this Good Samaritan (and I say that respectfully) could only see two white strangers standing by a car, enticing a lost young black boy to enter it. I can only imagine what that must have looked like from her perspective. Her mind completely dismissed what I had said to her, or that these two 'strangers' knew my name and in no way seemed unfamiliar or threatening to me. For all my assurances, she held my arm firmly like a mother lioness and refused to let go. This was fairly traumatic for me. From the perspective of a passer-by she looked more related to me and could have been my grandmother, but the truth was that she was the stranger in this scenario.

As well as calming down my distraught dad, my furious sister knocked on the door of one of the houses and had them ring the police, as a scene was developing and had started to get ugly. How had this weekend quest to find toys gone south so quickly and where had all this heightened emotion and drama come from? The police arrived, and after an interview between me and a friendly police officer the situation was defused. The next thing I experienced was the silent and tense car journey home. I'll never forget the look on my father's face, or the nervous anger of my sister, who was tempted to throttle the well-meaning Good Samaritan for doing what any responsible person might have done in that situation.

The well-meaning woman's 'crime' was that she refused to listen to a child and couldn't accept that some pockets of the world had moved on; that just like in *Diff'rent Strokes* it was possible, albeit unlikely, that a white family could have a black son — even one who didn't even realise what all the fuss was about.

There have been many awkward misunderstandings over the years, and Claire and I have learned to make a joke of the fact that people would predictably do a comedy double-take when told about our familial relationship. We have occasionally talked about that Saturday evening in 1991, and how for me it was the most aggressive realisation of how my role in the family looked to everyone bar us. Our strokes were undoubtedly different — in fact, we couldn't have looked more mismatched as a family if we'd tried — but the love was real. That was more than a consolation prize for the twelve-year-old going back to his loving home without a single Ninja Turtle prize in hand (on that occasion, at least).

CHAPTER FOUR

Bounty Bar Blues

'SHUT UP, YOU F****NG BOUNTY!' came the words, spat out like bullets into the atmosphere, aimed at my face. And that wasn't the only thing aimed at my face, as a swift right hook joined the party. My assailant then strutted off, job done, leaving my face swelling up like a water balloon, blood gushing from underneath my right eye.

I'd like to say that this was a new experience, but it was the second bloody eye I had received within a six-month period – though this was the most memorable blow. Like in the yard of a prison, tensions at St Joe's were always brewing among the testosterone-fuelled boys looking for a target on whom to unleash their frustrations. Boys can be territorial at the best of times. Add tribalism to the mix and you have trouble waiting to happen. As in prison, the tribes were often split along racial lines; the school had become predominantly black. The black boys not only out-numbered all the others but were physically dominant, too. There was an uneasy peace treaty at the best of times, and like Michael Jackson's 'Beat It' I found myself acting as piggy in the middle, defusing kick-offs.

Ironically, our uniform was a tranquil emerald-green blazer, though it would have been more fitting had it been red for danger.

My sentence at St.Joe's began in September 1990, when I was escorted to the gate by Claire. With no idea what I was going into, I was met by a friendly face in the same boat as myself. Alexander Mercier, a chubby black boy from New Cross with an infectious smile, reached out his hand to introduce himself. It was his first day, too, but he was upbeat, chirpy and excitedly talkative. We hit it off straight away and he became one of my closest friends throughout my brief stretch at that school. Through him I learned about video games such as *Street Fighter II*, the smash-hit arcade game that was the jewel in the crown at a fish and chip shop in Lewisham. The smell of stale vinegar and salty chips has always been associated with the game for me. We kept in touch sporadically after I left, bumping into each other on the street. Each time he had different-coloured hair and funky garments as he rose to become a prominent DJ and producer in the UK garage scene. Under his alias, 'Shy Cookie', he made a name for himself producing the music genre's greats, but he always stayed humble, remaining the same kind, good-natured boy at heart. I'm proud to still call him my friend. I'm also shocked that the school environment didn't corrupt him. I felt like Andy Dufresne, who escaped from Shawshank, but had to leave Red behind.

The school was increasingly becoming a ghetto while I was there. The mask of a respectable Catholic institution was being stripped away like the paint on the old building that housed it. My parents had been sold on the brochure and on the reputation that religious schools had for achievement and behaviour. We weren't the only ones who fell for it, as a few boys from my junior school joined me there, including my best friend Lee Bossler, until he and his family moved to Dartford, some fifteen miles away, leaving me without a wingman and protector. Lee could handle himself physically and had always protected me against any threatening characters on our estate. How I could have done with his help in the school playground that lunchtime, when my face felt the impact of a fist of fury.

I had been hanging in the lunch line with Kieron Gascoigne and David Humphreys, joking about an episode of *Harry Enfield* from the night before. Kieron was laid-back, and short but physically active due to taking karate classes. He was famous around school for sneaking a sai into the classroom – the same dagger wielded by the Ninja Turtle Raphael. David was the opposite: talkative, lanky and not physical in the slightest. What he had going for him, besides looking like the Milky Bar Kid, was his sense of humour. He always made me laugh. We were a funny trio, two white boys and a black boy, talking comic books and cartoons when it was still considered geeky. I was still in my chubby stage, which gave the impression that I could take care of myself. Growing up on an infamous council estate helped to expand on this myth, and I was physically bigger than some of my peers. But not the most feared boy in our school year.

I don't think Mike Tyson would be much bigger than this boy was. Built like a tank and almost predestined to be a heavy-weight boxer, he prowled around the playground like notorious music executive Suge Knight around young rappers. He was at the top of the food chain and we were several rungs below him. Leo wasn't just a gorilla but King Kong looming large over us mere chimpanzees in the jungle. The smell of greasy burgers and fries travelling through the canteen into the playground taunted us as much as the noise of those already inside eating away. The line was taking for ever to go down, and as pre-teenage boys we were feeling ravenous and impatient. None more so than Leo, who stormed past the queue like a whirlwind, indiscriminately knocking past people, including my friend David. David was spun on his axis as the force of nature knocked into him, sending his spectacles on an airborne trip across the playground.

I honestly don't know what possessed me in the moment that followed. As Leo came past me at full speed, a knee-jerk reflex caused me to react in a way that my mind would never have authorised. My leg flew out in perfect timing with his own, and this brute force of nature suddenly came tumbling down onto the concrete floor in full view of the hungry mob. These boys had a new hunger in their belly, and it was for blood. What had I done? I had publicly humiliated the alpha male of our school year, who would have no choice but to respond.

Time stood still as I waited for him to get up from the floor. I had no game plan and instinctively knew that I was going to get it.

'Who tripped me?' he growled, his ego bruised.

He didn't see me trip him? I thought to myself, believing for a moment that there was a chance I had got away with it. Until a sea of fingers came hurtling my way, outing me as the culprit, that was.

'Why did you trip me, bro?' Leo asked in rage and shock.

In an attempt to appeal to his sense of justice, I replied, 'Well...you barged past us and sent David flying.'

It was then that the opening line of this chapter came hurtling out of his mouth in conjunction with the furious fist. It was difficult to say which of the two hurt the most, as I also landed on the hard concrete floor with a fresh geyser of blood gushing from under my right eye. The bright red on my emerald-green blazer reminded me of Christmas – a strange thought in the moment. The blood from the cut was caused by the sovereign ring on the fist. My face hurt like fire, especially when the fresh tears met the fresh wound, causing it to sting sharply. Humiliated, beaten and bloody, I felt some comfort from the fact that I had stuck up for a friend, though the sting of my aggressor's words had cut deeper than his ring. I was a 'Bounty', which meant that I belonged to none of the tribes.

One of the most popular chocolate bars in England while I was growing up in the 1980s was the Bounty. It was made up of two equal-sized bars of coconut covered with either milk or plain chocolate. After the Mars bar, the Bounty was my favourite chocolate bar. It was ironic, then, that this fantastic treat could be used to hurl abuse and inflict emotional pain on me. This powerful imagery was used as a clear symbol of humiliation, affecting my life for many years to come. Like the American term

'Oreo', alluding to the chocolate cookie sandwich with a white cream filling, 'coconut' and the term 'Bounty' were used to describe a black person who was deemed to be 'white' on the inside, – specifically in terms of behavioural traits, tastes and mannerisms. As a black child raised in a white family, I guess I was destined to be labelled this way. Who decides what makes a person black enough anyway? I mean, what are the criteria?

Maybe there should have been a textbook or instruction manual, 'How to Be Black – An Idiot's Guide', available in all good book stores, while I was growing up. Only, I didn't find one in my local library. I wish I had, as it would have made my teen years a heck of a lot easier. Going through puberty is hard enough, with its outbreaks of acne and a constantly modulating voice box, without having to bear the burden of working through serious identity issues. No matter what I did, I wasn't black enough for some people. And no matter what I said, I wasn't ever going to be considered white, even though culturally at that time I had a lot more in common with the white kids on my estate than the black kids. In some ways I was the bridge-builder in the playground who brought black and white kids together in our little group. This was a lot harder in senior school, as boundaries based on our differences became more rigid among each camp. It's difficult for me to say which was harder: being the white coconut interior to my black friends, or being the chocolate coating to my white friends. Whatever the case, I realised that I would never be fully accepted in either camp, because I was the product of an unusual situation that very few could honestly relate to; a curious anomaly. And it was probably because of this that I learned to become a masterful chameleon.

* * *

When I was about five or six years old, I would stay behind at the school's children's club for activities and games. It was mainly for children whose parents worked and couldn't get there early enough to pick them up. For my mother, it was more about having a break from me and spending some time on her own. It was there that I first experienced racism, and it came from a person who should have known better.

Pudgy, white and sour-faced, Mrs Royale was in her early fifties. She rarely smiled, and spoke in a harsh domineering tone. She was in charge of the club and made sure everybody knew it, child or adult volunteer. For some reason she took an immediate dislike to me, which I wasn't used to, as teachers in the school generally liked me and I was popular among my peers. I was a friendly and placid child, who wasn't known for trouble or unpleasantness. I thought that if I was a good boy, I would be liked — that was what my mother had always taught me. Why then, did Mrs Royale, hate my guts? She constantly singled me out, shouted at me and made me stand in the corner by myself while everybody else played. Confusion set in about why she shouted at me for the slightest thing. My words were met with sharp abruptness when I asked her anything, her face filled with disgust. When all the other children got a boiled sweet, I didn't. While they played, I had to stand in the corner.

It never occurred to me that I was the only black kid in the club. This was 1985, a time when black and white people still lived fairly parallel lives in London, rarely crossing lanes. 'Nigger' would still be shouted on the road from a speeding car. But in my personal world, white people didn't have any problem with black people because they were black. Mum and Dad had always taught that we were all the same in God's eyes.

I still very much agree with the spirit of that lesson, despite being old enough to know that not everybody agrees with or cares what God thinks on the matter — if they even believe He, She or It exists. People gravitate towards other people like them. It's basic human nature and applies not only to skin colour but to class, occupation, nationality, and even sexuality. Birds of a feather flock together, as they say. Supporting the same football team can bond complete strangers on a rowdy drunken Friday night train journey home; people who would never have spoken to each other that same morning on their way to work. On a primal level, people seem to feel more comfortable with 'their own' kind. However, it has been said that comfort is the sworn enemy of progress.

Mrs Royale was a lot more comfortable with 'her own' kind, and took it upon herself to single me out and bully me. Why? Who knows? Maybe a black man or woman had looked at her the wrong way, or perhaps I reminded her of black comedian Lenny Henry and she was more of a Bernard Manning fan. She made me stand in the middle of the hall one evening, berating me and calling me stupid in front of all the other children, which left me feeling humiliated and ashamed. *I'm not stupid; I'm a clever boy*, I thought to myself, but I didn't dare say it openly for fear of receiving another dose of her wrath. This whole affair got back to Mum, who told my sister Claire. At eighteen, Claire was a pretty intimidating figure if you crossed her, with a mouth as big as Texas. My sister was very protective of her little brother and hit the roof when she heard about this woman's hate campaign against me.

Let's just say that, the situation vastly improved after a visit from Claire. Claire picked me up from the club the next day and had a talk with Mrs Royale, whose face turned ghostly pale when she discovered that Claire was my sister and I had a white family. How do I know this? Because she actually said, 'Oh, I didn't know Tony's family was white.' This roughly translates as, 'I wouldn't have bullied him – correction, wouldn't have *overtly* bullied him – if I'd known his family was one of us and could make life difficult for me at this school.' Reading between the lines, her logic was that I didn't come from a 'little immigrant family from Africa' who couldn't speak English and would therefore be unable to defend me against this abuse. Even at five years old it was obvious to me that something was wrong about this. As if by magic, she did a 180-degree turn from then on and was my new best friend. 'You all right, Tone? Would you like a boiled sweet?' I suddenly wasn't black any more, thanks to the insurance policy of being raised by a white family. Rather, my blackness was conveniently ignored. If I had a pound coin for all the times I heard, growing up in our area, 'I don't like black people, but you're all right, Tone', or variations on that theme, I would be competing with Bill Gates or Warren Buffett in the wealth stakes.

From this incident onwards I was famously known throughout school as the black boy with white parents. The subtext that came with the reputation was that they were very kind to have rescued me from a life of despair. I got this from teachers and my friends' parents, who at times even said to my face, 'It was really kind of your parents to take you in', as if I were a stray dog from one of those RSPCA ads or a Barnardo's orphan. What did they mean by 'take in'? I thought to myself. They had always been my family, and as far as I knew, my being with them was no different from any other child being with his or her family. Sometimes I glimpsed the relief in my white friends' families' faces as they saw that the parent bringing me to the children's party or day trip was just like them. They had narrowly avoided having to make awkward attempts at small talk with somebody different. Each time I progressed to a new teacher and class, the same routine started all over again, making me secretly dread parents' evening and sports day. The teacher always had to pretend not to be completely surprised. I may have been a child, but I wasn't stupid.

Claire often played the role of surrogate parent when I was growing up, due to my dad being constantly at work and my mum being mildly agoraphobic and later having further health issues. When Mum died in 1993, just months before my fourteenth birthday, my sister became a strange hybrid of parent and sibling, often with blurred lines. At twenty-five; she was young to be taking responsibility for a younger brother who had lived a charmed life up to this point, never having to do anything in the house. It was only once I grew up that I appreciated the pressure she had been under and the level of responsibility that I'm sure she partly resented, as anyone would. I don't blame her, to be honest. Instead of going out with her friends, she was often doing the washing and cooking, preparing meals for us and my dad, who came in late at night.

I can clearly see that such frustrations were behind her taking me to task over 'small' things, like leaving a plate on the side in the kitchen unwashed. It wasn't some military campaign against me. My teenage self resented her, as all I could see was another situation where I was feeling maligned and oppressed. We are very different people, I'm an idealist, whereas she's a realist, and very pragmatic. I believe in God and she doesn't. I see things as they could be, whereas she sees things as they are. You need both sets of eyes to experience the world for what it is, I think. We love and respect each other in these differences and they have never really stood in the way of our relationship. It's the fact that we are brother and sister that ties us together, as we don't have a great deal in common as adults. I am more than likely the only black person she has any relationship with, and even then she doesn't identify me as black in her head. She's known me since I was a handful of months old, and the first thing that comes to her mind isn't my skin colour.

We all have a primal fear of the other at some point in our lives. Embarrassingly, I was scared of Chinese people as a child. I wrongly associated them with the ultra-violent 1970s *Kung Fu* movies and was scared that I would get beaten up if I looked at them strangely. It was as if the random Chinese guy on the street could suddenly become Jackie Chan or Bruce Lee and crack my head open with nunchucks. Ridiculous, right? You couldn't convince me otherwise, though, when I was small. It's about as ridiculous as when I was constantly approached late at night on the street and asked if I had any 'weed' (marijuana), or any other drug, having never so much as smoked a cigarette in my life.

The more comfortable I became with identifying myself culturally as black, the more I tended to camouflage this with my white friends and family. This reinforced my role as a chameleon, changing colour depending on the environment, setting or players involved. We all do this to some extent. 'Code switching' is a part of everyday life. We have our phone voice, our friends and family voice, our office persona, and our Friday night down the pub or Saturday morning persona. For me it was a mild cockney or clipped middle-class accent with family and other white people, and either mock patois or subtle street slang with church or black friends. Maybe 'Coconut Chameleon' would have been an appropriate alternative title for this book, though with a name like that it would likely have been mistaken for a song title from a Boy George & Culture Club record.

The black community was always going to be the hardest nut for me to crack. They could smell a 'counterfeit brotha' from a mile away, and for several years my covert attempts at fitting in proved unfruitful. Does being unable to rap the *Fresh Prince of Bel Air* intro really disqualify you from the team? I had white friends who could do it in their sleep and they aren't honorary black people. It would have been much easier if I had been born thirty years later. You would find it hard to distinguish who was black and who was white among the youth of today if you closed your eyes, as both groups and everyone in-between speak 'urbanese'. This is a hybrid language originating among black British young people as a form of passed-down and evolved patois from their parents. Nowadays it's the predominant street lingo.

Truth is, listening to certain types of music and talking in a certain slang or language does not induct you into a racial group. However, there are details that unify and identify a group as coming from the same background, especially in a country where they are in the minority. I wanted more than anything to be a fully-fledged member of the black community, not just in appearance but in spirit, and it hurt me deeply to be considered an outsider.

Maybe I tried too hard, but the fact that I was trying at all was commendable, considering what the mountain I had to climb. To neither sound nor act how you look, or rather how you are *supposed* to sound and act, can be a very confusing thing – both for you and other people, and especially for those who look like you. The expectation from all directions is that I am black British, but where I really come from is the place of origin of my parents, one of whom was from Africa and the other from the Caribbean. I should have been able to pull from either rich cultural reservoir; to tap into perfect patois/pidgin at lightning speed, or even speak another tongue altogether. The most I could speak with confidence was mild cockney, and that was a stretch.

In the early 2000s, there was a contestant on the hugely successful reality TV series *Big Brother*, called Brian Belo. He went on to win that season, against all the odds. He was tall, skinny and black, but if you closed your eyes he sounded like a typical white bloke from Bermondsey. It wasn't just his accent but his mannerisms, speech and references that gave away that he too had been adopted by a white family and socialised predominantly with a white environment. Bello was the first black person in the UK to win the show, and up till that time black contestants had been either demonised or misrepresented. So maybe a black man who resembled a white man was more acceptable in a majority white country...if he wanted to win a reality TV show, at least. I wonder if Bello felt alienated by the black community like I did at times. It was my fellow black teens, after all, who christened me 'coconut', creating the link between me and the chocolate-covered coconut Bounty bar. It was their acceptance I craved the most, as I felt furthest from them. It was as if I were the movie character ET in a strange world, desperate to communicate and make meaningful contact.

'Alien' is an appropriate way to explain how I felt within the different worlds that I was trying to bridge, and it wasn't as simple as had been in the playground with little boys and girls. I was entering the treacherous world of adolescence. I was trying to follow a pride of lions who thought I was a tiger. In the wildlife programmes we are often told that the pack has rejected its fellow creature because it has been reared by humans and doesn't smell or act like them.

I found myself desperately trying to find the magic ingredients, that would make me blacker and hide my white background. Many people felt that my background was part of me and that I shouldn't need to chase a black identity. I felt like this too for some time, but it was far more complicated than they could imagine. If only I could have joined in with the jokes about the strictness of Nigerian or Jamaican parents; how they lived by the Bible's instruction to spare the rod and spoil the child when it came to physical discipline, ranging from being spanked with a slipper to being whacked with their father's belt. Disappointed that my parents never raised a finger against me? Disappointed to have missed out on a spanking? Crazy, right? That's how keen I was to identify. I didn't taste chicken with rice and peas for years after that early introduction at my neighbour's house. It was so long that I had almost forgotten the taste. The taste of African food didn't enter my mouth for many years to come. African culture was the most foreign and inaccessible to me., in fact West Indian culture was more than enough of a challenge without West African nuances thrown in for good measure.

If it hadn't been for my socialisation at church, I mght never have become comfortable in a predominantly black environment. Initially, I felt like an undercover white person in disguise, like Tom Cruise in *Mission Impossible* or Eddie Murphy in full character make-up. One day I'll get found out, I thought to myself as I tried to fit in inconspicuously. All I needed to do was come across more like *Fresh Prince* Will Smith and a lot less like his private-school, Tom Jones-loving cousin Carlton Banks. I was the equivalent of sugar-free cola: watered down or missing the key ingredient or X-factor of black swag.

At the same time, I was visually just another black teen, especially at the wrong place, wrong time. Such a wrong time (and arguably place) was an incident that took place in the leafy suburb of Blackheath. With its array of million-pound houses in 1994 money, an evening's walk home on a Friday night turned into a police incident, complete with blue flashing lights. At fifteen years old this was possibly the most eventful thing that had ever happened to me, and not in a good sense. Today it would likely have been caught on a smartphone and spread across social media, bringing me instant fame, shame or both. Unlike 50 Cent's anecdote of surviving a spray of bullets or escapades with the 'po-po', my most thrilling adventure up to that point was having my hand almost sliced off after bursting through a school glass door at full force a couple of years previously. My hand survived, even though I totalled the door, and I got out of trouble because I'd almost Luke Skywalker-ed an appendage.

My thrill-seeking 'criminal activity' that night was picking up horse chestnuts, or conkers, on the wrong side of town. It had escaped my knowledge that conkers were illegal contraband, but in truth what was threatening to the police and the numerous curtain-twitchers at the scene was my being there in the first place. Like something out of Dickens' *A Tale of Two Cities*, the differences between the Ferrier Estate and Blackheath, which was a mere couple of roads and a duck pond away, were fairly stark. One was a council estate, progressively run down, and the other was affluent, with mansion-like houses. I loved walking through Blackheath on my way to senior school or after youth club in nearby Lee as a more scenic shortcut. Besides having impressive houses and quiet roads, it had plenty of greenery and open space, in contrast to the Ferrier Estate which was largely made of concrete. It may have been home, but it sure was ugly, and I've always had a thing for aesthetic beauty. If something caught my eye, I pretty much had to have it, or figure out how to do so.

That included the conkers spread across the lawns of this leafy suburb. I had grown up with a huge horse chestnut tree in my front garden, and as kids we all loved the hard brown nuts that fell from it in season. The tree had been cut down by the time I was a teenager, but my affection for conkers never left me.

It was dark, but certainly before 10 p.m. when I was approached by three officers.

'Are you all right there?' one of them called out to me, hand held out authoritatively in front of him. The other hand was indicating to his colleagues to manoeuvre around me, blocking any potential exits. This was a bit overkill considering their large vehicle was doing a fairly effective job of blocking me in.

'Yes, officer. I'm just picking up some conkers,' was my nervous reply, which must have sounded like a surreal Monty Python sketch as comical, and absurd as it sounded. Being surrounded by police was a new experience for me and the way they were bracing themselves indicated that they were anticipating a hostile confrontation. Here I was, a kid walking home from youth club on a Friday night with conkers spilling out of his pockets, and I was being approached like Britain's Most Wanted.

'Do you live around here?' was the follow-up question, and although it was perfectly possible that I did, I and the officers knew what the answer was, and more importantly the subtext that sat underneath it: what on earth are you doing hanging around all these rich people's houses?

I didn't see the need for them to go through my pockets (filled with the prized horse chestnuts), and ask me a thousand questions, while also radio checking my details with the station, and keeping me standing in the street. This all played out in front of head-shaking onlookers for over an hour, and they still filed a report, despite having verified that I had only picked up conkers. Naively, I couldn't understand why they were taking so long to do the checks – presumably they were surprised that they had nothing suspicious on me – and I wondered why the police had been called out in the first place.

Then the penny dropped. I was a fish out of water in this place and my chameleon powers were irrelevant in this situation. The message was loud and clear: YOU DON'T BELONG HERE. You can walk through here as a shortcut during daylight hours, but under the cloak of darkness, you need to make yourself scarce, as the odds that you live here are remotely slim. If we find you lingering a bit too long, be sure that you will be removed swiftly, without question. I wasn't wearing a hoodie, or any other stereotypical attire that for some could justify the assumption that I did not belong there. The only contentious thing I was wearing that night was my brown skin, which suggested to both the police and the residents that I was an intruder.

This was no Trayvon Martin situation (one tragic night on an American street, a seventeen-year-old African-American youth was shot dead by a vigilante who had followed him, suspecting he was up to no good). I walked away unharmed, aside from being traumatised by the enthusiastic body search and the presumption that I was a criminal, while my polite protestations fell on deaf ears. But I did get to go home.

I arrived home significantly later than expected, and my sister wanted to know why, as she saw that I was shaking, and that I was uncharacteristically quiet and withdrawn. Dad was still at work, but I would not have told him had he been there, and neither would my sister, as we didn't want to burden him considering his delicate health.

Claire was livid and leapt to my defence against those who had unjustly antagonised me. Like Mrs Royale a decade earlier, the Lee Green police withstood a confrontation from my sister, who demanded that they take my details off their records and out of the system. After all, I had not been arrested and had never broken any laws, so why would they need my details? Just in case I started a criminal career and it saved them paperwork down the line? Safe to say I was no longer a person of interest across south-east London, and there was no sign of any conker cartel or illicit trade!

The whole episode was a firm reminder that however much time had passed, there would always be a Mrs Royale around the corner. They would become bigger and more powerful, and their dislike for those who looked like me would have devastating consequences. Fortunately, for me anyway, there would also always be 'Claires' in my corner too. Thankfully, Claire always stuck up for me. I wonder, whether the outcome of the Mrs Royale incident would have been different if my family had been black. And perhaps my details would still be in the police system to this day if Claire hadn't intervened. I try not to imagine what would have happened if I had put a foot out of place with them that evening. They were waiting for me to trip up so they would have an excuse to put me in that intimidating meat wagon and do goodness knows what behind the blackened windows. After all, I wasn't 'He's all right...he's black Tone' to them – the familiar black face that wasn't a threat and wasn't like the other black boys.

How I acted culturally was less important to them than how I looked through the curtains at 9.30 on a Friday night.

Anger aside, I finally had something in common with many of my black friends. Many were equally innocent of any crime, but the face still fit. Whatever I did, whoever I felt I was inside, I was still judged based on what I looked like on the outside. This went beyond teenage angst and growing pains. I had the blues and it was getting more difficult to see the sunshine through the dark clouds. I was at odds with my outer shell and wondered if there would ever be any satisfying accord between who I truly was and what people wanted me to be. Would I ever be accepted and even embraced, not as a curious oddity or as part of an inoffensive minority, but just as I was, with no strings attached? No 'Bounty', 'coconut' or 'chameleon'; simply me, Tony Aris?

CHAPTER FIVE

Pentecostal Preacher

'Anyone like to receive Jesus as their personal Lord and Saviour?' Harold asked the intimate crowd in a tiny backroom hall. It was a warm summer's evening in 1992, a couple months after my thirteenth birthday and bang in the middle of the school holidays.

This question caused my mind to race unexpectedly, reviewing everything I had experienced with these people over the preceding days across various events. Dawn, who had acted as my stewardess into this world and group of people, was sitting a couple of seats from me with her eyes closed, mumbling. I could tell that she was praying. I was a believer, but what I saw with these folks was something different. They actually 'spoke' with God and had a personal encounter, as if He were in the room, and front and centre of their lives. Me and 'the man upstairs' were tight, but not like this, and it intrigued me. Looking at this racially and generationally diverse bunch of people, the only thing they seemed to have in common was their love and devotion for this invisible being who was felt tangibly everywhere.

My heart raced to catch up with my mind, which had bolted off much earlier. It felt as if God, Jehovah, Jesus...whatever His name was, was talking to me and nudging me to stand at the front and make a decision to become a Christian. I had never been asked this question before and didn't know it was something people responded to, but I knew that it applied to me. I pondered what it would mean to officially become a Christian, but my arm beat me to the punch by shooting up uncontrollably, volunteering me in an instant. My arm and I had not finished discussing this, and I felt it had jumped the gun a bit.

Harold, who was the only one in the room with his eyes open, didn't miss a beat and asked me if I would join him and one other person upstairs in the prayer room. This was happening. What had I just done? My mind knew that instinct had taken over and committed me to something I must have wanted to do but was too overloaded with concerns to do anything about it consciously. I heard people thanking Jesus, and there was a loud mumbling in a funny language (which I would later learn was speaking in tongues) as I got out of the plastic chair and headed upstairs to the prayer room.

There was nothing fancy or mystical about this room with its soft cushioned chairs and smell of coffee that must have been drunk earlier that day. It was just as ordinary as what I was about to do was extraordinary. I repeated a prayer along the lines of 'Lord Jesus, I believe that You died for my sins. Come into my life as I accept You as my Lord and Saviour.' As I was saying this, I felt a wave of peace and love wash over me; a pervasive sense that my life had for ever been changed, despite there being no physical evidence. The room didn't shake and I didn't see a single angel descend, but things felt different. Harold shook my hand, and that was that. I was part of the 'God Squad'. I had not been pressurised or manipulated; it was my choice. Harold was just the midwife that night as I was reborn. He explained what being a Christian entailed and encouraged me to read the Bible, then congratulated me on joining the family of God. I was a newly born-again Christian and I was hungry.

This happened on 28th August 1992, at a little Pentecostal church on Lee High Road, south-east London. I wasn't just born again; I was a Pentecostal, part of an evangelical tradition characterised by fiery and dramatic oratory with the electricity of a power station. This version of church was very different from the Catholic Mass my father and I used to attend (once or twice a year) because it was a prerequisite for my attending the Catholic primary school, as one of the few non-Catholics enrolled. We used to fall asleep during those services, and I never understood what was going on. I believed in God, even from a tender age, and loved learning about Him and the Bible stories in school, although I lamented the fact that as a non-Catholic, I was never allowed to eat the 'bread' during school Mass. I wondered what that small wafer disc tasted like and was often tempted to grab a load from the priest and shove them into my mouth like the Cookie Monster from *Sesame Street*. Probably not appropriate when you consider it represents the literal body of Christ to Catholics. *If God loves me, then why can't I eat the wafer disc?* I thought to myself. It wasn't as if I didn't believe in Jesus or was a bad child. Issues of theology were far from my young mind, which is ironic seeing as I would spend a significant portion of my life studying the subject many years later.

The day I joined Team Jesus started off as ordinarily as any other. I said goodbye to my mum in the morning, went to school and didn't see any flashes of lightning or hear any thunderous voices on the way. My parents were not particularly religious but believed in God, and taught me to say my prayers every night before bedtime. I attended a church school, but that had very little to do with God and more to do with results and prestige, as it was the best school on our council estate. God never really came up in our family life in any significant way, but the fact that He existed, was like the sky being blue to me. I would talk to Him occasionally as a child and ask for things in an innocent way, as if He were a cosmic extension of my dad. There was no existential crisis; I'd never led a life of crime or amassed a multitude of 'sins' that required forgiveness, and at thirteen I wasn't looking for answers to the 'big questions' of life.

Dawn Brooks, a smiley, light-skinned black girl with thick-rimmed glasses, was a local girl I had shared a classroom with, and we were old friends. Towards the end of the term, as we were about to break for the summer, Dawn told me about some free events coming up on our estate.

She seemed to have her finger on the pulse much more than I did. Not having made any concrete plans, I was sold.

The first of these was a free BBQ on the field near the shopping area, one Friday night. In no time at all, a friendly, unassuming man dressed in jeans came forward from the small group serving a multitude of hungry locals and began to speak into a portable microphone. He wasn't the best speaker in the world, that was for sure, but he clearly meant every word that came out of his mouth, and that made an impact. I could tolerate boring, but even at that age I had developed an intolerance for insincerity and could smell it a mile away. There wasn't a whiff of it there.

The evening was soon over and the locals began to disperse just as quickly as the burgers and hot dogs. The team packed away and Dawn came over to invite me to yet another event. This was fast becoming a habit, and it felt a little like being asked out on a date...only without the actual romantic stuff. That would have felt icky, though, as we had known each other since we were six years old and weren't each other's type. She asked if I'd like to go to a gospel concert at Emmanuel Pentecostal Church that Saturday. I had nothing else on, so I said that of course I would. I loved gospel music, even though my only exposure to it had been in movies like *The Blues Brothers*, via the music group Sounds of Blackness and in the odd black American sitcom.

The first thing I noticed when I arrived at the church was how multi-racial and multigenerational the congregation was. This was 1992, it was heaving with diversity. This immediately spoke to me, given my unconventional background, but it would take more than a few uptempo gospel numbers expertly performed to enlist me as a signed-up member of the God Squad. I figured out that this was the overall agenda or plan of the week's events: to make fresh disciples and catch new fish in the net of the church. But even though the reason Dawn had become my new BFF was obvious to me, I had no reason to object and never felt that this came from a sinister place. People at this concert talked about finding a love in Jesus, and how it was the best thing in the world, and they that wanted to

PENTECOSTAL PREACHER | 73

share the experience with everyone. *There was nothing wrong with that*, I thought to myself.

At that time, there was a lot of negativity in the media about cults and fundamentalist religious sects gone rogue. An early 1990s storyline in Australian soap *Neighbours* followed one of the popular characters, Mark, who supposedly became a Christian after an accident and then became very extreme and borderline crazy. This reflected mainstream thinking: have your religious beliefs, but don't take them too seriously or bring them out in public. The character Mark was dating was arguably the hottest woman on TV, and he was about to marry her, but his 'crazy religious beliefs' caused him to jilt her at the altar, and he decided to become a priest instead. You couldn't have God and nice things, it seemed. According to soap lore, believing in God led to mental instability and becoming a danger to yourself and others. But these people at Emmanuel Pentecostal Church just looked happy. Besides, how could people be that bad if they were able to create great music?

The final 'date' Dawn asked me out on, with her little brother Kenton, was to her Friday night youth club, held weekly at the same church venue. Church on a Friday night? It didn't sound too appealing, considering that Sunday church during my childhood hadn't been very enjoyable. Friday night is sacred for a teenager and a few hours feel like days if it's boring. That said, compared with my childhood church experiences of my childhood, the last few events with this Pentecostal crew had been as different from what I was expecting as night was from day. One featured singing from a book in Latin with no instruments; the other used electric and acoustic guitars, a keyboard, and drums, at times singing in a strange language I couldn't understand, though the voices sounded great.

As I sat through the Friday-night-service, I felt a little bewildered. I looked around constantly, clocking the unusual sight of young people my age, younger and older, black, white and other, standing with their arms raised, singing to Jesus. Were they sure Jesus could hear them, and did it make a difference if your arms were up and your eyes closed? Some were very emotional and had their eyes closed, mumbling audibly. This was getting a little weird, and I began to wonder if I had stumbled upon a cult. I attempted to sing along as I took in everything I was witnessing, trying to make sense of it all.

The music – which was a cross between hymns and soft rock/pop fusion, so very different from the Saturday night gig – suddenly stopped, and the guy leading worship on the acoustic guitar began to make an impassioned plea to the audience of around thirty young people plus youth workers. This man was the aforementioned Harold, a tall, light-skinned black man with a medium-sized afro, glasses and outdated no-thrills trainers and jeans. He looked as if he was in his mid to late twenties and was as focused as a laser beam. He was joined by a slim white lady with medium brown hair, likely in her thirties, with warm eyes. At the front was a similar-looking lady with even longer brown hair, but younger. I would later learn that the ladies were sisters called Esther and Elizabeth respectively, and that Elizabeth and Harold were married. The talented bass player also caught my eye. He looked effortlessly cool with his neatly trimmed high-top haircut. He was black with a moustache and was noticeably senior to all of them. Trevor was his name, and he was part of the triumvirate of leadership in this youth group with Harold and Esther. There were a few other leaders, but these were the ones who stood out and played an active role on the night.

Finding this community was curiously well-timed, as it was less than a year before my mother died. My new-found faith would come in handy during this dark time, as I dealt with a world without a mother. I had never grieved before, so I never realised how deep the emotional wound would go, though I do know that having God in my life provided more than a superficial plaster. I had a deep sense of His love and comfort even though I was experiencing pain like never before. Outside my relationship with Dad, the church family was everything to me – the one place where I belonged and everything made sense.

My emotional and spiritual allegiances began to shift from the Aris family to my new-found church family. This inevitably rang alarm bells, and initially raised questions as to whether I had joined a cult. After all, I wasn't just attending the Friday night youth club, but Sundays and mid-week meetings as well. At night they might have heard me speaking in tongues from my bedroom, and the music I blasted out was not from the radio but from worship songs on my CD player. There was a whole new subculture to discover, and I was keen to explore it all: Christian bookshops, Christian rap, dance and pop music and Christian movies, all offering an alternative to the mainstream. I thrust myself into this world, learning the lingo, singing the songs and following the code. This was serious to me; not a passing fad or rebellion against my family, or a desperate attempt to be different and unique. Jesus was real, and it was as simple as that.

Maybe I took things a little too far in those early years, like burning many music CDs and a stack of vintage Marvel comic books – hundreds of issues, including *Uncanny X-Men* and *Iron Man* – on a bonfire in the church grounds, after an idea I suggested to Harold. I think he got carried away as well, because rather than talk it through with me, he ran with it and a number of the church youth brought their worldly offerings to the fire, while the others sniggered or looked aghast at what we were essentially throwing away. I think it was supposed to symbolise a rejection of negative outside influences; a sort of spiritual purge and cleansing, de-throning anything that had raised itself above the lordship of Christ. To non-believers (and to also some believers) this might sound completely bonkers and something that might be associated with hardline fundamentalists. I understand this, but to us it was like a form of radical monogamy. It was like making a commitment to one person above all and any other. It certainly didn't help to dispel the flashing red 'Tony's joined a cult' sign above my head in my friends' and family's eyes, however.

Emmanuel Pentecostal Church (EPC for short) was like nowhere I had ever been before or since. It was a social enigma; an odd but loving family with medical doctors worshipping alongside bus drivers and the unemployed; the elderly with teenagers; and the suburban with the urban. Nothing lasts for ever, and the church eventually began to buckle under the strain of its own diversity. As much as EPC tried to be like heaven, earth came crashing through too many times. As I grew older, I saw the strain and challenges within a community of very different people and cultures.

At EPC we never directly addressed race, culture or class. Those things were of the world and we were God's children. Senior Pastor Terry O'Neil, a tall old-school, white man in his sixties, had a posture and intensity that screamed fire and brimstone. He wasn't as intimidating as he seemed, away from the pulpit at least; in fact he was incredibly kind and conversational, if a little aloof. What he did struggle with was navigating the terrain of multicultural London. Ignoring the racial dynamics and complexities of the church was no different from what I was used to growing up in my household. Members of the church were just as badly equipped to deal with race issues outside the four walls of the church as I had been. Things were stirring in London, particularly in a small but significant town called Eltham near where I had grown up. This small town would become famous for all the wrong reasons.

In 1993, a young black teen named Stephen Lawrence was savagely knifed to death there by a gang of older white youths whose only motivation was racist hate. This major news event made headlines everywhere and not only inspired first national outrage, but years later led to changes across the whole Metropolitan Police Service, including amendments to their race relations policy. It was a horrific crime that hit far too close to home. I had been in that area countless times and had experienced racist insults, such as 'nigger' and 'black b*****d', shouted from cars and pubs. Once it started to get dark I would run to the bus stop like Linford Christie, leaving as quickly as possible in case I got chased.

But this was a different world from the soft padded walls of my church. You wouldn't have heard about this incident or any of these issues being addressed from our pulpit. In many ways it reminded me of my household, which had long shielded me from the harsh realities of the world and its dog-eat-dog nature. I needed to be in an environment where I could process this growing awareness of what it meant to be black in a racially turbulent London. My love for God was deep and my need to search for my identity was equally deep. I had to find a place that could reconcile both needs, or at least point me in the right direction.

It was around this time that I began visiting many 'It' churches throughout London. Churches such as the multiracial Kensington Temple in affluent Notting Hill, the dynamic Rhema Ministries in Croydon and the classically black Pentecostal New Testament Church of God (NTCOG), which was immediately next door to EPC. This was as awkward as it sounds. Visiting most other churches meant travelling to different areas, which could be done with some degree of anonymity. But there was no way to walk past my present church incognito in order to visit the church that was literally next door. For the three years I was a member of EPC, the only interaction the churches had with each other was to negotiate noise levels during services. NTCOG was very loud during its services, often interrupting our pastor's sermon at EPC, and the music could be heard all the way up the street. The NTCOG Lee branch was a lively, predominantly Jamaican congregation that was Pentecostal with a capital 'P'. That meant women wore hats and little to no make-up, men were clean-shaven, and everyone wore formal clothes to service. It was like the church in *The Blues Brothers*. EPC, which was much more reserved, rarely strayed from the traditional white sensibilities of its elders except for the occasional bit of ethnic seasoning. EPC may have been multiracial, but culturally, it was very 'English'.

I had never ventured next door before this period of searching, but it was clear to see that it had a large black congregation, as it exited service around the same time we did. The sea of big hats resembled the influx of satellite TV dishes that had begun to invade my estate. I wondered why the church was called the New Testament Church of God. Did they reject the Old Testament? All I knew was that they were loud and the congregation looked as though it were attending a wedding every week.

My understanding would broaden as 1995 came to a close. It had been a year of transition for me, having completed my GCSEs and graduated from secondary school. Turning sixteen, I felt as though I was ready to take on the world. I had informally left the Friday night youth group that summer. I say 'informally', as my sudden non-attendance was a consequence of starting a part-time job at McDonald's with my best mate Ashley. They worked me really hard on the restaurant floor, and I often had to take out the rubbish. At least loading up the rubbish-crushing machine gave me some alone time to contemplate my next move. Working at McDonald's on a Friday night gave me the perfect excuse to be absent from the group I was outgrowing. My natural tendency to question and be outspoken had caused friction between myself and Harold, whom I respected but increasingly disagreed with. He was a bit on the black-and-white spectrum perspective wise, while I liked the colours in-between. He was cautious and regimented, whereas I was inquisitive and fluid. I would always be grateful to him and to everyone there for showing me an incredible path, but I couldn't remain on the same one as before. It was tough to consider leaving my surrogate faith family, the very one I had been born into spiritually, but I had changed. The churches approach was to cushion and shelter us from the harsh world I was eager to explore and understand.

I continued to sporadically attend the dwindling Sunday services until my attendance became the odd cameo appearance. By Christmas 1995 I was conscious that I needed to start the New Year in a new spiritual home. Preferably this new home would be local, as the previous churches I had checked out were miles away and expensive to travel to on a regular basis.

I attended EPC for the New Year's Eve service, and caught up with old friends. One of them, Eska Mtungwazi, a black woman with large, soulful eyes, an infectious smile and bohemian Tracy Chapman vibes, was in attendance. This was a rare thing for her, being an in-demand, nomadic musician. I shared my plans with her and she understood. She was one of the few people who did. She remarked that after the clock struck midnight the service would be over, everyone would go home and we would be bored. The night was still young, we thought, and it dawned on us that the NTCOG was holding what it called a 'jamboree' next door. This was a praise party that went on till the early hours of New Year's Day and was a big, concert-like event. Neither of us had ever been before and we were beyond curious.

'Shall we?' Eska said, goading me with a smile.

'Yeah, why not?' I replied with a twinkle in my eye.

We were about to enter unknown territory. Though we were both black, this would be foreign ground for us. Eska was more of an artsy, hipster-like musician than one of the prim and proper, satellite-hat-wearing ladies we had seen piling in.

The New Year's Eve formal service had not quite finished when we entered, and the sermon was still in full swing. We were ushered into seats on the balcony, and I was struck by just how black the congregation was. Not a single white person in sight. The second thing that struck me was how the music dominated everything. The preacher was still in the pulpit, yet the music was playing. That would never have happened with Pastor O'Neil. He went up to the pulpit and the music stopped, no exception. Here, preacher and musicians were in sync. Such was the level of skill that the musicians seemed like session players for some big artist. It was an amazing night of music, humour and self-expression, with a distinct Caribbean flavour. So this was what it was like to be in a black church! My mind processed it all, my head bopping and body swaying rhythmically in sync with the choir. It was around this point that I decided I was going to be there for the next Sunday morning meeting, which just happened to be on New Year's Day, the very next morning.

I was drawn to the 'blackness' of this church as much as I had been attracted to the diversity of EPC three years previously. The fact that this church was not ashamed to express both its spirituality and its culture was liberating and empowering for me as a sixteen-year-old exploring his identity. It felt as though God was not just in the house but raising the roof off the walls. Unlike the more conservative crowd at EPC, people at NTCOG would regularly get 'swept away by the Spirit', which gave the appearance of drunkenness, with people either falling over or running around the sanctuary.

The master of proceedings was a middle-aged man of a light brown complexion, tall and portly with thick-rimmed glasses, wearing a clergy collar and suit. His name was Reverend Louie McLeod and he was seemingly responsible for this branch of a church network that I would learn spanned the country and was part of an even bigger denomination spread across the world with its headquarters in Cleveland, Tennessee.

Revd McLeod addressed the large crowd with a strong, melodic tone that reminded me of the old footage of Dr Martin Luther King Jnr I had seen in history class at school. His sermon would gradually rise till it reached a crescendo of rhythmic chanting, accompanied by an excited pianist stabbing the piano keys in time when the preacher took a large intake of breath. They call this 'whooping and hollering' in black preacher circles. Originating in the United States, it is as much a trademark as the gospel choirs in oversized gowns clapping left to right. I later learned that this tradition of church gave rise to artists like James Brown, Jackie Wilson and indirectly even Michael Jackson.

For me, this style of church was motivational and uplifting. The person speaking from the pulpit looked like me, and as a black person was not relegated to the musicians' corner or leading worship. I needed to be in an environment that could accept me for the person I was becoming and help me process my identity issues, and when the service ended I knew in my heart that my search was over. There was only one problem. Couldn't this new spiritual home be a little bit further down the street from the one I had just left behind? This was beyond awkward, as I didn't want to offend anyone. I felt as though I was betraying people who were dear to me, who had loved me and introduced me to Jesus. The problem was, they couldn't prepare me for my future and the man I was becoming. I was convinced that only this step forward would take me in that direction.

What better way to start a new year than a fresh start? I thought, and before long I was fast making new friends. The first of these met me at the door: a light-skinned, muscular usher called Julian. He looked a couple of years older than me and was friendly and inviting, with a trademark handshake that almost crushed my hand. Then there was a host of other young men who were much more streetwise than I was used to. In fact, it was this bunch of young men – Julian, Nicky, Paul, Patrick, Rico, Byron, Danny and Alan, who had become Christians and started coming to the church themselves – that sealed the deal for me. They were on fire and also far from sheltered, each having experienced the other side of life in urban London, ranging from rolling with gangs to womanising and fast living. They were as zealous as I was, but with more pre-Christian lived experience and a taste of street life that I could only have imagined. I became the young tag-along; a role I had perfected. I was always the youngest of any pack, as I was drawn to more mature groups, likely due to growing up in a household of adults.

I loved these guys and it was the highlight of my week when we got together midweek at church for the young men's meeting led by Andrew Simpson – a perfect mix of laughter, banter and spiritual sharing through each man's personal experience and perspective. This group steadily grew and grew to the point where the other departments started to get antsy and jealous, as the explosion of growth and vibrancy had not spread across the rest of the church. These young men were used to getting their hands dirty and taking part, and were not content to sit quietly in a corner. Men sat on one side of the church and ladies on the other, with young people on the balcony or outside chatting. It was like some form of segregation. Some of the young men tried to mix things up a bit and got seriously reprimanded. A common complaint was that they hadn't learned how this church worked yet and their street shenanigans were not welcome in the 'house of God'.

One brother who ruffled feathers was called Rico. Extremely popular, Rico was a bald-headed, dark-skinned, tall, athletically built man. All the women seemed to fawn over him, and many brothers secretly felt intimidated around him. Most importantly, he was a straight talker and a leader through and through. Having been involved in gang life he had the respect of the street, seemingly knowing everyone. He had a deep, pensive thought life that made him a kind of urban philosopher. He took his newfound faith very seriously and devoured Scripture like a hungry man, constantly asking questions and contemplating truth. Most of the time his questions were seen as an inconvenience, as he had no interest in following the script for its own sake. He would innocently ask the elders the most profound and challenging questions. Many times they did not have an answer but were too proud to admit it, and they felt undermined when Rico bluntly pointed this out. I remember cringing countless times when this happened. Deep down I and others enjoyed the drama, as he often said what the rest of us were thinking. Rico regularly cut my hair at his flat, and during this ritual we would chat, so we became good friends.

My heart broke after one such episode of conflict between the wider church and the young men. As much as Andrew, leader of the young men's group, tried to defend and cover us, the episode resulted in a rift. Being the hothead he was, Rico, left the church in protest, labelling the powers that be hypocrites and 'without love', which was a big issue for him. We kept in touch and a few of us attempted to persuade him to return but he found a new spiritual family that had the 'love' he felt was sorely lacking at NTCOG. According to Rico, these people who had recruited him on the street were like family. They called each other constantly, spent time together throughout the week and were all about intimacy. The problem with this 'loving' family was it turned out to be a pretty aggressive cult that systematically targeted people and take over their lives, while cutting them off from their friends and loved ones. This inevitably happened between our band of brothers and Rico. It went on for months, until we finally heard that he had broken free of this nefarious 'family' and given up the whole quest for God completely. This was my first taste of losing a brother in the spiritual sense, and I learned that faith journeys don't all have happy, enlightening endings.

The truth is that NTCOG Lee was neither a 'den of hypocrites and vipers' nor 'heaven on earth'. It was just a regular, flawed church filled with people from different walks of life, with different personalities and temperaments, trying their best to find spiritual direction and solace in the teachings of Christianity. This was good enough for me, as the pros far outweighed the cons, and the passion and fire of the place filled me with excitement and a sense of being on a mission. Especially given that so many of my contemporaries had left the church next door, and the fire there had seemingly been snuffed out.

A few months after joining the church, which was temporarily being led by Revd McLeod, I met the senior pastor of the congregation, who had been on extended leave in Jamaica. Enter Pastor Ulpian Simpson, a tan-skinned, grey-haired man in his fifties, with a small moustache and round face, who had a friendly but firm aura around him. He was welcomed back like a returning king, and it was pretty obvious that he was the one at the top of this food chain. Not that he seemed bossy or lorded it over people, but he had a quiet confidence that exuded from him. He was very different from my previous pastor, Terry O'Neil, besides the obvious point of one being white and the other black. They were both passionate in their own ways, but whereas Pastor O'Neil had seemed untouchable and aloof, Pastor Simpson was more of an everyman who didn't take himself too seriously.

I spent many afternoons with Pastor Simpson, seeing him as a father figure of sorts, as his office was always open, and he appreciated people who were zealous about the Lord and serving the church. I soon rose up the ranks, seizing any opportunity to get involved. I was there 24/7; at midweek meetings and morning prayer sessions in the week during the holidays. I practically lived at 370 Lee High Road. I asked Pastor Simpson a million questions about ministry and church, and perhaps he saw something in me that I hadn't even noticed myself. These chats evolved over the years and I had my first shot at preaching during the men's ministry meeting. It went so well I graduated to giving a brief message during the main Sunday service, then became a Sunday school teacher. It snowballed from there. The firm foundation I had been given at EPC made me stand out, and the fruit of it was increasing responsibilities being handed to me.

Another perk of being around Pastor Simpson was that if he liked someone, he looked after them. Fortunately, I was never in a position to find out what happened if he didn't like someone. He was always good to me, especially during our district church conventions – weekend-long services with a guest preacher, often from Jamaica, bringing our multiple congregations under one roof as the mother church. On the Sunday hot food would be served during the break. This food was an epic Caribbean dream: chicken and rice, curried goat, ackee-and-saltfish with plantain and dumpling. The memory of it causes my mouth to salivate even now.

When you talk about friends in high places you couldn't get a friend higher than the senior pastor. Whenever he saw me in the hall, he would tell me to fill my plate up and let the kitchen staff, the mothers of the church, know that they should take care of me, resulting in me receiving a plate of food fit for a king. I could see the eyes on me, or rather on my overflowing plate, as my hands juggled to prevent any food spillage. But who says favour is fair? I didn't have this type of food to go home to, so this was a treat.

I was far younger than the pastor's younger children, including Andrew, who not only led the young men's fellowship but was also the chief music director and gospel choir director. Pastor Simpson had an eye for spotting young talent in the sense of potential ministers, and I had caught his attention. He encouraged me along the way, but was also of two minds. He had been badly burned before, financing and promoting young people into church ministry, only to have their personal failings cause them to quit or provoke controversy, which was a great disappointment and embarrassment. One such situation had happened just before I came to the church, and the wound was still so sore that it was mentioned whenever the subject of supporting people in ministry came up. *I won't let you down*, I thought. *I'm different. I have the fire of God inside me, and I won't be distracted from the mission.* At this time in my life, it was less about pride and hubris and more about naivety. I genuinely only wanted to take my love of Jesus any and everywhere.

The day came one afternoon in Pastor Simpson's office when our casual chats about me going into ministry became serious and he asked me outright if I wanted to become a minister. This was like Obi-Wan Kenobi asking Luke Skywalker if he wished to become a Jedi. *Where do I sign?* I thought to myself in that small office. My eyes caught the sight of framed ministerial certificates and photographs of the pastor in clerical robes and the bookshelf full of Bibles and commentaries. Maybe I'd have an office like this someday, lead a congregation of more than five hundred people who will hang on my words from Mount Sinai...or Lee. This was the call to adventure I had been waiting for.

The more I grew in my faith, the more I felt a natural tug to preach and teach the gospel, and to inspire people to have a relationship with God. I wasn't the son of a preacher man, but this life style was calling out to me. Pastor Simpson told me about one of our movement's national treasures: a man by the name of Joel Edwards, now deceased, who was NTCOG clergy but also the head of a wider, predominantly white, Christian organisation called the Evangelical Alliance. *That's a mouthful*, I thought to myself as Pastor Simpson went on to inform me that NTCOG no longer had its own training facility, but that Revd Edwards had attended the leading mainstream evangelical seminary in the country many years earlier and might be able to tell me more about it. This wasn't quite the taking-my-father's-lightsaber moment I had been expecting, but it would do. A simple phone call would edge me that much closer to what seemed to be like my inevitable destiny.

I will always be grateful for the spiritual home NTCOG Lee gave me. By 1998, having had only been there a couple of years, I was already being embraced as an up-and-coming minister and was looking to be sponsored to go to Bible college – something that many had waited years for. Other hopefuls looked at me with bewildered eyes, wondering what made me so special. As I said earlier, favour is rarely fair, but this was for a life of servitude, not an all-expenses-paid education at Oxford or Cambridge.

Dad was initially unimpressed by all this. He was proud of me, but he had always envisioned me as a great artist or fulfilling my childhood dream of working for Walt Disney Animation Studios, or something equally creative. Becoming an ordained minister had not been on the horizon, though he respected the faith, he was disappointed that I was seemingly wasting the natural talents he had championed my whole life. I will never forget the times when Dad, Claire and my brother Martin's partner Maggie and her kids would come to my church at my invite, to hear me preach, only for 'the Spirit' to take over the service. This convenient occurrence was code for the musicians, chiefly the drummer when he got wind that Pastor Simpson wasn't preaching, to take over the service with music, as if it were their own personal concert. This got everybody excited – except me, who had been preparing to preach all week, and of course my family, who couldn't comprehend the idea of 'the Spirit' taking control of the service and wouldn't get to hear me preach after all. This happened on more than one occasion. No one has more power in a black church during the service, besides the pastor, than the musicians. King of all is the drummer; the Pied Piper at any black Pentecostal gathering.

Still, it was heart-warming to see my white family members swaying and clapping, having the time of their lives, to the vibrant gospel music. They played along when asked to introduce themselves and say who had invited them, although it was obvious as most people knew my background and therefore the association. Besides, it was beyond rare to see white faces in this congregation. It was a complete collision of cultures, but in a harmonious and sweet way; my church being nothing but warm and inviting to them and my family talking excitedly about the exuberant musical and cultural experience they had just had. I took it for granted how normal this church scenario was for me and how utterly alien it was for them; how unusual it would be for them to be in the minority racially and culturally in any situation. The fact that they didn't care, because they were there for me, touched my heart.

* * *

By the summer of 1998 I was all set to leave both camps behind for an adventure into the unknown. I had been working at Austin Reed, an old-school, formal-wear establishment in London like the fictitious Grace Brothers in the sitcom *Are You Being Served?*. My friend Winston Dubidad and I had applied together and successfully bagged jobs there, working tirelessly, under the crack of a whip, to fund our summer plans. It had been arranged that I would start Bible college in October, after a long conversation with Revd Joel Edwards and successfully getting past the interview stage.

I'm glad I went on holiday before starting, giving myself one last moment of carefreeness before the intense theological study. Rather than going to Ibiza or Disney World, my heart was set on going to the Holy Land, Israel. It was beyond surreal walking around places I had read about and knew existed. Actually being there felt like stepping into the pages of a book or inside a favourite movie. The intense heat, exotic smells and scenery were intoxicating. The only other foreign holiday I had experienced was Florida, which had been as artificial and constructed as Israel was ancient and authentic. The hotels were lavish and beautiful, just one of the perks of going on this package trip with members of my church.

The expedition was led and organised by Paul Pryce and Bishop Eric Brown, soon to be leader of the whole NTCOG movement. Both had made multiple trips to the Holy Land before and ensured we got our money's worth, including being baptised in the River Jordan, like in biblical days. I had been baptised before in less exotic Lee, so this was purely ceremonial, but a golden opportunity.

Israel was the most prescriptive place I'd ever been to, with a strict culture. One night, while having dinner in one of the five-star-hotel restaurants, I was helping myself to a buffet of meat with a little veg when the dessert table in the other room caught my gaze like something shiny to a magpie. My body launched itself in that same direction, where the most amazing ice-cream sundae stood before me. After taking it hostage and preparing to return to the dining room to add it to my meal, I was approached by a waiter with the urgency of an action movie hero. What was his problem? It wasn't as if I had forgotten to pay, as it was part of our upfront hotel expenses, so I wondered what he was calling out to me for. *Here we go again*, I thought. I tried not to go to the place I had been to many times before in my mind. *Is it because I'm...?*

I soon discovered just how seriously the Jewish people take their customs. Besides the lifts being on automatic during the Sabbath so no one had to touch the buttons, the dietary law of not mixing meat with dairy had to be upheld. This had completely escaped my mind, resulting in my having to eat my dripping ice-cream dessert before my main meal in the other room. Having grown up in largely secular England, this dedication to religious tradition really was an eye-opener, and perhaps a fitting precursor to my Bible college introduction, which would also be a baptism of fire.

Speaking of fiery baptisms, Israel was the location of one of the most profound and personal supernatural experiences I've ever had. Besides busting my gut in a clothes store that summer to earn some holiday cash, I had also spent a lot of carpet time praying and meditating in order to hear from God. This wasn't unusual for me, but what hit me for six was the stream of words that came to my mind and spirit on that carpet. I believe God was talking to me; giving me instruction about the future and reassuring me that I was making the right decision. Does that sound crazy? Some people thought I was loco enough for not pursuing a degree in art or going to drama school. They said I would never make a living as a professional 'God-botherer'. Even some Christians thought as much. But if I was ever in two minds before this encounter on my living room floor, I wasn't afterwards. I felt a surge of power flow through me and clear words forming in my mind.

Fast-forward several weeks and I was inside a hotel lobby in Israel. A group of Americans had just arrived, checking in with their usual blend of bold confidence. Apparently, renowned TV healing evangelist Benny Hinn was in town, and these guests were somehow connected to him. I looked over, curious to see this group gathered around with suitcases, when one particular man locked eyes with me and started walking towards me. He as a black man standing among a predominantly white group, so I assumed it was due to the secret connection minorities have in such situations that was drawing him my way. He reached out his hand for a handshake, and I politely took it. Then, within seconds of introducing himself, he started to speak in tongues. The tongues in no way bothered me. After all, I was a Pentecostal and spoke in tongues myself. But it seemed a weird thing for a stranger to do, and took me by complete surprise.

As I awkwardly kept hold of his firm handshake, my eyes searching for clues as to where this was going, he started to speak in English with an American twang. The words 'I see an image of you praying on the floor, crying out to God...that you are called to go to Bible college in the coming weeks...and that you heard His voice correctly' came out of his mouth. My own mouth was rendered speechless, jaw dangling on the floor. This random American had just read out my personal mail in front of me, having just that moment met me. He said some other things that will remain private, but to say that his prophetic message was accurate, would be an understatement and mind-blowing. I stood like a deer in headlights during the subsequent small talk. It went in one ear and out of the other while I continued to process his prophetic message. We parted ways then, but his words stuck with me. The realisation that God had actually observed my life and movements gave me comfort that I wasn't going crazy, and that the journey I was embarking on was neither a big mistake nor a colossal waste of time.

* * *

I was heading into the unknown of Bible college all alone. I had heard rumours that it was the type of place where you went in believing one thing and came out believing another – if anything at all. As much as I was supported in this endeavour by my local church, financially and otherwise, there was a not-so-subtle sense that studying theology and getting 'filled up with head knowledge' was a waste.

It initially felt a bit like being drafted into the army while still going through the application process. I had been called to interview in front of two lecturers, who quizzed me on a number of things in the style of 'good cop, bad cop' to see if I was made of the stuff they were looking for. The tag team of inquisitors consisted of a tall man with moustache, a side crop of wild, wiry, auburn hair and a stern face, who looked like a cross between an eccentric professor and a Socialist revolutionary. He was one of the lecturers at London Bible College and his name was Meic Pearse. He had a stern gaze, but with a twinkle that suggested he was being deliberately provocative and relished the proverbial 'bad cop' role assigned to him. His accomplice, the 'good cop', was a silver-haired lady with a kind face and a northern accent delivered in a softer, more relaxed fashion. She was also part of the faculty and her name was Mary Evans. They must have liked my answers, because I passed the test and ended up being taught by both.

This was a foreign world I was entering into; a kind of Hogwarts and *X-Men* School for Gifted Young People, only for Christians exploring their faith and ministry potential. To my delight, I found that I would not be entering this strange world of theology and Evangelicalism alone after all. An old acquaintance from three years earlier was also enlisted to

Christian Hogwarts. His name was Wayne Brown, and unlike myself he was a born and bred son of NTCOG; the actual son of Bishop Eric Brown, with whom I had just been to Israel. His father was a pretty big deal in NTCOG, and fitting the stereotype, this pastor's kid had been a bit of a wild child. Rebellious and headstrong, Wayne's enrolment was no doubt a part of his rehabilitation as much as a 'call from God'. Wayne was caramel brown with a super-slim, athletic build (read 'a few sandwiches short' compared to my 'too many sandwiches'). He was handsome and charismatic.

After a phone call confirming the rumour that we were heading to the same boot camp, we met outside Kentucky Fried Chicken in Catford, where we chatted and shared our thoughts and feelings. The KFC was OK, the chat was much better and the feeling of having a comrade on this adventure was an exciting prospect. We made a pact during that late summer of 1998 that we would stick together and be a support system for each other, because we would be in a double minority: black men in a very white institution and Pentecostals in predominantly Anglican and Baptist territory. We would be the only black Pentecostal folk many of our peers would have crossed paths with, so it would be refreshing to have someone to trade stories with at the end of the day after going under the microscope.

That first night on campus was rough. Wayne and I had agreed to be room-mates, and to our surprise we found ourselves in a tiny room with a musty smell. This made the worst first impression possible, given that I had genuine OCD tendencies. And then I discovered that the smell led to my new bed, which had a huge wet patch on it from a leak in the roof. I was deflated and irritable, while Wayne was in hysterics – a dynamic that would become typical between us. He was effortlessly laid-back whilst I was uptight and serious, although this could sometimes be diffused by a silly comment or face from Wayne the Jester. We were like an odd couple; loyal keepers of each other's secrets and brothers going through a journey of self-discovery as we matured into our twenties. Wayne was two years older than me, but I was often mistaken for the older brother. I had always wanted a brother-brother. Not an older person called 'brother' living in the same house, our lives rarely interacting, but a playmate and a confidant. Wayne had actual brothers, so the novelty was lost on him, whereas for me it was a new experience to bunk as though we were having a daily sleepover.

Many times I was woken in the early morning or prevented from sleeping due to Wayne practising his 'runs' – vocal exercises that imitated R&B singers like Brian McKnight and Frank McComb – in time to very loud music blasting from the CD player. I loved the music, but not when I was trying to sleep or unwind from a mind-numbing day of intense theology classes. I could never sleep with the light on and Wayne would always keep it on. It's a wonder we didn't throttle each other, such was the difference between us. But I think that's what made it work for the best part of three years. That pokey, damp-smelling box room in an old converted mansion on the campus grounds in leafy Northwood, just outside of London, was home.

There was practically nothing in the area except for the train station, a Chinese takeaway and an Indian restaurant, and of course the Silver Moon pub, aka the Second Campus of London Bible College. Many a deep existential conversation and theological debate was had in this pub over a pint. Regularly frequented by the students, it was like luring a couple of vampires into daylight when we were first invited, such was our piety. As a couple of Pentecostal boys, we had been taught that we should not find ourselves in such places as bars, clubs and public houses. For a time, we felt spiritually superior to our peers for this very reason. In truth, I was worried about being seen in such a place and it getting back to the church that was sponsoring me.

This stance, along with a few others, softened over time. We went from staunchly defending our theological and cultural positions to jettisoning them, and then finally finding a compromise between what we knew and what we came to know. Our peers eventually became friends and many went on to do big things in Christian circles, such as brash football fanatic Gavin Calver, who now leads the same Evangelical Alliance that both Joel Edwards and Calver's father previously did.

One of the closest friends we made during our first few days there was a blond-haired, blue-eyed guy named Luke Harding. I emphasise the 'blue-eyed' as he epitomised the trope of a young man exploring the world for the first time, all wide-eyed and excitable. He'd had quite a sheltered upbringing, with Christian missionary parents, but, like Wayne, he had been a bit of a naughty boy – or at least wanted to be – and was on a journey of being straightened out at Bible boot camp. Luke was often caught between the extremes of Wayne's flirtation with danger and being a bit rebellious, and my strait-laced piety – much like the old cartoons showing a demon and an angel on opposing shoulders.

We went on many adventures together outside the safe and sanitised bounds of Bible college. We often slipped out at night to far-out Watford, full of bars and nightclubs that lured us in, offering an antidote to the environment we sometimes felt a bit suffocated by. It was never a fall from grace, more of a flirtation with fire. Luke had a constant mischievous twinkle in his eye, as though he was always up to something, accompanied by a nervous laugh. He would have been a useless poker player, but he had a heart of gold and became like a brother to us. He would pretend to be useless at pool in the recreation room, however, but soon proved to be a hustler, fooling me time and time again, though thankfully there was never any money involved. He truly was a real-life Cool Hand Luke. We became an inseparable trio for most of the first year, until Luke being a Bible college student was too much for him and abandoned ship at the close of the final term. We missed him, but kept in touch, such was the deep bond established during that season.

We were young men in our early twenties, looking to change the world. At the same time, we were still learning about said world, or rather navigating between very different worlds. The world of LBC was completely different from the world of NTCOG, both aesthetically and in how they each did Christianity. When I returned to my home church, I had to hide away the things I was learning for fear of being labelled a heretic, and to borrow a phrase from *Ghostbusters* I couldn't possibly imagine, crossing the streams.

Naturally, at the age of twenty I was thinking about finding a girl-friend. Many people paired off at the place often nicknamed London Bridal College due to the number of couples starting out there and ending up married. It made sense, as it was a place filled with wannabe world-changers meeting like-minded people. For me, though, as much as the minds may have been alike, I was always aware that the world outside campus was completely different. Meeting someone there and translating that relationship into the other world would be tricky. I was mature enough to realise that feelings weren't enough. Perhaps having always been aware that I was a fish out of water made me sensitive to how diffi-cult it would be for someone who had never lived that life to be my girl-friend.

Every time I went back to Lee it felt as if I was a Vietnam veteran like John Rambo; a young soldier sent off to war fighting for his people, only to be misunderstood and regarded with suspicion when he returned. The odd shady comment was made from the pulpit about 'not having a PhD in Theology but a PhD in the Holy Ghost', suggesting the importance of spiritual power over head knowledge. This was confusing to me, as they were the ones who had sent me to this place of learning. *So why would they draw first blood?* If I felt isolated and alienated from the world I had come from due to this evolutionary process at college, then how much more isolated would a person I brought from my new world into the old one feel? Especially if she happened to be a white girl. No, dating and all that stuff would have to wait for a while. Maybe I would meet someone in the wider denomination or at Wayne's church, which I occasionally visited when I couldn't bring myself to make the pilgrimage back to south Lon-don at weekends.

Led by his father, Wayne's church was in Wood Green, north London, and though not exactly close to campus, it was certainly much closer than Lee. Music was a big deal at Wood Green, home to the highly regarded Wood Green Gospel Choir. The choir was known among many circles in London, with lead singers such as the legendary Michelle Dixon, who would become one of my closest friends in the church and spawned Highest Praise, the youth choir founded and run by Wayne. Of course, Wayne was my 'in' into Highest Praise. He knew I could carry a note, but more importantly he knew that as much as I loved music, I was drawn to something else entirely. I had flirted with the idea of joining the choir for around a year on and off, occasionally helping to fill in the sparse tenor section, but juggling full-time membership with the rigours of theological studies and travelling across town caused me to hit the brakes on this activity.

Until one spring day in the year 2000, that was, when my eye was captivated by a familiar sight during a Sunday morning service. *Hey, is that...It can't be. No. But it is,* I thought to myself as my mind raced back a few months to the beginning of the year and a brief encounter in Walthamstow, east London. Amid a sea of choir gowns, the spotlight shone brightly on one gowned individual. Was this my friend Darren's date singing on the platform in front of me – the one who had been on his arm at the Vanessa Bell Armstrong concert and taken my breath away?

As I recalled the night and scrutinised the face of the young woman singing on the platform, my mind acted like a police profiling system, frantically matching faces. The realisation came that they were indeed one and the same. I had no idea that she attended Wood Green or was part of NTCOG. More significantly, I didn't know whether she was single, still seeing my casual friend Darren, or anyone else for that matter. *What were the chances?* I thought to myself.

The song and the service ended, and I made a beeline to say hello and re-introduce myself. 'My name's Jahlene,'she replied. I had never heard that name before we first met in January; it sounded rather exotic, almost

French. It was far more interesting than my own name, Tony. Jahlene seemed younger than I remembered, still in her late teens compared to my almost twenty-one years, though perhaps due to my upbringing the age gap seemed larger. She certainly was beautiful, possessing a warm aura around her.

After some small talk - where I slyly established that she and Darren wasn't in a relationship, having only been on a blind date - I thought that maybe I was a bit too old and square for her. However, like a moth to a flame, I was drawn to her. Over the following weeks, we would casually talk after church services and choir rehearsals. Of course, she was a member of Highest Praise – and the spark to my renewed interest in choral singing all of a sudden.

CHAPTER SIX

Rib-Eyed

Jahlene had many potential suitors and I wasn't oblivious to this, or to the long shot it was that she would be interested in me. Unlike the more mature women in the church who were looking to settle down, she was eighteen and had plenty of time as well as options. There had been no lightning bolt for me either, yet I found the attraction energising and a great distraction from the mundaneness of seminary. I didn't invest too much in the friendship, but I did awkwardly ask for her phone number one Sunday after church.

Time seemed to slow right down as I watched her response like a hawk, focusing on every micro-movement of her body language before the sound from her mouth hit the atmosphere. What would I do if she said no? *Too late*, I thought, as the request had already left the stable like a wild horse.

'Sure, it's 077...' she slowly dictated, to my complete surprise, as I frantically pressed the raised keys of my flip phone, all stubby fingertips while trying to play it cool. Give me a pulpit from which to preach a sermon and I was as cool as a cucumber. Put me in front of a lady I liked and I was a shy, stammering idiot, all self-conscious and tongue-tied.

Giving me her phone number wasn't exactly a pledge of undying love, as I would soon find out. After a couple of laborious but brief chats on the phone, we arranged a date at a Pizza Hut in Walthamstow. I say 'date', as that's what it was in my mind, but it became clear that to Jahlene it was more about passing some time. Jahlene turned out to be an introvert. In Myers-Briggs language an ISFP to my ENFJ, which meant that I did the lion's share of the talking.

In spite of the absence of fireworks and flying cherubs playing harps, however, I had this strange notion flash through my mind and spirit that, unlikely as it seemed, I was sitting opposite my future wife. All this was going on as I tried to discreetly guzzle down a slice of pepperoni pizza. It was eerily similar to the flash I'd had in my living room back in the summer of 1998 – the Spider-Man's spider sense that I experienced just before my trip to Israel nearly two years previously. It couldn't have been a more unlikely notion, as this young lady sitting across from me looked bored out of her skull, and I felt I was talking into the vacuum of space. I think it was here that I learned the profound difference between prophetic promptings and what you see with your eyes and experience in real time. It would certainly need faith bigger than a mustard seed to believe that this 'date' would spawn a round two, let alone a relationship transitioning into marriage.

The evening ended and we said goodbye. I followed up with a phone call, which confirmed what I had suspected. She wasn't interested. Disappointment was a given, but I wasn't completely deterred. A quiet confidence bubbled up inside me, assuring me that if what I believed would happen was right, it *would* happen. No harm, no foul, we would simply become friends and make each other laugh on the phone. Jahlene was considerably more conversational in phone-land than in person, and she was funny, with a cheeky personality.

Wayne found this all very amusing and would tease me endlessly about the whole thing. He was used to my many crushes and how I got a little cranky and weird about romantic issues due to my melodramatic nature.

It turned out Jahlene and I had a lot more in common than we realised. We had both been brought up by surrogate parents, in her case by her paternal grandparents, both of us feeling as though no one really 'got' us.

We became genuine friends; I would even advise her on personal things, including romantic issues, such was the nature of the friendship. Over the months, a deep bond began to thread itself like a spider's web, subconsciously and organically. What had started as a fun distraction from the heavy cerebral study of theology at college became something more serious, whether I realised it or not.

* * *

After returning from a missionary trip to New York in the summer of 2000 with Ascension Trust, I had a catch-up phone call with Jahlene, during which she hit me with a full disclosure. She was interested in a relationship after all. Though I played it cool, the feeling was mutual. By this point Jahlene had gone back to her home town, Leicester, a hundred miles from London. It might as well have been on the edge of space considering how far and expensive a journey it was for this hard-up student to get there. She had been studying in London and staying with her aunt and uncle, who were prominent members of the Wood Green church. London can be a pretty intense city with so much going on, as in any major city of the world, and it got a bit much for a girl from a much smaller city. Her return to Leicester meant that our developing relationship had to be conducted through the written pages of letters and expensive phone calls, with bills mounting up during those early weeks and months.

It was a day trip from London to Leicester after that catch-up phone call that officially kick-started our relationship. Those coach trips were torturous. They amounted to almost four hours on the road, with just about the same amount of time actually spent together in Leicester before I had to jump back on the coach. Jahlene lived with her elderly grandparents, Mr and Mrs Wint, or Brother and Mother Wint, to use their church titles. There was no way I could go to their town and not report to them.

The first time I met them they were delightful, but very intimidating, in the sense that they were very old-school and close to sixty years our senior. They were from a completely different generation, one that couldn't understand the concept of a young man visiting a young woman without any romantic motivation. My first visit coincided with her nineteenth birthday, so there was a home-made cake at the house, lovingly prepared by her grandmother. The Wints were curious about me, clearly feeling me out. My ace in the hole was that I was a pastor-in-training. This gave me automatic brownie points, especially as Mother Wint had studied theology and Brother Wint was a faithful deacon in their church. It helped even more that they were long-time members of NTCOG, so my being part of the church plus a trainee pastor was the equivalent of a golden halo. At the very least it gave me the benefit of the doubt in their eyes. Mother Wint was very chatty and openly inquisitive, quoting scripture like bullets, eyes focused, scanning me like an x-ray machine. This was OK with me, as I'd had plenty of experience conversing with the many elderly mothers at my church, so had come prepared.

Jahlene was even quieter than usual, and Brother Wint sat in his chair humming to himself throughout. Until suddenly and randomly out of nowhere, while I had a mouthful of cake and was busy fielding questions from Mother Wint, Brother Wint spoke. He fired a question at me that cut the air like a machete: 'So...what are your intentions with my daughter?' There was no thinly veiled aggression behind the question, though I could tell that was firmly meant and demanded an answer. I had to respect that this was his house and his granddaughter/daughter, whose interests he was firmly looking out for.

Totally blindsided by the sudden forthrightness, and unexpectedly put on the spot, I attempted a diplomatic response. 'Ahhh...me and Jahlene are just good friends.' Again, this was factually true and as much as I felt comfortable disclosing at this point, in the most uncomfortable scenario to date.

It was received with a smile and a feeling for me that I had got off lightly. 'OK, Tone,' came the reply of the patriarch from his chair. I pondered the question and my reply all evening and the flash image of Jahlene going bright red, which was easy to spot given her much fairer complexion than everyone else's in the room. Time had stood still for that moment then suddenly raced by quickly, and before I knew it I was saying my goodbyes to her grandparents, and Jahlene was seeing me off to the coach back to London. We spoke and after going back and forth over what I had said in the house earlier, we rebranded the status of our relationship to 'going out', as if it were a Facebook update. With a few simple words and a sly kiss, we were a couple.

No one had told me how difficult a long-distance relationship can be and that speaking endlessly on the phone actually doesn't make it any better. It was the equivalent of constantly smelling hot food that triggers your appetite but you can't eat anything. For once I had something else occupying my head space other than the big questions in life and matters of the spirit. This was all new to me. Wayne was the one who always had romantic issues and queues of interested females. On the surface I had been shunning such things, focusing on our higher calling while secretly wishing I was in his position.

Being in this relationship was great, besides the distance and the growing pains of coming from different worlds. I did worry about what would happen if this relationship became known. Not that we were doing anything wrong, but the words of Bishop Simpson swirled in my head: 'Don't mess up.' One wrong move and my career would be over before it had begun. I was marked and identified as a future minister in my local church in front of hundreds of people and known within the wider denomination, all while under the tender age of twenty-one. I may have been a man with a calling, but I was still a very young man; mature but with a lot of growing up still to do. In many ways myself and Wayne being put forward for ministry at such a young age was deemed the role of a dice.

Wayne and I were joined by another young man from NTCOG during our last year of studies, bringing our status as a duo back to a trio. Reverend Otis Wilks was an even more serious and pious guy than me, making me the one in the middle between the laid-back jokester Wayne and the statesmanlike Otis. He had already studied at a German seminary before joining us and had also obtained his minister credentials. A caramel-complexioned black man with a sea of freckles, Otis was a walking A–Z of ecclesiastical knowledge and formality; the ultimate clergy in training. He also looked a little like the actor Laurence Fishburne.

The fact that we were all under the age of twenty-five was significant, as the average age of ministers with our denomination was forty-five, so we were an anomaly at this time, and in many ways a risky experiment that some may have been waiting to blow up in our faces. To put things in to perspective, our church movement was one in which grown men and women in their thirties with children and high-flying jobs were still considered part of the youth department. How we ended up being recognised and put forward for ministry in light of this I have no idea, and can only presume to have been the unstoppable will of God.

The trade-off was a huge burden of expectation upon us, with every move we made potentially under scrutiny. Just as well there was no CCTV footage leaked from the Silver Moon pub; we did nothing wrong, and didn't even drink, but just being near that building would have condemned us in some of our members' eyes. Imagine what would have run through the minds of such folk if they had known that one of us had a girlfriend. I'm not talking about secret rendezvous or inappropriate behaviour. Just the fact that someone was in a relationship while being clergy in training could be a major PR problem with the NTCOG. To be fair, it was more an issue within our church culture than a formal, organisation-wide issue. Marriage was seen as a good thing, and actually required of a pastor was one of the many expectations that came with the job. Perhaps your mind has jumped to the obvious question of how someone could be expected to marry someone else without first having a girlfriend or boyfriend. Who told you to bring logic to the party? That sounds far too sensible for this situation. No one discussed the transition process; in particular how young ministers were supposed to conduct themselves publicly in a romantic relationship, as romantic things were never discussed in church for the pre-wedded and only, occasionally for the post-wedded. Don't even bring up the 'S' word unless you mean 'sanctification'. Then you can continue as you were.

In some ways it was easier that Jahlene was a hundred miles away, as it lessened the chances of us being seen together. The odd times when she came to London or I went to Leicester and we were 'caught' together led to spy reports getting back to Pastor Simpson. This resulted in gentle reminders to not create any situation that would lead to a regret of all that investment in me, leading to very public embarrassment and worse still shame. I was so in love with God and the adventure of serving Him and reaching others that I was naive to the complications that such a life brought with it. Namely, the incredibly high standard and pedestal that you are placed on and from that same dizzying height the potential fall from grace and the nuclear fallout consequences. In the black church there is no position higher and more respected than that of pastor/minister, and to be granted the honour of being among this rank at such a young age came with a huge responsibility.

As a really young man, the way I dealt with this was to act many years older than I was until it was no longer an act but a default position. Like an inverse mid-life crisis, this exaggerated the gap between me and my young, carefree girlfriend. She later told me that when she first met me she thought I was in my late thirties and married with children, such was the vibe I was giving out. Truth is, she was not alone in making this mistake, as I was the epitome of an old soul trapped in a young body. My skin was becoming chaffed by the tight fit of the straitjacket of this young-old minister persona. I felt I had to project this identity to be well received in the role and to draw attention away from any areas of immaturity that came with being under twenty-five.

It seemed that I had acquired yet another mask and layer of chameleon skin. Suddenly I wasn't invisible. Suddenly I was on a pedestal and respected, and had a platform from which to express myself. But playing a role in other people's lives distracted me from dealing with the uncomfortable parts of my own. Give me the mountaintop experience like Moses had any day of the week. The problem with standing on mountaintops spouting words of wisdom or being a mouthpiece for 'the Most-High' is that people won't let you come back down the mountain and be regular, flawed and basically yourself. It doesn't switch off, or rather other people won't let you switch it off. Flashes of the inner me — cheeky, funny and irreverent — would slip out, only to be met with shock and scorn. Then the mask would be back up in a flash, the voice would assume more gravitas and the back would straighten, with Bible clenched underarm. It was showtime!

Graduating with a 2:1 in theology, despite experiencing the loss of my father in the middle of my studies, was an accomplishment I was proud of. It felt good to be received back at Lee NTCOG as a retuning hero, though settling back to life post-Bible college wasn't too smooth. My expectation was that I would be given a church and put on the ministry payroll like many of my peers at Bible college. This had been the idea when I spoke with the overseer of our denomination before completing the training. I had no other qualifications, and theology degrees were not too common or appreciated in most employment circles, so I had put all eggs in this church-shaped basket.

This was a mistake, as I was told during my pilgrimage to our HQ in Northampton that there were no vacancies. And even if there had been, I was too young and inexperienced to qualify, and would have had to serve an internship. It was off to the job centre for me, and I hoped Jesus was still in the business of multiplying bread and fish, as I couldn't feed myself on knowing Scripture and preaching on the occasional Sunday.

I went through all this with a smile on my face and my head held high, but inside I was confused, surprised and close to tears. This was not the outcome I had been preparing myself for. Being back home, church-wise, was nice, but I wasn't the same person any more, having grown more questioning and analytical on the inside. Outside I had grown more diplomatic and political to match the role. Though I wasn't given a church I was still a trainee minister, and if I played my cards right a church gig would surely come up soon, which would mean no more job centre.

In the summer of 2001, after graduating from Bible college, I became part of an elite group of candidates whisked off to Overstone. This was the Northampton-based HQ of the NTCOG, once the grounds of a Bible college that trained ministers within the movement. Here I would sit exams to attain the NTCOG ministers' licence. Without trying to sound arrogant, in comparison to three years of constant questioning and deeply theoretical, headache-inducing exploration, memorising a large binder of the NTCOG teachings and protocols was a relative piece of cake. This was the cherry in the three-year tiered cake; the culmination of all my hard work and sacrifice. I had done it. I had officially become a licenced 'preacher man', a legit 'Pentecostal preacher' recognised and endorsed by Global HQ in Tennessee, and all at the tender age of twenty-two. If only my parents could have seen me as a respectable young clergyman. I had successfully forged a new identity that would stick to me like glue, whether I liked it or not. Reverend Antony Aris was actually a thing, and I had to get used to the cut and feel of this newly tailored suit.

The only ones in the world who knew the real me were God and Jahlene, and with Jahlene it was only fragments of the subconscious leaking past the tightly held, controlled persona that I held up most of the time. It wasn't that I was deliberately deceptive; more that I thought this was the role I was supposed to play for the greater good. A life in service to others, to save souls at any cost. The truth was, I needed saving myself. Maybe not from a lost eternity, but from a prison of my own making that was suppressing the vibrant, creative and free parts of me.

God's love is unconditional. Human beings' love is not...with the possible exception of Jahlene. Time would tell. She didn't care about my ministry credentials or whether I would lead my own congregation someday. She was with me when I had no money and no roof over my head, when she could have had her pick of all the eligible bachelors. Why was she with me? She didn't need me to pray for or counsel her; to show up at endless church council meetings and play politician over whether we could purchase a new boiler or install new pews. No, this girl was just into *me*, whoever that was. I loved her simplicity and inherent goodness. There was no agenda with her, and she would have given you her last penny or stood beside you in the pouring rain, such was her loyalty. God was there, I knew that instinctively in my heart, but His presence was abstract and at times distant, whereas Jahlene was tangible and present. Her ways were not mysterious, but easy to understand. No theological training or Scripture knowledge was required to figure her out. She made me laugh, and we had each other's backs. What else could you ask for? The fact that she was the most beautiful woman I had ever met didn't exactly hurt either, though the most attractive people can soon appear ugly if their personality and character stink. Fortunately, my girlfriend was the full package, and after three years together, most of that time in a long-distance relationship, I took the plunge.

I surprised her one night in Blackheath, where I took her to an Italian restaurant called Bella Italia. She was wound up by my being cryptic all night, hinting that I had something important to tell her. For some reason she thought I was going to split up with her, which made what I said as we walked across the pier of nearby Greenwich even more explosive. She was probably wondering why I had taken her out near the river in the freezing cold, which added biting winds to the mix. It was a thirty-minute stroll across the muddy grass, mainly stepped in silence, which added to the anticipation, or in her case, unbeknown to me anxiety. Was I really going to break up with her after such a lovely meal and then this freezing cold trek across the grass to a windy, cold pier?

Upon reaching our destination I started to ramble on, awkwardly summarising our relationship journey up to this point, saying that change was inevitable and all good things had to come to an end. This was all building to the ultimate switcheroo. In hindsight, this probably only served to confirm her fear that I was ending the relationship. That couldn't have been further from the truth.

I can still feel the jagged stones from the pier under my knee as I went down on it in the traditional way. I slowly and dramatically brought forth a diamond engagement ring that I had spent all my wages on at a shop in Hatton Garden. I was working full time for a Christian charity in Pimlico after months of temp work and wasn't earning very much, but everything I had went to this special ring project. It was so worth it, as Jahlene was dumbfounded, and the look on her tear-filled face was priceless. If nothing else in my life at that time made sense, this surely did.

What if she says no? That thought hadn't really occurred to me beforehand, but there was a river in front of us. *I could jump in and hide my shame. OK, the tears are touching but you haven't replied yet. Now I'm the anxious one.*

'YES!' The word came ricocheting from Jahlene's mouth so loudly that the fish in the water could hear it. The rest was a whizz and a blur of emotions.

Before long, we were standing at the front of the Lee congregation dressed in our Sunday best, being presented as a newly engaged couple. Part of the protocol was having to place the ring on Jahlene's finger again, which was met with rapturous applause, wolf whistles and shouts of 'Hallelujah!' during the service. The two most important people to me, without question, were God and Jahlene, and I was looking forward to spending the rest of my life with them both. Who would have dreamt that walking up those stairs to that little room in Emmanuel Pentecostal Church in 1992, with its stale coffee aroma, would bring so many things into my life? Good and not so good things, but at the very best, amazing and irreplaceable things. Without that little room I probably wouldn't have accepted Jesus. I wouldn't have gone next door, and entered the world of the New Testament Church of God. There would have been no London Bible College, and many of the people I'm blessed to have in my life would be missing from it.

Who knew that one simple prayer, earnestly uttered at thirteen years old, would lead to crazy supernatural experiences, a global church family, preaching to thousands, helping countless people navigate painful life experiences and meeting the love of my life? Without meeting God nearly thirty years ago, I likely would never have met Jahlene. For that and count-less other reasons I would utter those very same words over and over again. I wouldn't change a single thing from that night or the journey it has taken me on, even through the valley of the shadow of death. Like the first man, Adam, I had eyed and found my missing rib. And like Adam, God saw that it was not good for me to be alone.

CHAPTER SEVEN

We Did!

Wedding Day, 19th June 2004. It was a chilly summer's afternoon on what had been forecasted to be a hot day. It was anything but hot, yet the day would have a wedding regardless and I was the groom.

I woke up somewhere in north London at the home of best man Wayne Brown's parents, which they had kindly vacated for us for the most important event in my life. I ate a full English breakfast but remember not enjoying it – nothing to do with its quality, but rather my inability to focus on it. An influx of nervous energy engulfed me, rendering all my senses, including taste, momentarily paralysed. I hadn't slept very well the night before, my mind racing. It wasn't so much the fear of losing my freedom, or cold feet. It was something much that was more likely to be a concern for the bride: my hair was a complete mess.

At that time I wore my hair in gel twists, which were styled for me by a lady in Tottenham, who also styled Wayne's hair and was a true talent. She was hair stylist to the stars, including UK soul singer Lamar and US R&B singer Usher. Being one of her clients put me not only in good hands, but among the ranks of other well-groomed, high-profile black men.

Typically, I had let my hair grow out between appointments. The last appointment she had told me she would be travelling for a few weeks, but would be back a couple of days before the wedding, and would be honoured to style my hair for this big occasion. I was assured that she would be available and willing to do it...only until she wasn't. She *was* back in the UK in time, as Wayne and I stood outside her house door trying to get hold of her for thirty minutes. She hadn't answered her phone at all, which was odd, and I was provisionally booked in for the day before my wedding. Cutting it fine, I know, and pretty unwise to leave myself with so little time to spare before such an important occasion. The truth was, this hairstyle was pretty exclusive and not many salons knew how to do it, let alone make it spotlight ready. I had no idea what I was going to do.

The prospect of having a dodgy hair cut or having it cut low and uninspiring plagued my mind. Traditionally, it's the prerogative of the bride to be late to the church, but my life has defied convention in so many ways. Wayne and I raced across north London in search of a black hair salon willing to take on this Herculean task. We finally found one, but we were up against it. It was as risky as it was unwise, but the vanity just about paid off. My hair was freshly styled and it was the gel twist look as planned.

Meanwhile, Jahlene had to circle around in the wedding car a few times so as not to walk up to an empty altar. It wasn't the greatest start to our big day for sure, but thankfully this was the only hurdle we had to face that day – or at least the only one we knew about. Jahlene arrived at the arched doors of the church on the arm of her biological father, and slowly began her march. Wayne gave me a jab in the ribs with a grin on his face, anticipating my shock and awe as my best friend, and soon-to-be wife embarked on her runway walk to the altar. The joy, awe and emotion were momentarily suspended as I noticed that Jahlene wasn't wearing a veil. This was yet another break from tradition, as the minimalist bun and light make-up had been eschewed for sleek long tresses, bejewelled tiara and a bindi on a photoshoot-ready face. This was all fantastic, but a surprising deviation from the original simple plan. That's what you get when your bride's glamorous stylist auntie gets involved!

Once my mind had taken in the bling, it went back to a place of contemplating what was happening in the moment. This boy was getting married. This was my wedding day. This beautiful woman was moving closer and closer, resplendent in a glowing white dress, skin glowing just as radiantly. The occasional glimmer of her diamond-studded tiara and excited white-teeth smile blinded my eyes. Her father looked slightly sheepish. I could tell he was finding this whole experience as surreal as I was, while the soon-to-be Mrs Aris was taking it all in her soon-to-be-arriving stride.

Within seconds, the live saxophone rendition of Stevie Wonder's 'Knocks Me off My Feet' came to a close and Jahlene was standing beside me. I stood with freshly twisted hair in a knee-length white wedding suit, waistcoat and lilac cravat, a black, silver-topped cane in hand. I looked the business. We were riding the early noughties American trend of bride and groom in matching white. This may have seemed ostentatious for some, but in my mind we were like a Hollywood couple. We were marrying on a modest budget but looking the part no less.

My heart was racing and Wayne seemed to enjoy seeing my normally cool and controlled composure turn to jelly. Other people wouldn't have noticed it so easily, but he knew me well enough to detect it. Jahlene's large eyes were looking into mine, and for a moment I had a flash of the future: our home together, our intertwined lives and our unborn children. Wow! This wasn't just my soon-to-be wife standing in front of me, but the future mother of my children. Who would they look like? Would they be brown like Daddy or caramel like Mummy? Would they have my classic forehead or their mother's large, slightly Asiatic eyes?

Jahlene came from a large family on her father's side and an intimate but above average-sized family on her mother's side, so the children were already blessed with at least half of their genetic ancestry. Though I believe love is not restricted by race, I was determined to marry a black woman because I had always wanted to get close to a black woman and create a bond. Mum wasn't black and neither were my sisters, and I didn't have any aunties or cousins black or otherwise, so there was a huge short-age of real kinsfolk in my life.

While I was dating Jahlene I gravitated towards her family, adopting them as the black family I never had. The Wints on her father's side, and to some degree the Gilchrists on her mother's, were more than just regu-lar in-laws. Through them I would experience what it was like to have a cousin or an auntie/uncle, even if it was vicariously through my wife. They accepted me on both sides, with the brief exception of her parents, who initially didn't want to let go of the idea of her being a little girl, having missed so much of her childhood. They'd had her very young and were not ready to be parents, so they had given her to those they felt qualified for the job: her paternal grandparents. Mr and Mrs Wint, were truly her parents, having raised her from eighteen months old, and they accepted me into their family early on, quickly seeing me as a son. Like a lot of modern couples, my wife's parents were never married and had other children after her from different relationships. Our wedding day was the first time my wife's seperate family halves had ever come together, and it was an emotional moment for her.

I finally had a 'black family' and my children would be legitimate branches of that family tree, and not grafted-on adoptees like I was. No one would question their place in the family, or point and stare and tell them how lucky they were to have been taken in like stray puppies lost in the rain. I felt guilty for feeling this way, but it was the truth. All my life I had wanted to 'belong' and I was finally able to give this gift to my chil-dren. I knew that one day I would have to explain to them why Daddy's family was white and why I looked nothing like them. Would I play the game with them that my parents had played with me all those years ago? 'They asked for a brown baby', volume two? Would I perpetuate the con-venient lie or break the cycle and tell them the inconvenient truth?

It wasn't so much the awkwardness of that question that bothered me but my inability to answer follow-up questions as to where my black par-ents and family were. These half- or quarter-Nigerian children would, for all I knew, be acquainted with and embrace their Caribbean heritage via interaction with my in-laws. It hurt me that my children's Nigerian roots would remain non-existent and unknowable unless I did something about it. What could I do? I honestly struggled to find an answer. My Nigerian heritage was as mysterious and foreign to me as it would be to them, and I was more directly connected to it. It wasn't my fault that I had been left thousands of miles away from my mother, her home country and her people all those years ago. It hadn't been my choice to sever the family link. And though I believed my mother must have loved me, I couldn't explain why she never came back for me or why I had been left in England.

What was I doing? My mind suddenly returned back to the present. I remembered I was standing in front of my bride, a crowd of guests and the officiating minister, rather than in the future world of my daydreams, playing happy families. That would have to wait, as I hadn't even crossed the threshold of 'You may kiss the bride' yet. We both knew that this was a profound moment and felt overwhelmed, even though we were not exchanging words, as the message was so clear. In Jahlene's face I saw the future and the exciting adventures that lay ahead. This future vision was so much sweeter than the challenges and pains of the past that often reared their ugly heads in my mind, and of course the constant question of my missing people.

There was a segment of the Aris family there to support me, but no one from my biological tree. But a new tree was sprouting. Looking into Jahlene's eyes, all I could think was that from this moment *she* was 'my people'. Together we would be family.

The vows came, then the exchange of rings and finally that all-important 'first kiss', which signalled that we were finally and officially 'one flesh'. Well, at least as much as was appropriate for such a public occasion. We were moving forward together into the unknown future and the expansion of our family. But first, we had to get through the rest of the day. The excitement of ending four years of chastity would have to wait.

CHAPTER EIGHT

'She Has My Nose'

'Tony ... it's time,' Jahlene shot at me, giving me the look as if she expected me to suddenly spring into action like a super-organised superhero.

'What...you mean like last time?' I replied, the very definition of loving concern and husbandly support.

She gave me an even harder version of 'the look', which indicated that of course this was the real thing and not a false alarm like the last time.

Part of me remembered this being the case the previous time as we grabbed Jahlene's pre-packed overnight bag and raced to the hospital. At the last minute, transcendent wisdom stopped my mouth from verbalising that thought. This was not the time! Adrenalin raced through us as we double and triple-checked the bag containing everything she needed as we went into rehearsed military mode.

It was Good Friday 2006, and moments before we had been doing our morning ritual of preparing breakfast with *The Jeremy Kyle Show* in the background. A British *Jerry Springer Show* mixed with *Maury*, it never failed to make our lives seem better in comparison to those of the guests on the show. In just a year this show had become must-watch TV for us in the car crash sense, and it had become a guilty pleasure whenever I started work late in the morning. I could have lingered to watch Jeremy Kyle read out someone's lie detector results for longer, as my wife seemed to mouth the words in seeming slow motion. My half-attentive mind decoding those words as a sign that our lives changing for ever. It's not that I wanted to watch the show to the end, as if it meant anything to my life. Rather it was a welcome distraction, as subconsciously I wasn't sure I was ready for this event. It was probably a bit late to be thinking that, but there's a difference between the idea of a thing and the right here, right now reality.

We were almost a week behind schedule and were beginning to wonder if Baby Aris was ever going to make his or her grand appearance. This little one had overstayed his or her tenancy by five days, like a defiant tenant ripping up eviction notices and erecting a barricade. Baby Aris had already disrupted our plan for the birth to take place in our home borough of Lewisham before we moved across town to east London. With all our medical files in our old location it wasn't ideal settling into a new location when Jahlene was about to give birth. Why did this baby have to be so laid-back? Maybe it got the 'mi soon come, irie' thing from its Jamaican side of the gene pool. I'm anything but laid-back, so it didn't come from me. Besides, there was only room for one diva in our household, and Mrs Aris can testify as to who this is, she is very patient and tolerant of my condition.

Joking aside, words could not describe how proud I was of Jahlene, or how grateful that she had gone through all this hard work to extend our family. You would have thought she was carrying the Messiah by the level of excitement and anticipation I was experiencing. We had already upgraded in life from an 'I' to a 'We' when Jahlene said 'I do', but this would be next-level profound. The book of Genesis in the Bible talks about a husband and wife becoming one flesh; a mystical union of spirit and body. This new arrival would literally be 'of my flesh'; a surreal experience and a bond I had never had before.

* * *

I didn't know who I looked like for twenty-seven years, whether it was my parents, grandparents, siblings or a hypothetical Great-aunt Doris twice removed on my mother's side. My face was an anomaly, a one-off that had only had me for company for nearly thirty years. I would stare at myself in the mirror, wondering whose broad and slightly triangular nose I had inherited; from whom I had got my Mount Everest forehead. These were ever-present burning questions, and unlike a contestant on *Who Wants to Be a Millionaire?* I couldn't 'phone a friend'. The only comical certainty was that I hadn't got my good looks from the people I had always called Mum and Dad. Even a joke about looking like the milkman wouldn't work in this context. People tend to take these things for granted. 'Oh, I look like my mum' or 'I look like Auntie Betty on my father's side' or 'Uncle Leroy on Mum's side'. They can search through their family tree and see a link somewhere; a resemblance that confirms them as a branch of the tree and establishes their roots. Most people know where they come from, and if not from both sides of their gene pool, then at least one side. Not having this created a feeling of isolation, as if I had just fallen out of the sky one day, deposited here from another planet, the mothership having forgotten where it dropped me off. The mirror image reflecting back at me was my sole family likeness; the only image to share the features that made me uniquely who I was.

This relationship with the mirror was difficult at times. Sometimes we were sworn enemies, constantly at war with each other, until one of us extended an olive branch. My forehead was way too big and shiny, and why did my hairline have to start so far up my head? Don't get me started on my hair itself, with its coarse and brittle terrain that was the battleground for my self-image for many years. My biggest embarrassment as a child was the casualty of war that was my hair, full of knots and uncontrollable. I still wince when I remember the pain and discomfort caused as the black Afro-comb of death literally dragged through my scalp. Shaving it all off would have been an obvious solution, but the strict Roman Catholic school I attended forbade low-cut hair. Apparently, it gave out the wrong impression and lowered the standards. Low-cropped hair was associated with thuggery and low aspiration for some reason, rather than just an easy to manage grooming choice.

Though my childhood was relatively happy, I had received my fair share of taunts about my appearance, and this affected the way I felt about myself. Overweight and non-athletic until I entered my mid-teens, I was always last to be picked for sports teams. I made up for this by being funny and friendly, but I was never the one the girls pined for in the playground. Boy, how I envied the athletic guys and longed to be pined for instead of being the one 'sweet boy' they let into their inner circle during break time. I didn't want to be 'sweet'; I wanted to be 'hot' and desirable. Being in the circle meant I had to listen to them fawn over my friends. I wasn't attractive enough, I concluded; too dark, too fat or just not 'enough'. It was torture.

I was twelve years old when I began to consider the possibility of there being other people out there who looked like me. That was when I was officially told I was adopted. Claire took me out to Pizza Hut in Catford, and broke it to me gently, after much protestation from our parents. Nothing smooths over difficult-to-hear news like the smell of hot, fresh-out-of-the-oven pizza, with its melted cheese and meat permeating the atmosphere. Bizarrely, my parents thought I would never find out I was adopted, and didn't consider that I might already have worked it out.

After that, I often daydreamed about what my real family looked like. Did I have my mother's or my father's smile? Did I have black brothers and sisters? My imagination was always wild and fantastical. Wide-eyed in nature, I gravitated to cartoons and films in which the central character was the last of his or her kind, like *Denver, the Last Dinosaur*, *ThunderCats* or *E.T.* The latter characters were extra-terrestrials stranded on another planet, estranged from their kind, living among people who were very different from them. Not that I too was an alien living in my house like in *ALF*, though it sure felt like that sometimes. All I wanted was to be beamed up to the mothership and whisked off to a planet where I was Mr Hot Stuff to make contact with my lost kin.

Once we found out about the pregnancy, I was intolerably curious and grew more and more impatient as the months turned into weeks and then days. That thin blue strip on the pregnancy test was to change my life for ever, as the realisation sank in that I wasn't alone any more in the biological sense, that I was going to have a flesh-and-blood connection with this little person, and that was going to be a day of celebration. As with a wedding day, you never know exactly how you are going to feel until the event happens unfolds. If my wedding day was like a slow-motion movie, then the birth of our child was like a flick book, with the animation slowly happening in front of my stunned eyes.

Fifteen years after first considering the question of there being more of me out there in the world, I made First Contact. I wasn't the only one of my kind any more and I had never even had to leave planet Earth. I had my own Close Encounter that would change my life for ever and I would no longer feel biologically alone in the universe. Jahlene had brought immense joy into my life, but she was from another planet. Venus, I believe, according to author John Gray, and we were learning to become one as most young couples do in the early years.

My universe changed that Good Friday evening at 5.15 p.m. in a hospital in Leytonstone, east London, as Tiani Georgia Anaya Osula Aris beamed down into our lives, weighing 7 lbs 8 ozs. In spite of being Venusian, this tiny being was also from my species and made an impact on my life like no other had ever done before. This little creature wasn't green, and neither did she have two heads or three eyes. She was chalk white, with thick, slightly blue lips that were sucking rigorously as her bulging brown eyes slowly surveyed the room, taking in the strange sight of the maternity ward and its even stranger inhabitants.

Tiani arrived a few hours earlier than expected; a swift delivery after a delayed start. She was just as stirred by the sight of us as we were of her. As her head emerged and then her crying body whooshed out into the midwife's hands, I looked and thought to myself, *So this is what it feels like to be a daddy.* My heart burst through my chest, as though I were John Hurt in *Alien,* as I looked at her in amazement. My rotund brown face, black-rimmed glasses dangling from my nose, and black, worm-like twists for hair must have been a shock for her as she came out the business end. It happened so quickly, and I was unbelievably proud of Jahlene for bringing our daughter into the world through the pain and craziness that is childbirth. No man, I thought to myself, could ever do that, even if it were biologically possible. The experience was just as moving and emotional for Jahlene as it was for me, but in a very different way. The sight of our new baby daughter was an overwhelming reality as I kept looking at her, transfixed and in awe.

Tia was exactly what we had hoped for and more. We knew we were having a little girl; not by medical confirmation but through intuitive prayer. We felt the Lord had given us that intuition, even though everybody and their pet monkey was trying to tell us, judging by the shape of the bump, that we were definitely having a boy. I had always wanted a little girl first. Deep down, I was intimidated by the prospect of raising a son, as I hadn't yet made peace with my own masculinity, and passing down my insecurities to a son seemed cruel. Having said that, I would have loved Baby Aris just as much if she had turned out to be a he. I hoped deep down that she would resemble me, but whatever way she had come out, whether abled or disabled, big or small, this was my child and I was overwhelmed by her arrival. God answered my little prayer and she undeniably came out with a tiny triangular nose, high receding forehead and puffy cheeks, but with fair, vernix-covered skin.

I couldn't take my eyes off Tiani. It was love at first sight. Her arrival left me emotionally stunned and in shock, but hypnotised by her presence. Intoxicated, I couldn't believe she was finally here after months of feeling her slither about through the skin of my wife's womb, weird and exciting at the same time. I was right there and saw everything, but it felt as if I was watching it all on camera and wasn't actually present in the room. The most important person in the world to me was about to usher in the second most important person in the world to me, and I felt like the luckiest man on earth. My very own family, and neither death nor tragedy was going to snatch it away from me this time. An intense wave of ecstatic joy and utter disbelief blended together like a smoothie, with a pinch of fear. When I held her, I felt magic flow through my arms. The belonging I had craved for all those years was partly cradled in my arms and partly lying flat out, exhausted, on the maternity bed beside me: mother and daughter staring back at me. The two ladies who made my life feel complete.

If only Mum and Dad could have seen me now, holding my own child, their granddaughter, in my arms. If only my biological mother Priscilla could have seen the beautiful little face of her firstborn son's firstborn daughter as she slept, oblivious to the new world she had just entered and the joy she had brought her parents. Maybe I had looked like this when I made my debut on planet Earth. Only one person would know, but I had no way of asking her or of telling her that she was a grandmother.

If I had been able to talk to her, I would have asked numerous questions about how to look after this tiny baby, but instead we just had to roll up our sleeves and figure this thing out for ourselves. *I mean, how hard can it be?* I naively thought to myself.

It wasn't long before Tia's lungs properly kicked in and were emitting a sound like a police siren amplified by two stadium-sized speakers turned up to the max. We looked at each other with faces that said, *Do you know what you're doing? Because I don't.* Each of us was hoping the other would have a sudden burst of know-how, but we simply had a few words of advice from the midwives to go on, and off we went the next day with the realisation that we had to take care of her, having no clue between us and no instruction manual in sight.

I had set our house just right the night before, after being kicked out of the hospital in order for mother and baby to get some rest. There was nowhere for me to sleep at the hospital anyway. I say 'sleep', but I didn't really get any that night as the adrenalin raced through my body with Olympic intensity, such was the excitement of everything I had just experienced and the feeling of being master of the universe. Nothing could have taken me out of that high as I repeatedly pinched myself to make sure I wasn't dreaming. Part of me subconsciously believed that if I went to sleep, Baby Tia wouldn't be there when I woke up.

Chocolate Easter eggs couldn't have been further from my mind the next day as I enthusiastically raced to the hospital for my next fix of first-time-daddy magic, so excited to set eyes on my daughter again, and of course the one who had made it all happen. Before we knew it, our new family of three was in a taxi, homeward bound to our flat. We were tired and eager to relax in an environment that didn't smell of disinfectant and where we could have some real privacy, although we had to wait for the privacy as there was an influx of friends and relatives, such is the nature of becoming first-time parents. Everyone and their pet monkey wants to see your bundle of joy.

One visitor we could have done without was the assigned duty midwife, who showed up at our door within forty-eight hours of our homecoming. It wasn't that we didn't have the stomach for another visitor, or that she was effectively a stranger; more the instinctive feeling that we were being investigated and assessed. The fact that she wasn't the warmest of people, stern and strictly business, didn't help matters at all. We knew she was just doing her job, but we felt as if we were on trial, such was the intensity of the bombardment of questions. The smoking gun materialised when, upon inspecting Tia, she asked us sternly if she had fed yet. She hadn't fed much since leaving the hospital, as breastfeeding was proving difficult. It was as if we had just confessed to killing JFK in this woman's eyes. Without missing a beat, she ordered me to the shop right away to get some formula milk. My wife tried to explain that our baby had not immediately taken to the breastfeeding thing, and that she had been advised at the hospital that it takes a bit of time and was normal, but this fell on deaf ears. She gave Jahlene some advice, but it was tinged with an air of 'these two young people have no clue what they are doing', and to be fair she was absolutely right. We had read everything available in advance and attended prenatal classes together, but theory is very different from practice. This was not a simulation but the real deal.

We were left feeling that we had missed the net and failed at our first shot. Our new instructions were to turn the thermostat up higher, wrap Tia in more layers and stock up on formula milk as a back-up for a while. We did what we were told in the best interests of Baby Aris and to avoid being labelled Britain's Worst New Parents. Don't tell the midwife, but we soon found out how virtually indestructible a baby is. Such as when they roll off the bed suddenly within seconds of your eyes going from them to the nappy beside them and other such heart-attack-inducing hi-jinks. These fall into the category of 'what people don't tell new parents', possibly with good reason. But as tough as they may be, they are not toy dolls.

Speaking of toy dolls, there was one time when I went out around town with my baby daughter in her sling she was actually mistaken for a toy doll. A lady approached us randomly, peaked into the sling on my chest to look at my sleeping baby and nonchalantly said, 'Oh, she's real! I thought she was a dolly.' This left me completely bemused. Did she think I looked the type to walk around with a toy baby attached to my chest, and if so why? Was I giving off that vibe or was she the one who wasn't quite the full sandwich? I didn't stick around long enough to find out, as my first priority was to my daughter and to find a safe spot – just in case. It's weird how people think they can get in your face when you have a baby.

Tia and I bonded a lot during her early months. I changed my work patterns to be around in the daytime, and Jahlene eventually went back to work, so we had lots of father–daughter time. That sling became ridiculously heavy in time, with Tia's pale little hands sticking out of the sides, bent over like the Emperor's in *Star Wars*. These pale hands also brought a fair share of attention our way when we were out and about. Tia was almost white in colour in her first few months of life, creating an ironic reversal of my own situation. After saying how cute the baby was, the boldest passers-by asked, 'How come she's so light-skinned? Is her mother white?'

First, none of your business; second, why does this matter? And third, still none of your business, complete stranger on the street. I wish I had been brave enough to actually say all that rather than just smile politely.

This happened the day she was born. After I'd gone home, the hospital staff rotated, so there were new nurses attending my wife and baby. After seeing her, a couple of nurses asked, 'Aww, she's so fair-skinned...is your husband white?' The look on their faces when I entered the ward and took Tia in my arms was oh-too-familiar, and a knowing smile crept across my face. The native name given to me by my mother, Ekundayo, meaning 'sorrow turned to joy', had prophetically come true. I was holding joy right in my chocolate-brown hands, and I was never letting go.

Despite having become a teenager, Tiani continuously brings joy to my heart, and she was soon joined by yet another love of my life. Her baby sister, Eva Alliyah Olamide Osula Aris, nicknamed 'cocoa' for many weeks, arrived just over two years later in 2008, on another sunny bank holiday weekend. The assumption was that it would be exactly the same experience so that the excitement and novelty wouldn't be there the second time. To my surprise, rather than déjà vu it felt completely different but just as special. Eva was beautiful and made another huge impact on my already weakened heart. Would I ever get over the shock of having to look after the three ladies in my life? My hands would certainly be full in a household with an ever-increasing oestrogen count.

Nothing could have prepared me for how different my two children would be from each other. Eva was a mocha-coloured baby. The tips of her ears were a chocolate colour, hinting at her eventual skin complexion. Her nose was smaller and flatter, her hair straighter, and she almost looked Indian. Eva was also very emotional. More of a crier and very clingy compared to Tiani, who was a laughing, sociable baby, and would go to almost anybody. As infants, Tia was loud, extroverted and confrontational; Eva was quieter, reserved and very sensitive. The leader and the observer was the best way to describe these sisters.

Eva brought her own share of joy to our little family, and though it took a lot longer for me to bond with her, I loved her deeply. Eva was and is a lot more of a mummy's girl. I wasn't at home as much during Eva's early months, as I was holding down two stressful jobs, coming home late at night and often tense and unhappy, with the weight of the world upon my shoulders. My heart was heavy having looked forward to seeing the smiling face of my baby only to be met by a trembling lip and a scrunched face filled with tears. I couldn't figure out why she was rejecting me when I went to pick her up and she cried. Looking back, the frustrated tone of my voice probably made her cry even more. For a time it was like a vicious cycle that I thought would never end. *So there's a downside to parenting?* I thought to myself as baby number two seemed to genuinely hate my guts. It was by no means the first time I had faced rejection, but it was the first time I had experienced it from my own flesh and blood, and as irrational as it sounds, it hurt deeply.

She eventually warmed up to me and gave me a second chance once she hit fourteen months. After the famine of affection, a minute never went by without Eva standing in front of me with her head tilted skyward, lips pursed, often Weetabix-covered, waiting for me to give her a kiss for the millionth time, before I went to work in the morning. Maybe she wanted compensation for the lost twelve months when I was the bogeyman who made her cry. I now had all three precious ladies in my life onside. *Will I ever experience the pleasure of having a son?*, I wondered to myself. Both strikes had produced girls thus far and could I face the prospect of being last man standing amid a female force of four?

* * *

I thought I would be OK once I had children of my own. For a while it felt like completion and the tying together of loose ends. But in time this new reality of having children began to slowly highlight the fact that I had no roots. Having no roots meant my children had no roots from my side of the gene pool and only a half-branch family tree. They would know their Jamaican roots but not their Nigerian ones, which, though better than the deal I'd had, was not the full package with the benefits I wanted for them.

When I saw my face in my little girl that Good Friday, was it my mother's face staring back at me, or maybe my father's? Who did I look like and whose mannerisms did I have? *I guess I'll never know*, I thought to myself in a bittersweet moment. The determination to get answers for myself and my children was firmly established in my heart; it just wasn't a priority at that time. Such matters would have to wait for an appointed time. Where I came from, though important, didn't matter more than my children having a fully committed and engaged father; one who celebrated the fact they were here regardless of how he himself had 'arrived'. Jahlene and I would have to be enough, tending to the loving nest the best way we could.

Jahlene and I loved the surrogate parents we had and would for ever be grateful for them and the love they gave us. Yet it wasn't lost on us that this parenthood thing gave us an opportunity to experience through our children something that had eluded us both: an organic sense of belonging and a close, blood-tied family the right side of normal. Whether Tiani, Eva or any other child to follow had my nose, hair texture, skin tone or sloped forehead, the one thing I knew is that they would have my blood and no one could take that away. I was no longer alone in the universe.

CHAPTER NINE

Epiphany

'Sweetheart, I'm home!' I call out as I enter through the door. Tired and relieved to be home, I put down my briefcase, inhaling the smell of cooked food arresting my senses. 'Aromatic chicken to-night, then,' I observe, the spices tingling in my nostrils, teasing my taste buds. *It's been a long and stressful day, but some good food, some wine and an enjoyable night with my wife can make all the difference,* I think to myself.

'Hey Babes, welcome home,' my wife calls out from another room, more than likely the kitchen, considering the aroma that's filling the air. As I slowly walk towards the source of these intoxicating aromas, I see our dining table laid out like a restaurant on Valentine's Day; all napkins, fine cutlery and wine. *What's the special occasion?* I think to myself. Then my eyes are caught by the more arresting vision of my wife dressed up looking like the Queen of Seduction. For a moment I'm not sure which meal I'm most hungry for.

Before I have the chance to say anything, my wife, almost reading my mind, leaps right in: 'I thought I'd do something special tonight. I know things have been a little difficult lately, so I wanted to treat you.'

OK, I think to myself, smiling, though somewhat suspicious. *Has she gone on some sort of spending spree and wants to smooth things over before I find out? What's the play here?*

Then she's standing behind me, taking off my coat in preparation for me to sit at the table.

'So, how did it go?' she says excitedly.

'Yeah, it was fine. I should know in a few days,' I reply, not really wanting to go into office life while I'm at home, trying to unwind.

'Well, I know it's going to be fine. I believe in you,' my wife sweetly replies with a smile. 'Now tuck in; you must be starving,' she urges.

I oblige, as I really am hungry and would rather fill my mouth with food than words about work shenanigans and possible promotions. For now, I just want to be blissfully transported in the realm of my senses, first through a mouthful of this enticing food and then… Well, I'll leave that to the imagination.

Wifey is giving me the eye, and I'm not sure if it's part of the romance or if she's eagerly waiting for my response to her food. Either way, it's a bit unsettling, as her eyes are transfixed, putting me on the spot.

'This is cold,' I tell her, spitting out the food in disgust. I can't believe that after all this effort she could drop the ball in such a spectacular way.

'I'm-I'm sorry… let me put it in the microwave,' she says nervously, her body shaking slightly.

What's her problem? I think to myself. *If anyone should be upset it's me, working hard all day, deserving some TLC — and then sitting at the table to eat stone-cold food? I should be shaking.* In fact I am, with rage, as I am bombarded with excuses from her as to why she couldn't get the food temperature right and how I'm over-reacting. *Forget this rubbish,* I'm thinking. The next thing I know I've thrown a plate across the room and my heart starts beating like that of a prize racehorse. I don't want to eat or do anything else right now. That ship has sailed. The evening's ruined and the one person who was supposed to make everything OK has let me down; betrayed me, even. How could she be so selfish and uncaring?

'Babes, what's wrong?' she whines, stammering in a pathetic voice.

I ignore it as I advance towards her. She starts to back up to the corner of the room. She's scared of me. Tears stream down her face as she starts to cower, lifting up her arms in submission.

'Why are you playing the victim? *I'm* the victim here. This is all your fault. You deserve this!' A red mist sweeps over me. I find my belt mysteriously in my hand as I raise it up in fury, unleashing my pent-up emotions in multiple strikes. Her screams are deafening, but somehow they don't register and in no way deter me.

Then deafening silence. The lights are snuffed out and it's all over.

'And…. SCENE!' comes a shout from out of nowhere.

The lights went back up as quickly as they had gone out and the tension was defused as the director came over to chat with us. The adrenalin was still pumping through my veins, as I'd given that scene everything. Silvano, my scene partner and the fellow actor playing my wife, was taking some time to get over the intensity of the scene and the real emotions it had triggered. I thought she should have been used to it by now. After all, she was the one who had written it!

* * *

I had wanted to be an actor since I was a teenager in drama class. I loved the process of becoming a character, expressing myself and my feelings in a make-believe situation. It came easily to me and felt like a natural path to follow.

It would be several years later when, aged twenty-eight, I was able to explore acting again and release my inner thespian. I had regularly come into contact with acting and the entertainment industry through my job working at a radio station, where I would occasionally be dispatched to do red-carpet interviews and press junkets for film. At the office they all knew that I adored film and entertainment, calling me 'Showbiz Tone'. They knew I would voluntarily throw myself at any and every opportunity to interview actors and attend press screenings in order to review them as a guest slot on presenters' shows. To me it was a way of getting closer to the flame without committing myself or running the risk of getting burnt; like being a commentator at an adrenalin-charged sports event who excitedly comments from the box while really wanting to be out on the pitch or in the ring.

It came as a big surprise to be thrust back into the world of acting when I volunteered to take part in a two-night play at my local church. In late 2006, Jahlene, Tia and I were attending a branch of our church organisation in Mile End, east London, called Epainos. It was a strange name to us too; you won't find it in the common English language as it's an ancient Greek word meaning 'praise'. Our pastor, Davey Johnson, was very much into praise and worship, having been a worship leader for many years, and he was even more heavily into the ancient Jewish and Greek roots of the faith. The name encapsulated both interests perfectly. It took a while to become accustomed to than the more basic 'Mile End New Testament Church of God', but we didn't have much choice, as the rebrand was Pastor Davey's conviction and we were full steam ahead going in that direction. Epainos had always been seen as a progressive, seeker-friendly and contemporary church by its sympathisers, but as compromised, worldly and liberal by its critics. Its former name, Mile End, was prophetically appropriate for us, seeing as it was the last NTCOG church we would attend before eventually leaving the denomination.

It was within this community of professionals – predominantly middle-class, more English than Caribbean in sensibilities – that I was able to reconcile the broad differences between the wider NTCOG denomination and my post-London Bible College self. The perfect halfway house after being exposed to the wider, predominantly white Christian world. At Epainos there was a bias towards creativity and contemporary ways of doing church. The DNA of this was partly a legacy passed down from the previous pastor, Joel Edwards; the same Joel who had personally recommended that I attend LBC, he himself an alumnus, when I felt the call to ministry at eighteen. Maybe it was some strange form of poetic justice that it was at Joel Edwards' former church that I would experience a new sense of purpose and life direction – ironically a road that would lead me back to the path I had abandoned years earlier.

Silvano Griffith was a short black lady in her twenties, with curly hair and small, piercing eyes with an intensity about them. She was supernaturally driven and abrupt, but only in the sense that she wanted to get from point A to point B quickly and not waste time. If she came across a bit short, then so be it, but she was far from cold. You just had to get to know her and see past the urgency.

The urgency in question was that she was a burgeoning playwright who had a vision to put on a play that would tackle controversial and taboo subjects, such as eating disorders, coming out and domestic abuse all within one family. There is nothing particularly shocking about this now, but at the time, and in the context of the black Pentecostal church, this was pretty ambitious and went against the grain. Silvano knew that a few of the roles would be tricky to play, and she wasn't casting seasoned actors, but amateurs from within the church.

One character she had written, Adrian, was the villain of the piece and would be hard to pull off. You hear stories of soap opera villains being approached in public by angry fans hurling abuse. This is both a compliment in terms of their abilities and a curse that comes with the job. The problem with Silvano's play was that, unlike the soap actor, the person taking on this role would be back in church the next day, seated among the people who had seen him 'beating up' his poor wife the day before. If he played the role too well, a portion of the audience would question just how much acting was going on. So when Silvano approached me with the script for her play and said she envisaged me playing the role, I didn't know how to take it. I was flattered to be asked, for sure, as I hadn't performed in anything for almost a decade and it was a key role. Part of me relished the idea of playing against type: the respected young minister, personable and kind, transformed into a violent, abusive monster, masterful in manipulation and control. It was a role to sink my teeth into and bring out the inner performer I had kept locked away for a long time. I took the script and told her I would read it and get back to her, but I had pretty much decided to do it, even though I was worried about what people would think of me after playing such a nasty character.

We met for rehearsal every Wednesday night in the church hall. Rehearsals were tough, as many of the cast members had never been in a play before and there were varying levels of commitment and enthusiasm from the actors. Silvano took it very seriously, as did her director Carl, who was a member of the church and a struggling actor. He was also a friend of mine, to whom I had confessed my interest in one day exploring acting again. Among the more passionate amateurs in this group was Nayden, the youngest of the cast, who was to play a teenage son who came out to his family as gay. He was very talented, but he seemed to be at a crossroads, not knowing which direction to take, as he was also a skilled singer, footballer and academic. Then there were the actors playing the ageing parents, the middle sister who was about to marry but hiding an eating disorder, and the got-everything-together big sister played by Silvano herself. Hidden behind her dark Prada sunglasses was the black eye given to her by her 'perfect husband', Adrian, played by yours truly. Jahlene had a very small role in the play, but acting wasn't really her thing. She just wanted to help out and have some fun.

Playing Adrian was a learning curve, and one that wasn't entirely pleasant. Though I had never been physically violent or abusive to my wife, it did bring back memories of angry moments in our relationship when I had lost my temper in the very early years. At times I had seen a red mist of rage and felt volatile over the slightest offence. No one had ever told me that I was a selfish person and that marriage would not be all about having my needs met in a state of perpetual bliss. Jahlene and I were in our early twenties when we married, and this was only three years on. What would people think about our marriage when they saw me being passive-aggressive and then all-out rage monster on stage? I felt I had to really go there in my mind in order to do this storyline justice. At times in rehearsal I saw genuine fear in Silvano's eyes and wondered if she was just really good at method acting or regretted casting me, as I was actually freaking her out. She later told me that there was something in my eyes that was real and malevolent, and after a while we seemed to just rush through the scenes.

It was somewhere between thumping my fist on the dining table and grabbing Silvano by the hair with my other arm raised that I tasted the strangely intoxicating cocktail of dramatic power. The knife-cutting tension in the air and the angry gasps of the audience confirmed to me that this was what I was born to do. Not hit women, of course, but be on a stage conveying emotions and ideas, blurring the lines between fact and fiction.

The play was Silvano's vision come to life. It was more than a little amateur production put on in the church hall. For all involved the message we were embodying was an important one. That one family might go through so much simultaneously seemed a bit far-fetched, but the aim was to drive people to explore and discuss the suppressed issues plaguing many people in church. As a preacher I could preach theoretically about domestic violence from the pulpit I occasionally borrowed from Pastor Davey. But seeing me embody a perpetrator of domestic violence showed it in a visceral way that must have felt painfully familiar to those who had lived through similar situations. There were tears and angry boos whenever I came on to the stage after my debut scene. The explosion of rage that erupted when I began to berate Silvano for the cold food, then for everything she said to try to divert my attention from it, was immensely powerful. My part wasn't large, but the impact was undeniable.

At the play's conclusion, when I received a blow to my head from my long-abused wife that put me into a vegetative state, the outburst of cathartic emotion from the crowd was deafening. The comeuppance of the domestic abuser won't work if the audience doesn't despise him, and boy did they celebrate his downfall! As I took a bow and absorbed the jeers and hisses, I knew there had been a reawakening. A part of me that I'd thought was long dead had been resurrected, and not only still lived but shone like a bright star. I will always be grateful for this catalyst that prompted the re-emergence of the actor inside – the artistic phoenix burning through the straitjacket of my serious clergy persona.

What did all this mean? I now had a hunger for acting, and was energised and fired up not to just tell stories but to embody them. I loved preaching and I also loved acting, but I had already committed eight years of my life to being a minister. You couldn't be a minister *and* an actor, right?

I had unleashed something from deep within, like a repressed personality scratching me from the inside, desperate for a chance to come out and play. But 'play' wasn't proper for a 'man of God'. Maybe a one-off was acceptable, but then I would have to return to more spiritual things and resume the lofty position the job required. Perhaps I was already in the role of my life, trapped in full method mode; lost in a persona that had increasingly become a prison. I knew I had been called by God to serve Him and His people; I just wasn't so sure how much of myself I was supposed to sacrifice in the process or whether I was really me any more.

Epainos was not short of talented and creative individuals. There was a heavy bent towards music, with some of the best singers and session musicians in the denomination residing in this medium-sized east London congregation. We had dance troupes, expressive flag-wavers and an increase in alternative performance, such as spoken-word poetry. We were only a stone's throw from Stratford, which was becoming another hub for a burgeoning community of young creatives spread across east London in areas such as Hackney, Dalston and Shoreditch, the 'hipster' capital. This influx of trendy young creatives mainly came from the universities in east London, and Epainos had a growing number of students attending services. The youth of the church started inviting their peers, as the arts offered something to hook them into.

One Sunday service a young woman in her late teens came to the altar to accept Jesus. She wasn't alone, but she stood out with her short-cropped hair and large eyes. Tears came streaming down her face and it reminded me of that night in 1992 when I had become a Christian as a teenager. Like myself, she and a few others clearly weren't church kids. This encounter with Jesus was a new experience for them, and it was radically different from the usual experience of a university or college student.

It turned out that this young girl with the red, swollen eyes was called Michaela. Bold and straight-talking, she was a breath of fresh air in a polite, middle-class, predominantly middle-aged environment like ours. She was definitely a leader amid this growing group of young urban students who were excited about their new-found faith and soon found themselves involved in dance troupes and organising out-of-the-box evangelism events. If I'm honest, I was both encouraged and jealous. Due to my age and position on the leadership team I couldn't be one of them, though a part of me would have loved that. Not everyone among this new generation was a dancer or a communicator, but Michaela was both. It soon became very clear that she was destined for a platform, and a big one at that. We probably thought it would be the pulpit at some stage, but it was very clearly a stage of some sort. I had a soft spot for Michaela as she was real and zealous about Jesus, which reminded me of myself. She was beyond inspiring, and seeing her explore her new-found faith was highly motivating.

Michaela soon became known throughout London for her spoken-word career. Some sang about Jesus, while Michaela rhymed about Him and other hard-hitting subjects from a Christian perspective. She was our hip young ambassador, released into London with cutting urban slang and Pentecostal zeal. We, the church, supported her all the way with her spoken-word projects: two albums' worth of witty, thought-provoking and provocative poems. In many ways these were a precursor to the contemporary 'woke' movement, especially among black student circles. She spoke about spirituality and transcendence in the midst of hedonism and promiscuity.

Michaela held an album launch at Epainos that was filled to the rafters with people, and not the usual church crowd. These attendees were significantly younger and more diverse. I couldn't have been prouder. The frustrated artist in me recognised that she was doing what I could only dream of: reconciling her art with her faith unapologetically and with great success. Michaela Coel, as she is now widely known, is a successful and accomplished actor, star of Channel 4's *Chewing Gum*, which she conceived and wrote, and a BAFTA award-winner. She is currently working on big-time American projects with Netflix, making her star shine even brighter overseas.

Michaela was still part of the church when my family and I left Epainos in 2008. I lost touch with her for several years, though I heard that she had gone to drama school. She also had a starring role in a short film called *Malachi*, directed by a close friend of mine, Shabazz L. Graham, about a sick boy with a video camera point of view of the world. Michaela played the boy's downtrodden but fierce young mother. It was her first role on screen, and it seems a lifetime ago from where she is now. I was happy to meet her again on my TV screen and read interviews with her online or in the newspaper. It was the most surreal experience to see her living the life I had foreseen for her many years earlier.

Well, part of the life. Reading her interviews, it became clear that she had moved away from the Christianity of her younger years, seeing it as a toxic form of religious fanaticism and unhealthily dogmatic. *Mile End?* I thought to myself as I read the article. If it had been Lee, where I spent my teen years, or countless other of the more traditional NTCOG churches, I would have understood, even if I didn't totally agree. But Epainos? Our church was the more contemporary black sheep of the family. We embraced expression and artistic freedom, and though traditionally evangelical we were more inclined to enter into dialogue and engage with people rather than judge them or ram our beliefs down their throats. Of course, we all see things from our own perspectives, and I'm sure if

Michaela read this she might remember things differently. But I saw her time with us as happy and inspirational, and she was held in high esteem.

The fear I'd had in my late teens when faced with the opportunity of going to drama school was that it would somehow seduce me away from my faith. Could you be an actor and a Christian at the same time? It seemed to me at the time, back in 1997, that the answer was no.

*　*　*

In January 2008, in the wake of my renewed passion for acting, I enrolled for the Introduction to Acting course at City Lit Adult Education Centre in central London. I was overwhelmed with a new sense of purpose, possibilities and excitement about what I could become, and what this might mean for the future. For the first time in years my life was rapidly beginning to change, as the buried creative persona burrowed its way through the rubble. A new lease of life was infusing my current one with new energy.

It was four years into my marriage and my wife could see this growing change. It must have been like living with a different person, like when they replace a long-time regular soap opera character with a new actor and think the audience won't notice. 'Today Antony will be played by...' It felt as if there were two versions of me negotiating for control, jostling for space and at times getting into internal conflict, like the good versus bad Superman in *Superman III*. There was no fight in a scrapyard, but at times I could feel the tug of war within me as different impulses were pulled in different directions. The more conservative, boy-scout Clark Kent, the epitome of restraint and control, versus the primal, impulse-driven but powerful Kal-El (Superman) who couldn't wait to express his new-found power and freedom. The task of keeping these impulses and the conflict within at bay was tough.

These feelings were momentarily held back by two demanding jobs and an expanding family, with the pending arrival of baby number two, Eva, but City Lit opened the door to a whole new world for me. I knew

I was marked by God for something, but the way I understood this was broadening. Maybe I wasn't only a clergyman after all. Either that was one of many roles I was to play or the result of a game of telephone gone wrong, with the message misunderstood.

With this new identity of actor came not only new experiences but also new relationships, which helped with the transition into my new self. Errol Servina, Liberty Blackburn, Charlie Ryall and I met on the Introduction to Acting course, though we were all at very different stages of the acting journey. We were also very different, and no one would have predicted that we would become friends, creating a bond that would see us through some challenging times. At twenty-eight I was keen to know for sure whether I had it or not, whatever 'it' was, and to see if my dabbling with acting at Epainos was just that or something more. It felt as if all four of us were at a similar place of wanting to know if we were serious contenders. Was my future in acting, or was I just trying to escape the feeling of being 'trapped' in my life, like having a premature mid-life crisis, where you look at your life and wonder what exactly you've done with it, and whether it's been worth the trip so far. I didn't regret putting Team Jesus first, but I felt I had become a religious martyr, locking up my artistic potential, sacrificing it at the altar in order to belong to a community with all of my pious work and young years spent undertaking a broad range of church activities. Surely that would look better in God's book of life than my 'prancing around on stage' doing Shakespeare or getting mired with oil paint and watercolours? The work of the Lord could not possibly include anything trivial like that, or anything that I deeply enjoyed or was gifted at. It couldn't be about my personal ambition or interests. Could it?

It would take some years, but the light bulb would eventually switch on. The epiphany finally came to me that I could be devoutly committed to Christ *and* a fulfilled creative. Even a professional artist, or dare I say actor? My mind was properly blown. Once I had succumbed to this truth in my heart and not just in my head, my journey towards becoming an artist began. I would chase this identity with the same vigour, tenacity and zealous focus I had years before with my enrolment into seminary.

The introductory course, which ran for eight weeks, helped confirmed that I wanted to pursue acting, and had lit a spark, but it was very basic and I was hungry for more. On the last night of the course, our teacher Terry, who was much more relaxed and outgoing once he had finished teaching, sat with a number of us at the pub across the street, having celebratory drinks. He shared with a few of us that he also taught at a more intense professional acting school for the seriously committed. If we were truly hungry and had caught the acting bug, we could join him there. It felt like being invited into a mysterious, exclusive club. All we had to do was sign up with him that night and we had a place at this mysterious acting school on his exclusive ticket. It was the easiest yes I'd ever said.

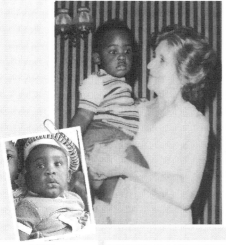

TOP ROW

1. The earliest and only baby photo I have in existence

2. Myself and Mum (Wynne Aris) at the family home in Kidbrooke circa 1980

3. Me with Dad (Albert Aris) during caravan holiday in Great Yarmouth

MIDDLE ROW

4. Baptism day aged 16 at Emmanuel Pentecostal Church with dodgy hairdo

5 & 6. Graduation Day, London Bible College with wing man Wayne Brown and with big sister Claire

BOTTOM ROW

7. Wedding Day in 2004, posing for photos in our hired vintage car

8. Throw back photo to early days of dating; our first photo as a couple

9. Birth of Tiani with proud mum Jahlene in the hospital

CHAPTER TEN

'I Want My Mummy'

Caravanserai was a very interesting place; a kind of Hogwarts for thespians that was not just an acting school but a community. It wasn't just a place of learning, but a movement, and in many ways a way of life for those who were at its core. It reminded me of church in the sense that people connected with an ideal that was bigger than them, and gave them the feeling of being 'called' to acting.

The acting centre was the brainchild of seasoned actor Giles Foreman, a flamboyant and expressive man, white, dark-haired and tall with steely eyes that not only looked right through you but suggested some serious life had lived behind them. He possessed a strong presence and an almost cult-leader-type aura that drew many young men and women to the altar of acting. He had an innate gift for drawing out truth from a person in their performance, even if it was painful. That said, he was likeable, and underneath the initially intimidating presence he was genuine and generous to a fault at times. I say 'generous to a fault', as it was a habit for many of the students to pay only a fraction of their tuition fees upfront and leave the rest outstanding for months on end. A seemingly endless line of credit was given to the actors who collectively owed enough to run a small country. Giles was much more of an artist than a businessman in that regard, and I'm sure the missing fees almost shut down the operation countless times. Giles was not in it for the money – that was clear.

At first, the continuing students from City Lit watched him from afar, as we started out being trained by Terry. Then for some unknown reason Terry very suddenly stopped teaching there, leaving us in the hands of a new teacher, Charlotte. Charlotte was kind, with red hair, freckles, big green eyes and the warmest smile, and was the most nurturing teacher I have ever had. An immensely talented actress herself with heaps of experience, she would teach me to trust my instincts, harnessing my emotional memories to use like a paintbrush giving life to a scene. She was setting a firm foundation, and my only regret is that we, the Beginners' Class, were in such a rush to get to the heavy stuff with Giles that we short-changed ourselves. If Charlotte was like the nurturing mother of the school, Giles was the distant father, prodding and provoking to push us to our limits.

I couldn't have faced this without my three closest acting friends from City Lit who took the leap into this new frontier with me. Errol Servina, a goateed Scotsman, was tall and slim but firmly built, and confident bordering on cocky. I had no idea that he was biracial for weeks, such was the fairness of his skin, though he did have a slightly ethnically ambiguous look about him. He was funny in a no-nonsense way, and was definitely the Alpha male of the group and likely most of the groups he found himself in. He reminded me of Sean Connery every time he spoke, and I thought he would make a great Bond one day. Errol and I developed a great camaraderie. We were brothers in arms and both had a lot to prove to ourselves, seeking confirmation that we had something as actors.

If Errol was the big brother, then Liberty Blackburn was the slightly hipster, avant-garde big sister Liberty stood out from the crowd. Slim and slender, with medium-black hair scrunched under a dark beanie hat, she would slip in and out of class like an enigma. She was biracial like Errol, and besides her model like appearance, she stood out with her choice of attire. Beneath the layers was a warm personality, and beneath that lay a strong woman, courageous and fiercely ambitious, having overcome a ton of obstacles to find herself in pursuit of a life she really wanted.

The last of the Musketeers was Charlotte 'Charlie' Ryall, the youngest of our bunch and arguably the most qualified with regards to acting, as it literally ran through her veins. Charlie was not only the youngest but the shortest. She was white and bespectacled with medium-length brown hair, and she spoke with a posh accent. She absolutely adored Shakespeare, and it wouldn't have shocked me to find that she was distantly related to him. The four of us were on our own paths, each having different obstacles to overcome. But we were bonded by our ambition, supporting each other on the journey like a kind of Fellowship of the Ring.

One of the benefits of being at an actors' studio like this was the reputation it had in the acting community, with its array of teachers, both on-staff and visiting 'guru' types. One such acting guru came to Caravanserai to teach an exclusive ten-day intensive class for only the most gifted and committed students in the Advanced Class. You couldn't just get on this list; you had to be chosen. There were whispers that this acting coach was a big deal in Hollywood, serving actors like Juliette Binoche, Tom Cruise and Nicole Kidman. The latter had allegedly thanked said coach personally at the Oscars while clutching the gold man in her hands.

All I heard was 'Oscars' and I was in! There was only one problem: I wasn't in the Advanced Class. Actually, two problems, as the workshop would cost hundreds of pounds at a time when I was strapped for cash. Eva had arrived by this time and, having been at Caravanserai less than a handful of months, I was still in Charlotte's Beginners' Class, far away from Giles's qualifying eyes.

Whatever happened, I knew Liberty would be in that workshop even if she had to rob a bank and audition a thousand times, standing on her head. Errol wasn't overly fussed and wasn't as convinced by the guru-following, pretentious side of the acting world. He preferred to make his own steady progress in his own time. Charlie and I were both inspired by the persuasive energy that Liberty emitted, and before long we had followed her in writing our names on the crumpled piece of paper going around to gauge interest. It was a million-to-one shot, and I instantly felt foolish for putting my name down. We were never going to get a place on this workshop, which had only fourteen places reserved for the most promising actors Caravanserai had to offer.

What I didn't know was that we had Charlotte firmly in our corner. She gave Giles a glowing referral, convincing him that the three of us had talent worthy of the opportunity. Charlotte had faith in us and knew we could rise to the challenge, having seen something in each of us in the few months she had been teaching us. Part of me secretly wanted to be left out, as the classes would be brutal, starting at 9 p.m. and finishing at midnight on a weekday, not to mention the sting to the wallet. With my day job and a teething baby to contend with, the idea of getting even less sleep wasn't too enticing either. Living on the other side of London made it a logistical nightmare too. Sometimes in life, though, you are faced with a major opportunity – one that terrifies you to the core – and if you can find some Dutch courage and ignore those negative voices in your head and walk through that door, your life will never be the same.

Against all odds, the three of us got onto the course with the big Hollywood acting coach. I couldn't believe it. This was the perfect validation that I wasn't misleading myself with this acting thing; that I wasn't a 'wannabe' but a 'could-be' if I really wanted it. This was the opportunity of a lifetime. What I didn't know, and couldn't possibly have known, was just how much this woman and her workshop would alter the course of my life – and not in the way I expected.

Susan Batson was a petite, gravelly voiced, energetic African-American of mature years, who for a woman so small held court with effortless authority in the studio. Her big, soulful eyes scanned the young actors in the room, sizing us up and evaluating the material she had to work with like a sculptor feeling the clay. Maybe it was her reputation as an actor who had sat under the infamous Lee Strasberg, the original Hollywood coach to the stars, or her natural aura and self-confidence that had us magnetised and hanging on her every word. I had never been in the presence of a Hollywood acting coach before and didn't know what to expect.

Susan soon let us know that she was not messing around on this course; that she expected excellence, and nothing but blood from our veins and tears from our tear ducts. Nothing less would do. She cursed unapologetically, which took me aback as I had never heard a lady of her age speak like that before. No judgement – it just came as a real surprise. She was feisty and no-nonsense, but simultaneously nurturing and maternal with us, her temporary students. When I felt out of my depth and a little overwhelmed, I could feel her eyes willing me on, like proverbial hands pulling me up from the ground and affirming me. I'm sure everyone felt this at some point, cementing her genius as a teacher and her innate ability to draw out what was inside of us.

She had asked us all to work on the same scene, paired up, with each pair playing the two main characters from Lillian Hellman's *The Children's Hour*. The fact that both leads were female was irrelevant to her selection process, it seemed. Once I got over the shock of this, we were told that we would play the characters according to our own gender and were paired up with the same gender counterpart. My partner Jason was in Giles's class; one of the few black men not only on the workshop but in the entire school. He was as pleasant as he was talented, quieter than me and deeply serious about the whole thing. It wasn't his first rodeo performing in front of directors and coaches. He was calm and collected, while I was anxious almost to the point of neurosis. It meant a lot to me and I didn't want to screw this up.

Susan used methods I had never thought of before. These methods would push us beyond our comfort zones, sometimes defying our expectations. I often heard the bemused mumblings of students questioning what they had signed themselves up for. One of the tools Susan introduced us to was an exercise that involved us finding a personal space in the studio and tapping into an emotionally vulnerable place. The 'Mummy Exercise' was sold as an effective way to reach into our vulnerable raw emotional state and then use it to serve the scene. Nothing is more sacred than the mother-child relationship, and the idea was that it houses a wellspring of feelings. No one can love us or screw us up quite like Mummy. There are many theories in the mysterious world of acting that have their roots in modern psychoanalysis, and this one had a distinct 'Dr Phil' and 'Oprah' vibe all over it. The need for 'Mother' was a golden key of sorts, as it was a primal portal into our emotional core; the place where our need lives.

As a typical Brit, I was sceptical and uncomfortable with this at first. We had to find a space on the floor and cry out, 'Mummy… I NEED YOU! I WANT MY MUMMY!' over and over again, like a mantra, or a lost two-year-old at a shopping mall. I felt ridiculous, like a prize idiot. *How much have I spent and sacrificed to be part of this workshop?* I asked myself, feeling tired and embarrassed. *Errol would have a field day witnessing the three of us on the cold, sweaty wooden floor doing this,* I thought.

I told myself to shut up and continue with the infantile mantra. Then something hit me like a brick wall. Something happened. Out of nowhere, a tidal wave of emotion overwhelmed me. My eyes began watering and a gnawing pain twanged in my stomach. *What the heck is going on?* My body was paralysed; not by self-awareness, as it had been earlier, but by an inexplicable emotion that had taken over me. I had hit an emotional nerve, as though I had struck oil in the ground. Suddenly, this wasn't a silly exercise any more. It was real and I was an emotional wreck. I rarely thought of either my mother Wynne or my biological mother Priscilla in everyday life, but I instinctively knew that regardless of how much I loved and missed Wynne, it was Priscilla who was causing me this distress. A primal connection powered this moment before conscious thought kicked in.

One of my mothers had been dead for almost fifteen years, the other was AWOL. I had always wondered if I would ever see my missing mother again and hoped to find her one day. Who knew what I would say to her? With almost thirty years to account for, it wouldn't be an easy conversation. This was the baby Tony calling out of the adult Tony's mouth – calling out to the woman who had disappeared off the face of the earth, never to be seen again. For a moment the infant and adult versions of myself were one and the same on that wooden floor, fused by a traumatic experience that triggered a charged cocktail of yearning, loss and unfiltered rage. Wow, this acting lark sure was heavy! There was no reassurance that Mummy would come, however many times I asked her to. The only thing that came to meet me was disappointment and loneliness.

It took me longer than everyone else to snap out of this strange trance. I stumbled into the next exercise, hung over with what I had just experienced and in a state of shock. I was shocked that this experiment had actually worked and by what it had done to me... or perhaps I should say was *still* doing to me. Who would have thought that the biggest turning point and breakthrough in my acting career would be deeply connected to unexpressed feelings for my long-absent mother? I hadn't seen that coming.

Susan looked over at me with tear-brimmed eyes, intuiting that this had hit me harder and more uniquely than it had the other students. Liberty's eyes also met mine as she mouthed, 'Are you OK?' from across the room. I remember her and Charlie giving me an empathetic hug during our break, both knowing something of my past and seeing me in a state that was as foreign to them as it had been to me. The lesson of the day was that however make-believe the circumstances may be in acting, the feelings are very real – at least they are when it comes to good, meaningful acting.

Susan had almost become a kind of mother figure to the group herself. Perhaps this was part of the plan, as we were all in a post-'crying for our mummies' state, so were liable to latch on to the closest thing in the room. She certainly managed to nurture us into a place where we could handle a two-hand scene that would be performed in front of the school at the end of the course.

The actual skill we were learning in this whole process was called script analysis, which means breaking down the dialogue of the scene into beats: moments in the text that range from emotional intention to mere prescription. We were forbidden to memorise any lines. If we were to graduate from this workshop, we would need to learn the skill of fusing text with emotion and action that naturally sprung forth on the night of performance because it was ingrained deep in our psyche. I struggle with learning lines, but I found myself recalling large chunks of dialogue during this process because it was so embedded with emotion and movement that it felt lived rather than learned 'by numbers'. A strong emotional connection was needed, as the character I was playing was Martha, friend and fellow teacher to Karen. After their lives were ruined by gossip, Martha finally confessed her hidden feelings for Karen. I initially found this difficult to get into as a straight man until I discovered that the context was irrelevant, as I needed to draw the feelings from a different, real place and substitute the moment.

It was soon time for me and Jason to enter the stage. This was the culmination of an exhausting and challenging experience that would either land in triumph or crash in failure. Make no mistake, Ms Batson did not hold back when it came to her critiques. From the moment I first stepped on to the stage I was 'Marty', my version of Martha, and there was no trace of Antony to be seen, except for the feelings, which were painfully real. This guy knew his way through the valley of rejection, so there was plenty for me to draw from. The role helped me discover what it truly meant to act; to be so given over to the moment that it wasn't about the audience any more, however prestigious its members were – even with Susan and Giles sitting in the front row and my more experienced peers behind them. At the point when I was rejected by Karl (Karen) it felt as though I had been knifed in the gut. As I said goodnight and made my way off stage and out of the scene, I was carrying that rejection in every fibre of my body.

The next thing I remember after being brought back out and hearing applause that signified both the end of our scene and the approval of our peers, was Susan's big, teared-up eyes as she customarily nodded her head in approval. She started by praising Jason first, which I expected, as he had been brilliant. I was preparing myself for some harsh criticism. Throughout the nights of training, I had been told that I was almost there but not quite landing. That I was too much in my head or overly dramatic; indicating my intention to the audience rather than just trusting my instincts and *being*.

Then Susan turned to me and spoke. I couldn't believe my ears as she told me my beautiful performance had moved her to tears. At that moment I knew I had finally made a connection with my art. If I wasn't already shocked enough, Giles stepped in and gave his feedback. They had disagreed with each other a lot over the course of the evening in terms of who they liked and what they saw as areas of improvement for each actor, but in my case they were unanimous with their feedback. I couldn't believe what I was hearing, and felt euphoric with relief and happiness. It seemed I was legit after all, and that this had been my baptism by fire. Lib and Charlie, who had received similar feedback, were also triumphant, and there was no need for any emotional first aid this time.

I had brought along my copy of Susan's book to have her sign it as a memento of what had been a huge chapter in my potential career. She took my pen and wrote on the opening page:

Dearest Tony,
Your growth as an actor touched me deeply!
You have greatness as a performer and power and vulnerability as a wonderful actor!!
Stay in the Dream – Always in The Art!
With love and encouragement,
Susan

Wow! This was living proof, in pen and ink, that I'd come, I'd seen and I'd conquered. Hollywood had given me an open invitation to pack my bags and come and take my spot. At least, that was how I felt with all the adrenalin racing through me!

This was the biggest public affirmation I'd ever had, certainly as a performer, and I felt genuinely chuffed and empowered. So why did I also feel hollow inside, with a growing twinge that felt like a small itch starting somewhere in my body but spreading like wildfire? It soon became clear that the source of my new-found acting powers, the raw emotion and my connection to it, had left an exposed nerve. The Mummy Exercise had successfully connected me to my character's 'need' as intended, but it had also gifted me with an urgency regarding my own hitherto unexpressed 'need'. This would certainly come under the category of ironic plot twist in the book of my life. Something had been awakened inside of me and, like a genie released from its bottle, it couldn't easily be put back in.

The need for my mother was more than an exercise in an acting class. It represented a lifelong mystery; the constantly missing piece of a jigsaw puzzle that haunted my subconscious mind. Wanting my mummy wasn't about sustenance or nurture; it held the key to understanding who I was and where I came from. This primal need I had to belong had been a part of me since I started recording memories in my head. If I found her I would have concrete answers and therefore some kind of solace.

Where on earth are you? I thought, wondering if I would ever hold this mother-shaped puzzle piece in my hand; whether perhaps somewhere out there she was having the same guttural conversation, crying into the ether, 'I WANT MY SON!'

CHAPTER ELEVEN

A Barber, a Cleaner and a Security Guard

As the year 2009 unfolded, it was shaping up to be a significant one for me. I had reached a milestone accomplishment with my acting, resigned from my post as an NTCOG minister after much soul-searching and was to turn thirty in the summer. Of the three life events, turning thirty was the scariest, as it signified becoming a proper grown-up. Yikes! I knew I was officially an adult with a wife and two children, but at this junction called 'thirty' I was supposed to have my life together and have put all the lessons learned in my twenties into practice. The stakes were higher now, as what had been forgiven in my twenties would not be in my thirties – as if it were some magic number. This would be a big birthday. I needed to celebrate it in a big way, as I had nine years earlier with my twenty-first. I had thrown a space-age-themed party back then, playing on the fact that I had turned twenty-one in the twenty-first century.

The most adventurous thing I ended up doing for my thirtieth was booking our first family trip abroad, to Florida, in the same month as my birthday. Hardly slumming it, but not the epic party an extrovert like me had craved. Sure, I did have a much smaller-scale party with a handful of friends at a swanky bar in London, but it wasn't a match for my previous milestone birthday bash. One thing I've noticed is that when you get married and start having children your social life takes a hit and the herd of friends starts to thin. Back in the day I could draw together small crowds; at this time I struggled to get a handful of people to leave their house on a Friday night or choose me over the next best thing. *Yay! Welcome to my thirties,* I thought.

One of the few constant things in my life was my continued employment at Premier Christian Radio. I had joined the company five years previously as a junior audio editor for speech-based programming and was pretty much in the same position. This career rut, though frustrating, was at least convenient, as I had negotiated flexible hours and days while I juggled a second job in magazine sales, and had the space to attend auditions and book acting jobs. This was a godsend for me, as there weren't many jobs that would allow you to attend auditions at a moment's notice and be flexible enough to accommodate a burgeoning acting career. Acting isn't ideally suited to family types with domestic responsibilities, but more to adventurous, free-spirited individuals who only have themselves to support, usually by doing bar work or shifts at call centres. I was grateful to have a job that was at least remotely creative and gave me access to people in the media and entertainment industry, however sporadic.

A lot of the time I worked late into the night at the station by myself. I would sit at my desk, often the only person in any of the offices, feeling it was a heavy price to pay for my freedom and a flexible work schedule. But alas, this was the arrangement, and like clockwork I would do my shift, take the lift down to reception and strike up an exit conversation with the building's security guard.

Laurence was heavy set, over six feet tall and bald-headed – a Nigerian who loved to talk and was generally very jolly. Loud and rambunctious, he was much friendlier than any security guard I had previously come across. He was often the only other person in the building after hours and carried out regular patrols. I liked talking to Laurence, in spite of the countless times he caused me to miss my bus after I had left exactly the right amount of time to get from my desk to the bus stop near the front of the building. What could I say? I'm a sucker for banter, and who was I kidding? I was never going to make that bus, as I never factored 'chat with Laurence' into my calculations.

'No way you're Nigerian! You're Jamaican, o!' said Laurence in disbelief.

I told him I was Nigerian, or at least half-Nigerian as far as I knew from my mother's side, and he said with absolute certainty, 'No! You are a Jamaican!'

I knew that I wasn't stereotypically African in my demeanour, but neither was I Caribbean, so I couldn't place his protest. On and on this went until he asked me what my surname was. I had told him my given name, 'Aris', was my legal name through adoption, and that my born name was 'Osula'. He had never heard of the name 'Osula', so I told him the little I had discovered: that it was a 'Bini' name originating from Benin City in Edo state. Benin Kingdom was one of the grandest kingdoms in Africa (not to be confused with the nation Republic of Benin, which was formerly called Dahomey and was once a province of the kingdom, renaming itself in 1975 in honour of its heritage).

He looked surprised and then told me that one of the cleaners in the office, Anne, was from Benin City and might be able to find out some information for me. Laurence himself grew very excited about my story, as he didn't know I was adopted or that my biological family originated from Nigeria. He believed it would be very straightforward to find them, as I could trace my family tree using my last name.

After a couple of weeks, Laurence called me down to reception to meet with Anne for the first time. She was very pleasant and intrigued by the story of my being a long-lost son from her hometown. First and foremost, she had not only heard of the name Osula, but she said that it belonged to a very large and influential family who just so happened to be Benin royalty, directly tied to the Oba (monarch of Benin) himself. I knew the name was from Benin and belonged to a well-known clan, but the royalty part was news to me. She also said that the Osula family were very important in Nigeria, and that her mother knew them personally, and particularly a Chief Osula. *Say what now?* This was great news, and my first hot lead for sure. She agreed to ask her mother to make enquiries and then report back to me. After asking her a few basic questions we ended it there.

Like two buses coming at once, Laurence told me about a barber shop in Hackney, east London, whose owner and workers hailed from Benin and might provide another possible lead. Apparently, they also knew of the Osula family and had confirmed that it was indeed a well-known and important family. That was two positive reports so far, but something felt stuck, like a bone in the throat. If I was part of such an important family, why hadn't I been important enough for someone to seek me out? Why was the effort all mine? Maybe I would get to ask them if everything came together.

Laurence and I arranged to visit the barber's one Friday evening after I'd finished work. Before the meeting took place, Laurence said that the woman had told him about an ex-wife of Chief Osula's who was living in London and might also be able to help with my enquiries. My expectation was that this would be part of the visit, or at the very least be brought up in the conversation, and I said as much to Claire beforehand as I shared with her the excitement of a new lead.

Laurence and I met at Liverpool Street station and drove down to the barber's, my stomach churning in anticipation. When we arrived, I sat for what seemed like an age amid the barbers cutting hair. Dressed in a suit, I was formally prepared for whatever was to come my way, which I was hoping would at least be a solid lead. Wearing a suit to a barbershop was unconventional, but I was desperate to make a strong first impression and show that I meant business, especially if there was any truth in the rumour that I came from an important family.

After thirty long minutes the owner came over with her small boy attached to her leg, and Laurence introduced us. I stood and shook her hand as I nervously pondered, *Could this be it? The answers to the big questions I've been carrying around for the best part of thirty years?*

She unsubtly looked me up and down, sizing me up, then touched her forehead to signify that I had an obvious Osula family trait. That was one mystery solved, at least. She asked me several questions and I answered, telling her about my mother and the circumstances I knew of relating to my birth. The barber claimed to know the family fairly well and in particular Chief Osula, whom she referred to as my uncle, 'the musician'. Unfortunately, she had not heard of my mother, either by the name Priscilla or by her native name, Omosede.

This didn't seem like a good start. If she knew the family as intimately as she had said, why didn't she know my mother or react straight away at the mention of her name? She glanced at the information I had been asked to bring, with details of my mum's last known address and a photo of myself as a baby with my surrogate mother, which would prove my identity to my birth mother once she was found. As she took it all in, I couldn't help but notice that she seemed a little suspicious or overly cautious, as if she had to be absolutely sure that this was the real deal and not some kind of elaborate hoax. She was guarded whenever I asked a direct question about the family, often replying with, 'Don't worry. You'll soon find your mum.' What exactly did she know, and was she withholding information from me?

I was beyond anxious. I was also growing suspicious and wondering whether I had done the right thing in giving her so much sensitive information about me. But I was in a desperate situation. While I was thinking this on the inside, I had to present a different face on the outside, smiling, gesturing and doing whatever it took to gain her trust and encourage her to feel enough compassion to help me – if she really did have the connections to the Osula family she claimed to have.

We were told she would be travelling to Nigeria in the next couple of weeks and that she would have a talk with the family and give them the envelope containing all my details. In hindsight, it was fairly naive to give her such private information, especially with it travelling to Nigeria, home to some of the most inventive scams known to mankind. But I had to take the risk if it meant finding my mother.

The evening ended with a handshake and a promise of future correspondence. To be honest, I was left feeling disappointed and a little apprehensive about the whole affair, and I wondered where this was all leading – if anywhere at all. We left the barbershop in Hackney in the hope that the 'Barber from Benin' would embark on her journey and give us good news from the other side. I felt a bit silly when I told Claire over the phone that the information was vague at best, and that the details I had been given about the former Mrs Chief Osula were merely speculative, and I had no way of contacting her. This certainly hadn't been the eureka moment I'd expected, but at least I had something to grasp on to, even if it would turn out to be a straw.

Laurence drove me back home to Catford after the meeting. Sitting in the passenger seat, I pretended to have retained the same level of enthusiasm as when I first sat down in the car at the start of our journey. I didn't want to seem ungrateful; he had gone well out of his way for me, even dropping me back home to the other side of London. I said my thanks as I got out of the car, readying myself for the bombardment of questions from my wife, who had been anxiously waiting for an update.

We're still waiting for that update, as I never heard from the 'Barber from Benin' again. I discovered that she never took that trip to Nigeria or sent my details across to Chief Osula. I did eventually get my information package back, fortunately, but the truth of behind whole evening remains a mystery. Was it a complete waste of time or a necessary step in the right direction?

After a few weeks, sometime in mid-May, I received an excited phone call at work one evening from reception. It was Laurence excitedly telling me to come down immediately. I knew it could only be about one thing, and that perhaps this was going to be the best news I had received in a long time. Hurrying down the stairs, I saw Laurence standing at the reception desk with Anne, speaking into a mobile phone in her native tongue. I presumed the conversation was being undertaken for my benefit due to the fact that I had been summoned, even though I had no idea what she was saying.

She ended the call and began to explain that she had just been speaking to Chief Osula, the man presumed to be my uncle, with whom her mother had made contact on our behalf. Anne's mother had told him about me, and Anne had given him further details and acquired his phone number, which she gave to me, though she suggested not calling straight away as he was preparing for a meeting. My heart started to race as it dawned on me that I might have finally found a firm lead; that I was just a phone call away from the end of my search. I would finally be striking gold and not tin. It was only afterwards that I questioned the importance of a meeting that would take precedence for my uncle over a phone reunion with his long-lost nephew. Red flag alert or was I being over-sensitive? Nonetheless, I thanked her and took the piece of paper with the number on it, and then we said our goodbyes.

Laurence and I looked at each other like two men who had just discovered oil in our back garden. We both knew what the other was thinking; we needed to make that phone call NOW. Forget busy! How busy could you be if your long-lost nephew suddenly came back into your life and was but a phone call away?

We called the chief within minutes and waited as the phone rang and rang. It was answered after what seemed like an eternity. Chief Osula – the man who could be my mother's brother – was on the other end of the line. I knew my grandfather was a Chief Osula and that as he would likely be dead by now, the title would have passed down to his son. That much of the culture I knew.

The phone line was terrible and we struggled to understand each other between the bad signal and the different accents. Even Laurence found it difficult to hold a conversation on this call. After several attempts at talking, we decided to exchange email and contact details, and I was to send him all the details I had about my mother. I found it strange that after mentioning my mother's name there was no reaction from him. Not even a glimmer or an inflection of recognition in his voice. Perhaps this was the result of a polygamous home; that my grandfather had so many children they didn't all know each other. In the letters I had from my mother, she had only mentioned her mother, my grandmother. There had been no mention of her father. This gave me the impression that she had grown up with only her mother, and perhaps without her siblings. This was one of the questions I hoped to find answers to after sending my email to the chief, which I did straight away. Typically, I was obsessively detailed and thorough, and was anxious for a swift reply.

I checked my email inbox daily but found no reply. I resent the email just to make sure it had been received. After all, it could be sitting in the heaving inbox of an important man, and this was Nigeria we're talking about, where time and haste are relative to each person. Despite this, I was growing frustrated. It was worse than the not knowing anything or the empty leads, as I knew the information I craved was just around the corner, teasing my patience and dragging its heels. I needed a distraction, and fortunately that came in the shape of a two-week family holiday to Orlando, Florida. There would definitely be enough to occupy me there, with the wife, kids, the Binns family – friends from the UK with whom we had planned our trip and shared our hotel – and beautiful sunshine. By the time I returned I should have all the answers I needed, and then some.

While in Florida, I made frequent trips to the internet room in the hotel lobby to see whether the chief had made contact. Patience was a virtue I had missed out on when it was handed out, and I thought it couldn't do any harm to check my mail once in a while on vacation. Maybe this was not such a good idea, because as it turned out I received zero correspondence from Chief Osula during the whole two-week period of my family holiday – not even confirmation that he had received my first or second email. I was having an amazing time with Jahlene, the girls and the Binns. But regardless of the fun the two families were having, I couldn't shake this nagging feeling at the back of my mind that was making me anxious. *How can I have come so far yet still have no answers?* I tried to suppress these thoughts until I got back to England, as it wasn't fair to let it spoil the holiday. The issue would still be there in a few days' time, so it was best to try taking my mind off it.

Jahlene had a few 'off' days while we were in Florida, feeling nauseous and a little giddy at times. It was extremely hot and sticky, especially outside the air-conditioned areas, and little Eva was ratty half the time. It got so hot that Jahlene even fainted at Sea World. It was strange that the rest of us didn't, but I figured she was more sensitive to the heat or something. She also complained of feeling bloated, but I put that down to the stodgy fast food we were regularly consuming. All the signs were there; I was just too preoccupied to pick up on them.

Once we returned to England on 25th June, I started to ponder another of the major distractions on the horizon: the event of the year; the 'This Is It' Michael Jackson concerts that were to start in just two weeks' time. My wife and I had been talking about it non-stop with our fellow vacationers, as we had tickets for the shows. I am a Michael Jackson fan and have been for the majority of my life, but this would be the first time I would get to see him perform live, and it was billed as the last time anyone would do so. Tickets had just been too expensive when I was growing up, and who would have taken me anyway? My workaholic dad?

That evening I went out for a walk, trying to adjust to being home and fighting the jet lag. En route I received a text from a work friend of mine called Karoline. The text simply stated: 'MICHAEL JACKSON HAS DIED!' *What? Don't even joke about that.*

I instantly dismissed the text as nonsense, as that particular story had been around once before and proved to be a hoax. Then Karoline followed up to ask if I was OK, knowing how big a fan I was. OK, this was getting a bit out of hand now. Within minutes I received a text from another work colleague saying the same thing. My heart began to sink as I pondered what I was reading and what it all meant. I raced home to check the television.

CNN, Fox News and Sky News all confirmed the worst in unison. My heart was broken. How can you mourn a man you'd never really known, yet spent your whole life invested in? Jahlene and I had danced to his 2001 classic 'Butterflies' at our wedding as our first dance. Michael Jackson had been such an important figure in my life as the most accessible and influential black person to me in a white household, yet he was someone I had never met until a few months previously, super briefly, sometime after his concert announcement.

I had been at the O2 Arena the day Jackson announced his new tour, and later that day found myself outside the prestigious Dorchester Hotel, alongside journalists and fans. I not only managed to get MJ's attention but something close to what I had dreamt about since a small boy happened: I received a handshake from the King of Pop himself. It wasn't a photo opportunity, but I was grateful for what I got, especially as mere months later he would be dead.

The magic died that night on 25th June 2009, as did my dream of collaborating creatively with him some day or bagging an interview. Shaking his hand was more than millions of fans got a chance to do, so that was something. It had been quite a year, with the advent of America's first black or biracial president in Barack Obama (which I'd celebrated with others at a party in London's Docklands), and now the loss of Michael Jackson, the first to tunefully assert that it didn't really matter whether people are black or white after all.

How things could be all sunshine and hope one day, and storm clouds the next was truly puzzling. I walked the streets of Catford in a sombre mood. Not just because days before I had been on sunny International Drive in Orlando, which was beyond comparison, but that everywhere I stepped I could hear Jackson's music blaring out of speeding cars, houses and shops as a communal tribute to a fallen star. I liked walking. It took my mind off situations like this one and the many stockpiled in my head, such as the Bini chief who was too busy to correspond.

It would turn out that I, or rather we, would have a bigger situation to occupy our minds than Jackson and Bini chiefs, however. The symptoms that had plagued Jahlene in Florida intensified in London, and it turned out that it wasn't the sunshine or junk food after all. It was baby number three. After having enough of feeling weird, Jahlene took herself to the doctor for checks and was told the news.

I got back from acting class that night to be given the update. 'Wow! Are you sure?' came the dumbest question ever to spill out of my mouth. It came as a complete shock to us both; a pleasant one, but a shock nonetheless. Father to three children? The stakes had just been raised and I needed some news from Nigeria more than ever. Nothing brings families together better than a new baby, they say. Well, hopefully I'd find out.

I continued to check my email inbox religiously over the next few weeks, each time hoping I'd hit the jackpot of personal revelations and long-awaited answers. The aerial silence was killing me inside. I prayed constantly that something would happen; for some exciting moment that would be a game-changer. Nothing. So I finally took matters into my own hands and called the chief directly.

As the phone started to ring, seconds felt like hours and my heart galloped like a racehorse in first position. If I got the news I was hoping for it would be like winning the Grand National, *American Idol* and all the lotteries on the planet at once, and then some. At the other end of the phone was the one who held the answers to my most important question of all. In that brief moment my mind wondered what it would be like to say hello to her. To share my life so far – heck, to introduce her to my wife and kids.

I was getting ahead of myself as the phone rang for what felt like forever. *Compose yourself, Tony*, I thought to myself. *Get it together and breathe.* This was a dignified older gentleman I was about to speak to, after all, and a chief at that, which means a great deal in African culture. They don't deal with the currency of sentiment in that culture, but respect; fail to trade with that and you will have problems. The fact that this was possibly either my uncle or, less likely, my very elderly grandfather was irrelevant at this time. I had to play things exactly right, or else I would blow the whole operation in one conversation. It would be like that situation in the movies when the hero has to defuse the bomb that will blow up a building full of people and has to carefully cut the red or blue wire to disarm it, but isn't one hundred per cent sure which. As my shaking hand held the phone close to my ear, my random thoughts were interrupted as the ringing abruptly stopped, and a deep-toned voice said hello.

'Good evening, Sir. This is Antony Osula,' I said with confidence and warmth.

This was met with a pause, as if he had been caught off guard or was confused. Had I just snipped the wrong wire? Then a muffled sound confirmed that he was still on the line. It was clear that he initially had no idea who I was, and suddenly then realised I was the young man from England he had spoken to weeks previously. There was a shift in enthusiasm in his voice, yet he still sounded laid-back and coy, allowing me to do all the talking.

I politely mentioned the emails I had sent to him, trying to keep my anxiety at bay and mask my frustration with regard to his lack of urgency. *Why haven't I heard from you?* is what I felt like saying. Busy or not, if the roles were reversed and he were my long-lost nephew or grandson I would have put him out of his misery by now. If I were him, I would have been eager to get this family reunion in full swing. Maybe they did things differently in Nigeria, or perhaps, being part of a very large and prominent family, this wasn't the first time this scenario had played out.

As the initial small talk subsided and things headed towards the matter at hand, I became increasingly confused. The chief sounded as if he had no idea who I was talking about when I frequently referred to my mother, which was strange. This confirmed to me that he was more likely a distant uncle, as a father would never have forgotten his own child. I knew that my grandfather, Chief Osula Senior, had likely been polygamous, having many children by many women, but surely siblings would have at least heard about each other, no matter how many of them there might be… right?

'Her name is PRISCILLA OMOSEDE OSULA, Uncle,' I reiterated for the second or third time.

In return for my efforts, I got the reply, 'Oh, yes! I know your mum. If you will invite me and my family, we can discuss things further.'

I was puzzled. *Invite?* I thought to myself. *As in, to a birthday party or something?* The emphasis on the word 'invite' made no sense to me whatsoever, especially at a time like this. "Sorry, Uncle. Invite…' I began.

'Yes. If you invite me and my children to the UK, we can talk.'

Again, was there some kind of magic word or action I was supposed to say or do? I held my tongue, but now wish I had said, *I'm sure at some point my wife and I would be delighted to host you and your family, but surely this is not the time to be discussing this.* I would much later come to understand that an 'invitation' or 'invitation letter' was something requested by a visitor from country A requiring a visa to gain entry into country B, like the UK or USA, which would include the invitee's commitment to financially support and look after the visitor during their stay, effectively taking full responsibility for them.

After the chief had carefully spelled out his request – that he wanted to come over to London with his wife and sons by my invitation – it finally dawned on me that this was some form of negotiation. I give him an invitation and he gives me access to, or at least information about, my mum. I finally understood. *How could I have been so stupid?* I was a meal ticket, an opportunity ripe for exploitation, and I couldn't understand how I had been so gullible.

Feeling duped and misled, my world began to unravel, and the realisation that I was on a not-so-cheap phone call from London to Nigeria that was a complete waste of time began to sink in. If this *was* my mother's brother, or any sort of relation, I wasn't sure this was the kind of family I wanted to be part of. I made an excuse to end the conversation as quickly and politely as I could, in spite of wanting to erupt like a volcano.

Everything was falling apart. My plan to find my mother had gone to pot. All the leads I had gathered had come to nothing and were, in truth, barren. I had no other connections in Nigeria, and most Nigerians I knew in the UK acted as if they were in exile, holding no ties to their country of origin. Out of luck and options, I had rolled the dice and they had flown off the table and vanished into thin air. In short, I had come to the end of the road.

CHAPTER TWELVE

Fatebook

While surfing through Facebook one day in the summer of 2009 following the bitter disappointment of my unsuccessful family investigation, the idea came to me to look up the Osula name and reach out to whomever I thought looked trustworthy. As a Westerner, I had been groomed to think that any contact with Nigeria and Nigerians was a dangerous game of Russian roulette. I felt secure, however, in the distance Facebook provided. It wasn't the real world, but a virtual one.

The following criteria and method might sound strange, but I restricted my contact to women bearing the same surname who looked to be between the ages of twenty and thirty, and who seemed educated and reasonably affluent. I felt women might feel more empathetic about my cause and were less likely to be involved in fraud. I was not going to be anybody's mark or meal ticket, and I wasn't going to fall for any more tricks or schemes.

I had nothing to lose, and although Facebook is about keeping in touch with friends and family, it also offers a way to send private messages to strangers, thus creating the possibility of estranged family reunions. I let my wife know that I would be searching the profiles of women who happened to have the same original surname as myself and that I would be reaching out to them. Maybe I'd have better luck this time, or maybe not, but at least I was taking matters into my own hands, asking questions and making contacts. If it were God's will for me to find my mother, He would guide my steps, right?

It was on the 7th of July that I sent several internal mail messages to various 'Ms Osulas' on the platform. I simply introduced myself like this: 'We may be cousins. My surname is also Osula and I'm trying to trace family in Nigeria and would appreciate any contact information and see what happens. Hope you will accept my friend request. Thanks. Tony.' It was a simple but straight-to-the-point request. This was my bait, cast into the sea to see if there would be any bites tugging at the end of the line.

The very next day I got that bite; not from one fish, but *two*. They were from presumed cousins by the names of Ukinebo Osula and Eronmwon 'Emmy' Osula. I already knew that the Osula clan was massive, so I had no doubt that we shared DNA. The real issue was how much DNA and how much they knew or could access, information-wise, from others in the know. Of these two ladies, the first reply came from Ukinebo: 'Yes, we are cousins. OSULA is one big family. I base in Nigeria but I can help.' This was short and simple but heartening. The next was from Emmy: 'Hi yes, we Osulas are one family. Don't worry, you'll find your way back home. No problem.'

Of the two leads, Emmy seemed to offer the best chance of success, as she went on to say that she would speak with her older sister about me and report back with any news. I knew the Osula family was one large unit, but I had no idea just how close my two young leads were to each other in the family tree. Unbelievably, they turned out to be half-sisters who shared the same father. In fact, they were just two out of twenty or so siblings – or half-siblings –from the same father. The degree of sepa-ration was becoming ever smaller. Emmy took ages to get back to me and wasn't really switched on about the urgency of the situation, failing to grasp that this meant everything to me. I had no choice but to be patient and not come across as too insistent in the email correspondence, which might jeopardise the whole operation. Ukinebo was still a back-up card for, but burning bridges with one sibling would likely spread to the other, and then I would be back to square one.

The days that followed this first contact felt like years. In truth, it had only been three days when I got a message from Emmy requesting my phone number, with the promise of exciting news from her older sister. I was literally shaking as I looked at my computer on the morning of the 10th of July and saw the first real potential lead of the summer. Breakfast didn't taste the same that day, as my full attention was on the prospect of what might be and the anxiety of waiting that followed. I really hoped she wouldn't drag her feet.

Emmy was a fair-skinned woman in her early twenties, who besides looking as though she knew how to enjoy life and was glamorously put together like a model, had a very similar cheekbone, forehead and eye composition to mine. I initially thought that she was my auntie, as after doing some research on the internet before making contact with her I had come across records of a Chief Valentine Edobor Osula. He had been a well-known, prominent figure in Nigerian society, and I assumed he was my late grandfather. When I chatted to Emmy about my research and mentioned him, I discovered he was her late father. By deduction, I assumed that my mother was one of the twenty or so siblings Emmy simply didn't know about. I remember seeing a photo among her Facebook photo albums of herself, Ukinebo and another girl, whom I discovered was their younger sister Izegbe, at a function. They looked vibrant and beautiful. How cool it would be to have these women as my aunties, I thought to myself, seeing an increasing similarity between us that was deeply impactful. At the very least we were related, and at best they would become firm family overnight. The more I dwelt on it, the more I found myself silently begging Emmy to pick up her phone and put me out of my misery.

∗ ∗ ∗

The phone call came late one night in mid-July. The soft lilt with a Nigerian accent gave away the fact that it was Emmy. Her intonation suggested she had some very important news to get across to me. This was it; the countdown to the moment I had been waiting for; the season finale of the longest, most angst-ridden summer of my life.

'Hey, Emmy, how are you?' I answered with standard phone etiquette.

Emmy was more to the point. "I have news about your mum…' She paused. I could actually feel the phone shake up against my cheek. 'She's late.'

As in, she's on her way but hasn't got to the phone yet? I thought as I grappled with the term 'late'.

'But don't worry…'

Wait a minute. My mother's late? I let the words sink in for a few seconds until the penny finally dropped. 'You mean… she's *dead*?' I said with chilling matter-of-factness and the hope that I had misunderstood what she had said.

'Yes. She's passed, but don't worry.'

Don't worry? DON'T WORRY?! I'm hearing that the woman who gave birth to me – my biological mother, whom I've never met but have thought about for years, whom I had hoped to meet one day – isn't alive any more, and I shouldn't worry? I felt as though I had just been kicked in the teeth and punched in the stomach all at once. Who knew that mere words could have such a devastating effect? This scenario had never played out in my head. This was not how the movie was supposed to end. Having faced great adversity, the protagonist should have been rewarded with a triumphant happy ending, complete with resolutions, with the 'journey' having made them a better person. Hollywood had clearly lied.

I'm sure Emmy continued talking, but my mind was somewhere else entirely. I tried to process this news and make sense of it all. This explained why Priscilla had never come back for me all these years and effectively let her off the hook. A mother who had wanted to come back for her son but couldn't from beyond the grave was a much more loving narrative than a mother who had simply carried on with her life apart from her firstborn, never once seeking him out. But I was beyond gutted.

In that moment I would have preferred to have an awkward conversation with a long-lost, dead-beat mum, however uncomfortable it felt, rather than deal with arguably the greatest disappointment of my life.

My eyes darted across the dark living room, lit only by the light flickering from the TV and PC screens, as I tried to calm my heart rate. *Is this it? The end of my journey? A complete dead-end void of answers and a face from the void that I now knew would never gaze back and make contact with my own eyes?* That void was too far gone into another realm. The only possible reunion now would be in death, which was a bridge I hoped not to cross for many more years to come.

Emmy was still on the phone. I knew this, as although I was adrift in a world of thoughts and emotions, I could faintly hear her asking if I was OK, which drew me back to reality.

'Sorry. Yes, I'm here,' I replied.

'OK, there's more. Your grandpa's name is Basula. He's late, too, but don't worry!'

It took everything I had not to slam down the phone and scream. Was any of my immediate family still alive? Not that I hadn't expected my grandfather to have passed already; it was just that hearing it confirmed was a double whammy, and it stung. By this point I was angry. Not with Emmy (though the frequent use of the term 'Don't worry' was fast becoming a trigger for my inner wrath), but because I had lost two close family members in one long-distance phone conversation, and I wasn't sure what the point of any of this was any more. I kept my cool, however, and committed to hearing out the rest of what she had to say, even though it felt as if I had invited the Grim Reaper around to my house for dinner.

'Hold on for my big sister Nauna,' Emmy said after trying to reassure me that in spite of these two big blows there was something positive to come out of all this. I waited, resisting the urge to hang up and trash everything in my immediate vicinity like an overgrown toddler. Childish? Perhaps, but this whole situation had reduced me to the state of a helpless child emotionally and psychologically, as at a primal level I felt the sharp edge of abandonment and then the realisation that the people I would have wanted to come back for me never could.

'Hello, Tony,' I heard another Nigerian-accented voice softly say. This voice was slightly deeper, and more authoritative and mature.

'Hi there, Auntie… Nauna?' In African culture everyone older than you is either Uncle or Auntie. I knew that much. I would later learn that her full name was Naruna, but she was affectionately called Nauna.

'Oh Tony, this is your Auntie Nauna. I'm your mum's cousin and we were very close. We grew up together, and she was the first-born girl of your grandpa. We called her Egbon.'

I came to know that 'Egbon' means 'senior' in Yoruba and was applied to my mum as the eldest girl in the family compound. I was intrigued. This auntie had my full attention.

'Tony, I'm so sorry your mum died. She flew to the UK already pregnant with you. She was so happy, and she told me all about you. She loved you very much, Tony.'

Those last few words cut like a knife's razor-sharp edge. 'What happened?' I asked nervously.

'Your mum made a mistake, Tony. She went on a trip to Paris, leaving you with the nanny in London, but she violated her visa, so they detained her once she got back to the UK. They deported her to Nigeria, but she couldn't take you with her. It broke her heart.'

This was the first time I had heard the full story, like why she was deported, and it was a lot to take in. The people who could have told me, namely my parents, were not around any more to verify the details. 'So my mother was deported?' I asked, appealing for more information.

'Yes, Tony. Then not long after she came back to Nigeria she went downhill, took sick and passed. Your grandpa found out and was devastated.'

There was so much to take in. 'My grandpa?'

She replied, 'Chief Alfred Basigie Osula. He was a very important man. The head of our family. He died sometime in the 80s.'

The name Basula, which Emmy had used earlier, was an abbreviation of his given names and derived from the fact that my grandpa owned a prominent bar in Lagos with that name. As a society man it had been frequented by high-profile people and many Western visitors to what was the capital back then.

Auntie Nauna told me everything that had happened and about all the family connections over the course of this long and expensive phone call. It was huge for me, as it put everything into context, and for the first time I had an understanding of my origins. Of course, this was all from one person's perspective, but it was a significant step beyond my own imagi-nation and could very well all be true, or at least partially true if not. Auntie Nauna referred to certain things that rang true about my situation and could only be explained by her being as close to my mother as she claimed. Either that or she had hired a private international investigator, which was beyond improbable.

No, the simplest answer in this case was the right one. She not only knew my mum, but importantly knew some of her secrets. She spoke as if she knew me, and in one sense she did. She had actually travelled to London once and met me as a baby, which came as a real surprise to me. For some reason I'd had the impression that I was a family secret and that no family member besides my mother had ever clapped eyes on me. It turned out I couldn't have been more wrong. My aunt, who was techni-cally my cousin, informed me that 'everybody' in the family, or at least everybody from her generation and the one above, knew about the late Omosede's 'lost infant son'. It was I who had never heard of them, but this was about to dramatically change.

Emmy had hooked me up good and proper. In spite of delivering the most devastating news ever in the most deadpan and understated manner possible, she had connected me to someone with solid insider infor-mation and who had actually known my mother, which was priceless. There were no scams this time, no requests for 'invitations' or any other form of transaction. This was just an excited, emotional family member rejoicing in the fact that a long-hoped-for day had finally come to pass. A piece of the past had finally found some resolution.

'May Omosede *finally* rest in peace, o!' Nauna said in celebratory relief. She confided to me that she felt she had let my mother down as a family go-between, because when Priscilla returned to Nigeria she was still estranged from the family, having left Benin pre-pregnancy to become an independent woman and then them finding out about me for the first time, particularly my grandfather. After her death there were seemingly no clues as to my whereabouts abroad on the Osula side. It was a double tragedy.

I was numb, emotionally drained and overwhelmed by the end of the phone conversation with my new-found aunt. She had told me not to worry (a favourite family expression, it seemed); she would be going straight to my immediate aunts, uncles (my mother's siblings) and great-aunts and uncles (my grandfather's siblings) to inform them about me. She assured me that upon hearing the news they would be overjoyed and very keen to reach out to me, so I should be prepared for this.

Prepared? OK. How should I prepare for something like this? I had no idea how to feel about speaking to immediate blood family – people who were either my mother's siblings or her own aunts and uncles. This was beyond surreal. But I knew that I'd better decide, as they would be ringing my number pretty soon and I would have to say something.

'Something' was a lot harder than I had estimated, as the phone started to ring a few hours later and didn't stop ringing for some days, as if my home had become the Nigerian Embassy. I got to speak to a variety of family members over that time, but the most important person I had to speak to straight away was Jahlene.

She was waiting on the staircase, listening in – there to support me if I needed it, but giving me space to deal with whatever was to come my way. She knew how important this whole thing was to me and was devastated I was to hear that my mother was dead and that I would never have that reunion, at least in this lifetime here on earth. Her eyes were filled with tears as she embraced me the moment I hung up the phone. Her baby bump pressed up against me, as if two people were comforting me. She didn't know what to say, but her embrace communicated that she felt my pain and was with me through this; that she had my back and was a constant in my life. No matter how difficult this road became, we were on this path together. I would always be her family.

CHAPTER THIRTEEN

Coming to Nigeria

My all-time favourite comedy movie is *Coming to America*: the 1988 classic directed by *American Werewolf in London* and *Thriller* music director John Landis, and starring *the* movie star of the 80s, Eddie Murphy. Murphy plays Prince Akeem of the fictional African nation Zamunda. It's an urban fairy tale about an African prince rejecting his father's plans for an arranged marriage, and instead flying to America to find his queen in the New York region of Queens, of all places. It is a typical fish-out-of-water scenario, with the very privileged African future monarch and his aide Semmi bumbling around in disguise as poor students in gritty, straight-talking New York City. It is as politically incorrect as they come, but in a harmless way that simply observes, sharply, the differences in culture, class and the black American experience in a witty, gut-busting series of scenes and interactions that only Eddie Murphy could get away with. In many ways, *Coming to America* is a celebration of black American culture, depicting a lot of its stereotypes, from the barbershop to over-the-top clergy to the running in-joke hair product commercial of 'Soul Glo', which satirises the wet-look, jheri-curl hairstyle I narrowly avoided as a child.

What truly sets this film apart, though, is its depiction of this rich culture through the eyes of an African from an Africa that isn't war-torn or ravaged by poverty. Prince Akeem isn't upgrading or improving his life by coming to America. This is a prince who knows who he is and walks with confidence, secure in his heritage, regardless of people's perceptions of him while he moves about incognito.

I wasn't from Zamunda, but Nigeria was just as fantastical in my mind, and I had heard almost every story about the nation imaginable without ever having travelled there. Nigeria had developed a bad reputation for its legendary email fraud schemes known as '419'. This infamous con job usually works along the lines of receiving an email about the next-of-kin or representative of a deceased wealthy individual needing a bank account to transfer wealth into, with the promise of a cut given to the kind person able to assist with their bank details.

The problem is that Nigeria, one of the wealthiest countries in the African continent, has suffered from terrible inequality. The majority of its two hundred million plus population are living in poverty or struggling to get by. A super-elite one per cent live like kings and queens as inheritors from the oil boom, due to corruption in government or from an intricate network of internal favours which ensures that wealth only travels through a limited, controlled stream. That stream often flows out of the country into Swiss bank accounts or through overseas investments, though the main point is that the wealth of Nigeria rarely ends up in Nigerian hands. Hence the endlessly inventive schemes some Nigerian natives concoct to make their money. But nothing can hinder the Nigerian spirit, it seems; the nation's inhabitants once topped a poll of the world's happiest people in spite of the many injustices they face in life.

Nigerians who came to the UK in the 1970s and 1980s were traditionally from the middle classes. They came to further their education and fill out the workforce as doctors and nurses, such was the high regard for England and its opportunities. The stereotypical Nigerian used to be the perpetual student and academic, endlessly studying at university and acquiring countless educational accomplishments, well read, philosophical and willing to get into frequent debates and passionate arguments.

I don't know when this changed to a depiction of the average Nigerian as a fraudulent con artist, scamming people for money online and thus becoming the new prevalent stereotype. Even the Nigerians I knew who lived in the UK were suspicious of anyone coming from Nigeria, and many had severed ties with their relatives and other people back home. Unlike most immigrants, those I knew who came from Nigeria rarely travelled back there and their children had often never been to their parents' homeland. A lot of kids I thought were Caribbean while I was growing up were actually Nigerians in disguise, having adopted the Jamaican swagger, patois slang and dress sense. Why was this the case? Maybe they were simply adapting to the majority black culture. Those from Africa couldn't pass as white, for sure. They could, however, assimilate the culture of the Caribbeans, who had been in the country for almost two decades and seemed to have been accepted, at the very least for their contributions to the NHS, entertainment and sport – a 'you can entertain us with your reggae and soul music and play in our premier football clubs, but do not live next door to us or date our children' kind of deal. So to avoid standing out as foreigners, I guess these freshly migrated Africans had worn the trappings of their slightly more tolerated cousins, and for a while this strategy stuck.

I remember classmates who, when asked if they were African, be it Ghanaian, Nigerian or other, would swear blind they were not. It was like Saint Peter denying Christ, except rather than the cock crowing it was the very African mum showing up at the school gate at home time in native attire and with a thick accent, shouting out the name of said classmate! I knew all about the potentially embarrassing home-time collection routine for different reasons, though I remember wondering why anyone would want to pretend to be anything other than who they were.

But being African or of African heritage was a contentious issue for some black kids. From Live Aid to the crises in Rwanda and the continuous charity adverts on TV, depicting malnourished African children covered in swarms of flies, this was the last thing an African child would want to be associated with. The playground diss of 'Your mum's a starving African off the telly' was a very real insult and would stab like a knife, leaving wounds of shame, humiliation and inferiority deep in the flesh. The only time I heard about the continent as a child was through news coverage of famines and plagues, charity adverts or in reference to the transatlantic slave trade once in a while. Black children were torn between being part of a world full of war-torn poverty on the one hand and descended from slaves on the other. What an enticing, soul-affirming choice.

If I hadn't met any of my new biological family before embarking on a trip to Nigeria, I might have been reluctant. Spending time with my great-aunt Marcellin and her daughter, my cousin once removed Jennifer, in north London smoothed things enough for me to know they were good, genuine people, and after spending hours in their presence there wasn't the slightest alarm bell raised. I then met Aunt Marcellin's son Julian in a luxurious flat in London's West End, where he told me stories and got to know me better, still struggling to believe that I was Omosede's long-lost son. I, on the other hand, was taken by how fancy his flat was and that it was positioned in the heart of a very expensive city. This family was far from a '419' threat, so why were people passionately trying to dissuade me from taking a trip to Nigeria? Anyone would think I was planning on taking a holiday to Afghanistan or Iraq circa 2003, such were the warnings and concerns. Nigeria was a dangerous and volatile place, or so I was led to believe. 'Go there at your own peril, and whatever you do make sure you don't go there alone,' I was told repeatedly.

I had always wanted to go, and now I had a reason to make this pilgrimage to my biological mother's land after meeting her family over the phone and via internet. But unlike when I went to Ghana, I did not have a Robert Kwami to guide me through this unfamiliar land. Though both West African countries, Ghana and Nigeria are very different animals with their own dynamics, the former being calmer and more predictable and the latter being more tumultuous. So I was in two minds. I wanted to explore the land my mother (and most likely my father) had come from, and put faces to the many voices I had heard over the phone, but I was also worried. Meeting members of the Osula family in England had been good, but would I be tempting fate by moving the reunion to foreign turf? What if I didn't like the rest of the family? Or even worse… they didn't like me? I had only spoken to those I would meet over there by phone, and I would be flying out alone, at the mercy of their hospitality.

Jahlene was worried too, but she knew how much this trip meant to me, so she encouraged me to have faith and take the plunge. She knew I would regret it if I didn't follow my gut. It had long been decided in my heart that Jahlene and the children were not just my priority but all the family I needed, when push came to shove. The idea of extending these borders was a profoundly deep and heavy prospect that I wasn't sure how to process.

Claire was also supportive, and curious of what I would find at the other side, having been gripped by the unfolding story. She had only been twelve when I came along, but she remembered my mother and the deportation situation very well. She was equally keen to learn the story from the other side and for me to get some form of closure, reminding me that whatever happened she would be in my corner. She encouraged me to go down the rabbit hole and not to worry too much about the 'what ifs', as I wasn't obligated to anyone but myself and my immediate family, so I could shout 'time out' at any point if I felt uncomfortable or didn't like what I was experiencing.

Even so, I honestly considered dropping the whole thing and being content with just knowing what had happened to my mother and where I came from. Some people in my circles echoed that sentiment, querying why I would want to dig and explore further, wondering what I would gain. I believed I would gain peace of mind and the chance to establish a connection with a long-severed root, if not for me, for my children. I owed it to them to take this trip and to establish whatever kind of relationship and connection I could with the Osula family. The past couldn't be changed, but I felt I could charter a new future.

It was late September 2009, just two months after that fateful evening when my past came crashing into my present, revealing my long-hidden origin story and family connections. The time to move the story along was nigh. I booked my flight with Dutch airline KLM, which meant a stop-off in Amsterdam for a few hours before boarding another plane to Lagos. It would be a long journey, but was the cheapest way to travel, so it seemed to be my best option.

I struggled to sleep the night before travelling, due to a strange mix of excitement and fear. I literally had no idea what would meet me at the other end, with flashbacks of my time at Accra airport in Ghana flooding my tired mind, and how far south that whole experience could have gone. There was only myself to worry about back then, with little else to lose, but things were very different by this point. I had a wife, two beautiful children and another on the way, so any misstep over there would affect my loved ones deeply. But there was no point entertaining these thoughts, so I prayed and forced myself to sleep as best I could before the big day ahead. Nigeria would see my face and the ground would welcome my feet. I owed it to myself, my children and my late mother Priscilla to close the loop.

All I possessed from Priscilla were the letters she had penned to my mum, Wynne Aris, from an address in Lagos that could only just be read on the almost thirty-year-old pieces of faded paper. One of the letters mentioned Priscilla's mother, my grandmother, in the strongest of terms, stating that I should be sent to Lagos to be with my grandmother 'over her [Priscilla's] dead body'. Priscilla stated that I would be bored and un-stimulated at the family home, as my grandmother was a busy business-woman who would be doing anything but nanny duties. This picture of how the family dynamics worked was as much as I knew about my mother's maternal side of the family. Although my grandmother would unlikely still be alive or living at the same house all these years later, maybe this address would provide some clues in tracking down other family members on my trip.

With bags packed, and after giving Jahlene some heartfelt reassurances, we clung to one another in an embrace that seemed to last for ever. We were both unsure what the outcome would be and what things would be like when we next embraced, if we ever did. I was going to the 'Wild West' of African nations, after all. I hadn't made a will or anything dramatic (or sensible) like that; we had faith that everything would be fine and that I would return in one piece. I made sure I had a visa sorted out and was cleared to travel this time, having learned from the mistake I had made exactly ten years previously. No, this time I would be super-prepared, having done my homework and had all my injections on schedule.

The flights were fine. I recall thinking how much had changed since the last time I had travelled to Africa and also considering the great contrast between this trip and the one I had taken just three months previously to Florida with my family. There would be no theme park in sight this time, as this trip was strictly personal business. If there was any fun to be had, that would be icing on the cake with a cherry on top. There was some turbulence as we made our descent onto the tarmac of Murtala Muhammed International Airport, so I wasn't sure whether my anxiety was a physical reaction to the bumpiness and sudden jolt in the air, or a growing awareness that the journey I had been thinking about for many years was about to become a reality. It was night-time in Lagos, so I would naturally need to be even more alert and aware of my surroundings.

After disembarking and working my way through the arduous customs process, punctuated by continuous requests for 'gifts', I finally reached the pick-up point feeling drained and vulnerable. I was on the lookout for a face I had never met before. The plan, as arranged by my great-uncle Ephraim, the elderly head of my family clan and mastermind of this mission, was for me to stay overnight with his son Julian, whom I had visited in London. I would be collected by his driver at the airport, who would hold up the clichéd handwritten sign to identify himself to me among the throbbing crowd.

Judging by its international airport, Nigeria seemed more rough-and-tumble than the parts of Ghana I had seen. There was a constant sense that anything could kick off at any given moment. Arguments erupted among taxi drivers over who would collect customers, and there was a real sense of people acting exactly the way they felt rather than by the agreed social norms I was used to back in England, or rather at the very formal Heathrow Airport. I would have preferred the face greeting me at the airport to have been Julian's, but after scanning the sign I had spotted a number of times to be one hundred per cent sure, I decided the driver's face would do. He kindly took my luggage and we made our way to the car.

After what felt like for ever getting to the car park and then out of it, my eyes seized the moment to observe my new environment, and I made a mental note that I had actually done it; I was finally in Nigeria! It wasn't too dissimilar to Ghana after all, just dialled up by ten in terms of action and volume. There was an even bigger sea of black faces everywhere than on my previous trip to Africa, and I noted that I hadn't experienced a deeply dramatic connection to the land yet. But I was only a couple of hours into my trip, and at a crowded airport to boot, so expectations had to be held firmly in check.

Nothing, however, prepared me for what we encountered on the long drive from the airport to my cousin Julian's abode in Victoria Island. Though the darkness, I clearly saw out of the passenger window what looked to be a pile of inanimate bodies scattered along the roadside. What I was seeing was a field of dead men and women, strewn out in various directions, covered in blood. As my mind processed what my disbelieving eyes had sent it, I uttered, between gasping breaths, 'Did I just see what I think I saw?' I hoped my mind was playing tricks on me through tiredness, or perhaps as a strange side-effect of the travel medication I had taken before flying.

'Oh, you mean the dead bodies? Ha! Welcome to Nigeria!' came the nonchalant reply, as if I had simply spotted a cow or goat. How anyone could be so dismissive of dead bodies was beyond me. Further still, they didn't look fresh, so I wondered where on earth the emergency services had got to.

Only later would I learn how naive I had been and what 'Welcome to Nigeria' really meant. Life and death hangs on a knife edge for many in this part of the world, which forces people to take the rough with the smooth. Survival mode desensitises them to the imminent possibility of death and suffering which would be unheard of in the West. Bad stuff happens in the Western world all the time, but it isn't a distinct possibility each time you step outside of your house, like a real-life version of Russian roulette. This was a foreign concept to my thoroughly Westernised mind and life experience. I had never seen a dead body aside from that of my father after his peaceful passing, and that was a far cry from the grim scene I had seen through the car window.

The moment passed quickly as the scenery changed. But the memory was already carved into my mind. I started praying, first that my eyes would experience much more pleasant sights moving forward, and second that, bearing in mind the speed we were doing along these dodgy, uneven roads, we would not be joining the pile of bodies. *Surely this adventure called my life isn't destined to end on a roadside somewhere in Lagos*, I thought as I continued this surreal journey.

The landscape around me was changing as the scenes became more developed and urban, with buildings and houses appearing, giving the emerging sense of a densely populated city. Though it was the early hours of the morning, many people were still awake, and the bustle on the street suggested just how crazy things would be during daylight hours. This was more like it; a bustling African city with a lively buzz rather than a shadow of death. The buildings looked very old, almost derelict, giving the impression that the city had been neglected over many years, its infrastructure literally hanging together by its bricks. *So this is Lagos, one of the continent's most famous cities?* I wasn't impressed.

I fought with everything I had to stay awake, as I wanted to drink in the sights of Lagos on this maiden voyage, taking in every possible detail, but this proved to be an uphill struggle. One minute I was alert and observing everything around me, the next I was out of it in the realm of sleep. This cycle was on constant repeat throughout the very long drive to Julian's home, and at one point I assumed we were in another country, such was the duration of this drive. My eyes flickered open to see big, lavish buildings that looked totally different from what I'd seen before. Had we driven so far that we had reached America? Honestly, the contrast of wherever the heck we were with where we had been earlier was like night and day. Much more like a modern city, with its neon lights, smoother roads and huge banks, it was generally more pleasing to the eye.

'Where are we, please?' I asked.

'This is Victoria Island,' came the reply.

It was the upmarket, wealthier district of Lagos, where all the development had taken place, likely at the expense of the old part of Lagos, which had lost none of its charm even if it had lost its shine.

We soon approached my cousin's home within the exclusive gated community for Lagosians who had money and wanted to keep it that way. There was a security guard who needed to check the particulars of my driver, and after a few moments we were allowed through the barrier and climbing up towards a row of modern-looking suburban houses.

This was all too much for me. The contrasts I had already seen in this country were beyond overwhelming, as literally each time I opened my eyes it felt as though I were in an entirely different location; from poverty-stricken villages to a gated community that could rival those in Beverly Hills. I had a lot to learn on this trip, but in the meantime I was just glad to have finally arrived at my destination. All I wanted to do was sleep.

Despite having caught a glimpse of how my much older cousin Julian rolled in London, I was still taken aback by how lavish his Lagos home was. He enjoyed the finer things in life, that much was certain. Let's just say that, judging by this set-up, the revelation that I was part of a royal family made a ton of sense, as this was a lifestyle fit for a king. Julian, or 'Uncle Julian' given that we were in Nigeria, was very welcoming and enthusiastic about showing me his home which he was very proud of. I could easily have stayed there for the duration of my three-week stay, but the plan was to catch a flight to Benin City in a few hours' time to be received by the bulk of the family there.

After a good night's sleep, which thankfully didn't feature dead bodies or anything unpleasant, I was refreshed enough to continue the journey. Julian wouldn't be joining me for the flight to Benin, but he rode in the car with me while his driver took us back the way we had come hours previously, and this time I got to take a look at Lagos by day.

Julian helpfully told me what to expect when I arrived at Benin and let me know that it was a very different place from Lagos: less hustle and bustle and much more traditional. It was good of him to spend this time with me, as I quickly figured out that Lagos was a busy place. With the nightmarish traffic situation, I understood just how much of a sacrifice giving up his time was. A simple drive to the airport was invariably a day-trip. It was nice to see a familiar face in a very foreign environment, and one thing was abundantly clear: there was no way on earth Uncle Julian needed any money from this Western tourist. All the warnings about guarding my money while in Nigeria or about being harassed for cash, at least within my family circles, were utterly redundant and misguided. Outside of paying for my overseas flights, all my expenses were taken care of by the family, and their hospitality was second to none.

Before long, Julian was wishing me all the best as it was time to board a local flight to Benin City from a different airport in Lagos. The flight was with local airline Aero, which made me nervous, as Nigeria was a place where accidents happened, and people would simply shrug their shoulders at the news of a plane crashing or a similar event. I was beginning to wonder how high their standards were when it came to keeping people alive. Pushing such thoughts to the back of my mind, I boarded the afternoon flight and was in Benin City within a couple of hours.

I didn't exactly kiss the ground when I arrived, but I was elated that it had been an incident-free flight and that I was on the cusp of experiencing what I had travelled all these miles for. My auntie, Tonia 'Esohe' Osula, had constantly been on the other end of the phone with me since that memorable night in July, and I had seen pictures of her on Facebook, so I knew I would be able to spot her in a line-up. Just as well, as she was the only family member I recognised among the convoy that came to the airport to meet me.

Auntie Esohe was nearly six feet tall with a healthy, solid structure that fit the standard of a mature African woman. She was slightly darker in tone than me, with long, braided hair, big cheeks and a face so warm it could melt polar ice caps. She wore a bright white top with large sun-glasses hanging off the side and a flowing black skirt, with huge, hooped earrings; much more modern than the traditional native auntie look I was expecting, but I liked it and she looked like a ton of fun. The family re-semblance was clear; namely the high forehead, prominent cheeks and twinkle in the smiling eyes, which was as eerie as it was welcoming. I glimpsed her face from across the concourse of the airport, her infectious smile drawing my line of sight like a magnet, followed by a hearty laugh of joy and possibly relief from her end. As I raced to meet her with a big bear hug, a sudden and unexpected swell of joy and relief came over me, too. This was more what I had been expecting when I arrived in the coun-try hours earlier.

The hug felt like it went on for ever, and in the intense heat we were both sweaty and sticky, but neither of us cared. This was a genuine family moment and possibly the closest I would ever get to the mother and son reunion I had craved. There were no tears, but a deep sense of joy and contentment, so much so that I didn't notice when we first unlocked our-selves from the bear hug that Auntie Esohe wasn't alone. There were more family members present, ready to receive this long-lost son.

One by one, Auntie Esohe introduced them: 'Tony, dis is your uncle, Father Babs... dis is your auntie Grace... dis is your cousin Osas... and dis is your cousin Alfred.' What made things confusing was that in Nigerian culture anyone senior to you was either auntie or uncle, so it took a minute to work out the precise family relationship with people I was being introduced to. Aunties Esohe and Grace were both in their fifties and had the same skin tone and familial features – the forehead, eyes and smile – to the point that it became more and more overwhelming the longer I was in their presence.

I saw the resemblance especially strongly in Father Babs, called 'Father' as he was a Catholic priest, who was wearing a grey khaki shirt and clerical collar at the time of our first meeting. *A fellow God-botherer*, I thought, excited to have something in common with a family member, before later realising I would have been the anomaly if I hadn't believed in God. I came from a family of Christians, ranging from Catholic to Pentecostal. Who would have known? He was more formal than the others – friendly but aware of his station as elder and minister, and the polar opposite of the excitable and informal Auntie Esohe.

Auntie Grace was somewhere in between. Wearing native attire, she was a vision of bright orange from the top of her headscarf to her flowing dress. She also gave a great hug and had the broadest tooth-brimmed smile I had ever seen, which wrapped around her whole face, exaggerated by her comparatively small eyes. Her jolly, fast-talking demeanour belied a no-nonsense, don't-mess energy that I soon witnessed first hand in the few times I rode in her car on the rowdy roads of Benin. In contrast, Auntie Esohe was a big softie, who wore her heart on her sleeve, very much like me. I wondered if I had been named after her, as her full name was 'Anthonia' and she was my mother's immediate junior sister.

Next in line was my younger cousin Alfred, who was a lively, funny young man, eager to entertain. In his late teens, he had a slender frame and a grin like a Cheshire cat on acid. Alfred was almost as excited to be there as Auntie Esohe, and he was super-enthusiastic about gaining a brand-new first cousin, having heard all about me.

The line-up was concluded by Alfred's younger brother Osamudein, Osas for short, who, like Alfred, was the son of my mother's elder brother, Uncle Ayo Osula, who I would meet him later. Alfred and Osas both had that distinct trademark family look, but Osas was heavier set build-wise than me and Alfred, with broader features. He was incredibly polite and laid-back, friendly but reserved, likely because he was in the company of elders and was the very youngest of this family entourage.

After some small talk had taken place, the main thing on everyone's mind was food, and we swiftly made our way to find somewhere to sit, talk and most importantly eat. *This should be interesting,* I thought to myself. Anyone who knows me knows that I'm notoriously fussy about what I eat, and the very sight of food that doesn't measure up to my standards can make me feel uncontrollably nauseous. I wasn't exactly a connoisseur of Nigerian cuisine. The most I had consumed at this point was jollof rice with inexplicably dry and chewy chicken, so I was secretly worried when we stopped off at some roadside eatery. Everyone looked excited about eating, while I was nervous. *What if I hated the food and can't eat it? What sort of first impression will that give?* Thoughts of retching, moments after eating, flooded my anxious mind as a host of enthusiastic suggestions for what I should eat came thick and fast. My freshly met relatives were beyond ex-cited to initiate me in their eating traditions, each suggesting a meal I should eat first, with names such as 'egusi soup' and 'amala' being bandied about, which were all foreign to this hungry but extremely cautious British boy's palette.

As I looked through the menu, puzzled, Father Babs grew impatient and decided on my behalf. I was to have pounded yam and egusi soup, which sounded… interesting. When it came, it looked like something you might find at the bottom of the ocean, all green and seaweedy with meat mixed in and a green sauce. It was accompanied by a mound of solid white mashed potato-like substance rolled into a ball in cling film at the side of the plate. I noticed there was no knife and fork, and before I tried to get the attention of the server, I realised none of my family had cutlery either and there was a bowl of water beside my meal. *Oh, so we eat with our hands then. Well, when in Rome…* I thought as I looked intensely at my strange-looking plate.

Auntie Esohe explained the culinary rules of engagement. I was to use the mashed potato-like food (pounded yam) to soak up the egusi soup with my hands –simple as that. I nodded my head and was about to get started when I saw the smiling faces of my family members who had stopped what they were doing to watch me like hawks. It was as if they were watching a baby take its first steps. My camera was in Cousin Osas's hand and he was taking a photograph of this historic moment. Yes, Tony would be eating his first local meal in Nigeria, and more specifically in his ancestral hometown of Benin – a true photo opportunity.

As I took my yam in hand and swooped down into the green egusi sea, I hoped to high heaven that this food tasted better than it looked and smelled. One chew, two chews, three chews… hmm, this wasn't too bad, according to the memo my taste buds were shooting to my brain. It wasn't Nando's, but it wasn't horrid either, and I successfully passed the Nigerian test with this eating exercise. It felt as though I was under a microscope, though, with eyes continuously on me. By looking at me I was clearly part of their family, but I was also a foreigner with very peculiar ways and something of a fascination – a walking experiment of nature versus nurture.

With lunch out the way we were on the move again, and looking through the car window I saw a lot of agriculture, much more than in Lagos, and flat buildings that were less stacked up high and more spread out. So far, Benin seemed more like a country town than a modern city; much more like the African experience I had been hoping for. The sun was oppressive, however, and unlike in Florida, which was equally hot, there was no air-conditioned respite to escape its effects.

The drive was bumpy in Auntie Grace's car and she was taking no prisoners as she fearlessly screeched 'Ideee-ot!' through the window at passing drivers who obstructed her in any way. The fact that some of the male drivers in question were imposingly large and intimidating made no difference to her, which confirmed to me that this cousin/auntie was truly 'gangsta'. Auntie Grace was chatty, loud and straight to the point, so conversation was entertaining, and her swagger suggested a confidence akin to that of an alpha male.

I have a similarly explosive temper when agitated and a serious, composed side, heart worn openly on my sleeve, so I could see an aspect of myself in each of my senior relatives in how they initially came across. I sat next to Auntie Esohe, who was as excited as a child on Christmas morning just chatting to me and telling me about all the family members she wanted to show me off to like a proud new mother.

We were on our way to what I was told was called Lagos Street, an area of Benin where the ancestral home of the Osulas was to be found. This was exciting, as I discovered the Osula family was huge, spanning into the thousands, with even my immediate line amounting to the size of a small village. That's polygamy plus no TV for you! Evidently the Osula men had no trouble on the procreation front, with the full family tree resembling something of a forest.

I don't know what I was expecting as the car suddenly slowed down on a rowdy, market-like road and pulled up alongside a basic-looking, plastered brick building with a little shop at the side. Judging by the sudden stopping of the car and everyone getting out I figured we had reached our destination, but where was the ancient-looking complex that had housed the very first Osula and his clan? This was, after all, the home of the head of the family, Chief Osula, who had at one time been my grandfather, then my uncle and was now my first cousin. I came to understand that the Chief Osula I had been liaising with that summer over the phone was a distant cousin, and though a legit chief of sorts was not *the* Chief Osula of our hereditary line. Incidentally, his own residence was down the road, but for now we were staring at the main family estate. The way Auntie Esohe had described it and its significance, I had half expected something like Castle Grayskull from *Masters of the Universe* meets *Shaka*

Zulu rather than the uninspiring brick storefront that stood before us. I would soon learn that my auntie got excited about things with much more regularity and lower criteria than myself, to put it diplomatically, and I often needed to abandon all expectation and take things as they came.

As I got out of the car, unravelling my squashed frame, I looked up and out. After examining the exterior, my mind jumped to what was to come next: an audience with the elders of my family who had gathered to formally receive me into the fold. As I walked through the archway, I took a deep breath in to control the anxiety that had begun to race through my body. This was the moment of truth.

Awaiting me on the other side was a walkway that led into a square arena that acted as the concourse of a building that had rooms all around it with a ground level and a second floor. This came as a surprise, as the complex was far larger than it had first appeared from its tiny front entrance. There was an additional bungalow across the courtyard, which was separate from the building within the concourse. It looked like a later addition, and it turned out that was where we were headed.

The famous Lagos Street was starting to become more interesting, and as we walked through a set of doors, we suddenly found ourselves in the home of Chief Iyeke 'Curtis' Osula: the head of this clan and son of my mother's late brother, Chief Biola Osula, my uncle. He had died several years previously – another missed opportunity to meet my flesh and blood due to an untimely death. For reasons unclear to myself, my cousin had only recently taken the hereditary mantle of chief, as the ceremonial head of our infinitely large family, and he was a year or so younger than me. Still, this was not only his domain but his home, so I planned to be as respectful to him as I would have been to a senior uncle according to culture and tradition.

As we entered the bungalow it led straight into the living room, where a council of seven or so senior family members were seated (a few others stood around the room and outside), including the young Chief Osula. The elders in the room were my immediate uncle Ayo; my great-great-uncle, youngest brother of my great-grandfather Chief Idugboe Osula; Great-Uncle Blessing; and finally the mastermind of the assembly, my great-uncle Ephraim. I could finally put a face to a voice I had heard several times on the phone. My great-uncle Ephraim radiated a seniority and gravitas even simply sitting down on the sofa as he led the proceedings, asking each present family member to introduce themselves and explain their place within the family tree. The formality made it feel like a cross between a court hearing and a church service, but I didn't mind as it made the whole situation more eventful, and my cousin Osas had kindly offered to film the whole thing on my brand-new Sony camcorder, the living journal I would use to record everything and anything I experienced on this epic adventure.

Uncle Ephraim was dressed in a casual but smart dark native suit and was easily in his early seventies, with greying hair and a noticeably lighter skin tone. He led the room with his deep, gravelly voice and reserved politician-like manner. His gestures were far more controlled and relaxed than those of most of the Nigerian men I had come across so far. He was a statesman, and I intuitively knew he was the most respected person in the room and would be the decision-maker for all that happened in the two weeks I was there.

On the other side of the room was his younger brother, my great-uncle Osaetin Osula, also known as 'Blessing'. He was similarly lighter skinned, short but heavier set and strong with a bolder, more extroverted composition than his elder brother. Like my other family members, he wore a broad smile across his bespectacled face. Ephraim and Osaetin were the younger brothers of my grandfather, Chief Alfred Basigie Osula, so as my mother's immediate uncles they would have known her very well and could give a full family perspective, alongside other members in the room such as my mother's brother Ayo Osula, her sister Esohe, her cousins Grace and Father Babs and, to my pleasant surprise, Auntie Nauna.

Nauna stood out in the room. A lady in her fifties, tall and strong in stature with caramel skin and wearing bright yellow native attire, she couldn't have blended into the background if she had tried. I was overcome in that moment as my eyes spied her, very much aware that none of this would have been possible without her, as she had brought the news of my existence to the family and set the ball rolling for this inevitable reunion. It was she who had first told me about my mother and that I was part of a large, prestigious family that would receive me with wide open arms, constantly reassuring me of this fact as my trip drew closer. Her words were proved true as I stood before a small but important delegation of our large royal family in this small living space.

Nauna took to the floor and addressed the group, sharing the testimony of how this had all come about, her involvement and how she could rest freely now that she had played a part in fulfilling the promise she had made to her cousin about looking out for me. It turned out that nobody knew where I was in England, at least for the majority of the time, so rather than them finding me, they had had to wait for me to find them. I learned through asking questions that the 'Edobor' name that Nauna and her siblings used in front of Osula was the Edo name of their late father and a way of distinguishing their immediate lineage, which I came to understand was of almost political importance in this culture.

Auntie Nauna's sister, Mary-Rose, was also in attendance and had the same likeness, though she was much slimmer and even taller. Glasses covered a warm face with expressive eyes that were obviously welcoming me into this inner circle. My uncle Ayo, a large, physically imposing man, sat silently in black native wear with a serious and stern disposition that gave nothing away. I couldn't work out whether he was happy to see me or how he felt about the whole affair, but he was present and I could see the family likeness even though he was much darker and more muscular than anyone else.

I was actually taken aback by the diversity of appearance in the room. There were different shades as well as different heights and frames, yet we all had a common physical thread which made it clear that we came from the same gene pool. Drinking in these details was important to me, as it was the first time I had ever had such a large sample of blood relatives to study. I had to balance my observations with trying to avoid looking as though I was staring rudely.

After a number of speeches, the elders raised a small bowl containing a kola nut: a nut like a cashew dissected into pieces that we were each to eat alongside a small thimbleful of gin. I had no idea what this signified and was slightly confused until Uncle Ephraim, as if anticipating what I was thinking, explained that what we were about to do was an Edo tradition of welcoming. It was like a form of communion, where you eat then drink as one, culminating in a prayer led by my cousin, the family priest, to formally initiate me into the fold.

Sounds simple, I thought, until I tasted the kola nut and almost retched, such was its bitter taste. As a non-drinker, the gin wasn't any better. The face I made told the whole story. This did not go unnoticed, as I heard a couple of laughs and saw some smiles, but it was something that had to be done.

When it was all over, the meeting was finished and there were hugs all round. It was clear that the majority of those present loved to talk and tell stories; it was a consistent thread. Each member took to the floor to deliver a monologue – even my junior cousin Alfred. It made a great deal of sense that I was related to these people, as there's never been a spotlight I've run away from or words I've failed to speak when given the opportunity.

Of the whole group, Chief Osula, the family figurehead and my cousin, was the quietest. Even my previously mute uncle Ayo had livened up, giving me a hug and expressing how much I looked like his late sister, while I was busy thinking, *Wow! This guy is huge!* Chief was a young man of few words and was clearly an introvert among extroverts who gave very little away. He did, however, seem pleased to meet me, and after all he was opening up his home during my stay in Benin.

My young cousins and I were to bunk in one of the flats above the courtyard. It had a mattress and some basic furniture, and more importantly a mosquito net, which would be very important come night-time. I had never stayed in an ancestral home before. This one had been in the family for a couple of hundred years, and though it wasn't the Ritz by any stretch, the thought that this humble accommodation had housed generations of Osulas, including my mother, made it special enough for me.

After the initiation ceremony and a good night's rest, Auntie Esohe and my cousins Alfred and Osas were to be my constant companions, taking me around Benin to visit tourist sites and many extended family members. It was fun and all a bit of an adventure, though a lot to take in within a short space of time and thoroughly exhausting. Names and faces started to bleed into each other as Auntie Esohe frequently said to me, 'This is your auntie… uncle… cousin…' Rinse, wash and repeat. Uncle Ephraim had suggested to his niece that she cram as much into my schedule as possible leading up to the big day on Saturday, which would be exactly eight days since I arrived in Benin.

You're probably wondering what was to happen on Saturday and why I needed to mention the number of days until it arrived. Well, in Nigerian culture, and especially Edo tradition, everything has a meaning and significance. On the eighth day after a baby is born, the family traditionally gathers around the newborn and parents to offer up a name for the little one. This event is called a naming ceremony. The child's parents are not obligated to choose a name suggested by the family, but it's a customary ritual and the full chosen names are pronounced, and henceforth the boy or girl is known to the world by the names given there and then.

That forthcoming Saturday was to be my very own naming cere-mony… aged thirty years old! I already had a name and was very used to it, but it was pointed out to me that this was a true initiation ritual into the Osula clan. This would be the ceremony I never had, having been born in England, and I would be given an Edo moniker to go with my English and Yoruba ones. And if they were insisting on throwing me my own personal party, then why not? Besides, it would be rude to turn it down or be a no-show at an event in my honour held at the Lagos Street residence itself. This was a big deal and word would soon travel around Benin, and possibly further, that a lost son had returned. Within such a large family as the Osula clan, this was unlikely to have been the first time a missing family member had emerged from somewhere, but I wasn't just any random individual. I was the first grandson of the most notorious Chief Osula, whose influence and benevolence was legendary. My grandfather had done a lot for many people in the family, and this was an opportunity to honour him as much as to roll out a welcoming red carpet for his grandson.

Besides being introduced to every single person in Benin carrying the last name Osula by Auntie Esohe, I tried to learn as much as possible in the run-up to the naming ceremony. There was so much catching up to do, and I tried to be like a sponge, absorbing every drop of detail available. Auntie Esohe was an encyclopaedia of family connections and a walking black book of contacts, though there were other points of contact for useful information.

Great-Uncle Ephraim was the unofficial head and patriarch of my immediate family there. His home acted as HQ for many of the gatherings and discussions; not just regarding my trip, but for a multitude of family matters. Uncle Ephraim carried natural authority and gravitas. As huge as my uncle Ayo was in stature, he still humbly took direction from his much smaller uncle. Staying at his home after a few days in Lagos Street was not only a comfortable upgrade but gave me personal access to the families head. That access would have saved me a lot of mosquito bites if it had come earlier, but I took what I was given.

Uncle Ephraim's home had everything I was used to comfort-wise, including satellite television and the all-important aircon. Having servants in the house took some getting used to, especially as I was accustomed to taking my own plate to the kitchen and making myself a drink. Having someone wait on you might sound great in theory, but it felt somewhat uncomfortable in practice, as I couldn't help imagining that if things had been different that might have been me. Not that the staff were ill-treated, but it was clear that in Nigeria the lifestyle you had was based on a sort of lottery. You were either born lucky or you were not, and the likelihood of ever escaping your lot in life was very slim.

Talking with Uncle Ephraim was a pleasure, as he had great wisdom. Being a man in his seventies, he had a broad depth of experience to share and could give me an overview of family and Benin histories. He had looked up to his older brother, my grandpa, and had been helped by him during his youth by way of sponsorship to London to pursue accountancy studies. He spoke of his late brother with real affection and respect, though he lamented the vices that had contributed to his unnecessary demise. He made a point of explaining how growing up in a polygamous home was not a good thing, with multiple siblings from multiple mothers in the family compound. Naturally, the full-blooded siblings were the closest, and I'm sure much political manoeuvring was learned through these delicate childhood interactions with half-siblings. The pain caused by this family dynamic had clearly left its wounds on the children, and Uncle Ephraim was adamant that this wasn't the best environment for young ones.

Spending time with Uncle Ephraim reminded me of the times I had spent with my father. Both men were wise and deeply philosophical, and both enjoyed passing down their wisdom to this inquisitive mind. I lived for that kind of talk, and the more I was able to learn about the intricacies of our family history the better. Being around him was the closest thing I had to having my grandfather present, and he was tangibly manifested through various anecdotes.

One afternoon I met with Uncle Ephraim at his printing press, which he had set up when he retired many years previously. In the absence of a stable economy, Nigerians had to be entrepreneurial by necessity. It was here that he proudly introduced me to his proudest print project: his self-produced autobiography. It was bright yellow, with the face of a familiar but very young man on the front printed in thick black ink. At first, I found the idea of writing and self-publishing your own life story a little ostentatious, but perhaps that was the English mentality coming through. On reflection I began to see the value of putting your story down on paper, especially if you had lived through interesting times. Uncle Ephraim had done so and then some.

Every time I spoke with him, I was in awe of how he had overcome so many obstacles in turbulent situations. Losing businesses, surviving military coups, the Biafran war breaking out around him, all with a young family, his life had been no walk in the park. He was keen to teach me that no matter how prestigious the name Osula was or the royal blood we possessed, it had been no meal ticket through life. Each of us had to stand on our own two feet and make a name for ourselves. We each had to make our own mark in life; no one would do it for us. This was probably one of the earliest lessons learned in a polygamous household, each child having to fight for their place in the compound to get what was theirs.

'Tony, remember… *this* is your home. Wherever you are in the world *this* is your root and nobody can take it away from you,' Uncle Ephraim said with stern conviction. Most Nigerians are proud people, but the Edo people of Benin City are notorious for their pride and their ability to stand up to anyone with their heads held high.

'You come from a royal family and from the immediate line of the chiefs,' he continued, referring to his father and then his elder brother, my grandpa. 'Know where you come from, but you have to make your own path in life.' The firmness of his admonition intrigued me. 'Here, take a copy of this.'

Uncle handed me the yellow book containing his life story, which felt like being handed a key to an old mystery box. I had always liked history in school, but that was general, whereas this was deeply personal. My curiosity level was through the roof at this point. Thumbing through the pages, I was immediately drawn to photographs of my great-grandparents, Grandpa and his siblings, which transported my mind through time and space. A couple of months earlier I had never seen my own mother's face;

now I was seeing those she was descended from in this book. I felt like Indiana Jones with the holy grail in his hand.

The first thing that struck me was how much I looked like my grand-father's brother, Victor Osula. It was like looking at selfies twenty years into the future. The second thing was just how giant Grandpa was, stand-ing over six feet tall in his chieftain garments, all bare-chested with beads. He oozed regality and self-assuredness in the shot, rather than looking like the fun-loving guy I had heard about. His father, Chief Idugboe, was much shorter and had a lighter complexion than Grandpa, who had dark mahogany skin, and Chief Idugboe was stern-faced, lacking the warm smile of his son. I not only gained all this information from two flat im-ages on a page, but had it confirmed by Uncle Ephraim as he spoke of them. Ephraim Osula had certainly inherited the stern look of his late father, a court judge, and shared his no-nonsense outlook on life and per-sonal discipline. The resemblance, it appeared, was multifaceted.

I made sure to let my uncle know just how much of an honour it was to receive the book in my hand and hear his narration of our shared leg-acy. It was genuine, and I also appreciated his self-controlled demeanour and quiet authority in an environment in which everyone shouted and postured. Even for an extrovert like myself this had become tiresome af-ter a while, so Uncle Ephraim's company was a very welcome refuge from all the noise and high-octane activity. He was an elderly statesman through and through; a distinguished gentleman from a bygone era yet still with us.

While the clock counted down for my naming ceremony, I sat with this book every chance I had, drinking in its details. The life of Ephraim Nakaru Osula was interesting enough, but it was the roots of the tree I was poring over. After all, it's not every day that you discover the back-story of your mother's regal lineage. Reading the first few pages reminded me of the genealogies in the Bible, with all the begottens and begettings. The Osula family tree read as follows:

Chief Obasuyi Osula
the father of
Chief Ekhaguere Osula
the father of
Chief Herbert Idugboe Osula
the father of
Chief Alfred Basigie Osula
the father of
Priscilla Omosede Osula
the MOTHER of
Antony Ekundayo Osula

In truth, the last two entries are my own adaptation, indicating where my mother and I enter the picture. We are both intruders on the list, in that women are not supposed to be the permanent name-bearers (or on the list) and their child would normally carry the father's last name. My mother and I were both exceptional in that she gave birth to me unwed and gave me her family name. I distracted myself from dwelling on that fact, which agitated my own ongoing paternity question, by contemplating how a man could sire thirty children in one lifetime. That was my great-grandfather's personal record, with my grandpa's attempts landing at the fourteen mark. There would need to be a lot of trees if more family members were to write their own autobiographies with similar numbers. I am the sole only child of my grandfather's children, so my name looks pretty lonely on the branch compared to the rest.

Wait, I'm royal on two sides? I inwardly reacted as I read that my great-grandmother hadn't just married a royal descendent; she was a royal in her own right. Hailing from the Itsekiri people of Warri, Madam Beatrice Ajogo, daughter of Chief John Ogbe, was part of the Itsekiri royal family. You could literally use my blood to form a genetic map of Nigeria, with its Edo, Itsekiri and Yoruba content flowing together. Hopefully long life was in the genes, too, as Great-Grandma Beatrice, affectionately known as 'Mamma Bini', lived into her mid-nineties, sadly passing in 1995. It hit me that I could have had my great-grandmother in my life at sixteen years old, which would have been remarkable. I was thousands of miles away when she passed, oblivious to it and her very existence.

Trying not to feel resentful, I continued with my homework, filling in the missing pieces and painting an elaborate picture with my imagination. Having images and names as well as broader context made the tree more real and easier to track. Auntie Esohe was great at filling in the gaps and taking me on family meet-and-greet tours. This book was so much more official, however, and was just the legacy manual I hadn't known I was looking for.

* * *

The big day had arrived; the eighth day after my 'birth' was upon us. All roads led to Lagos Street, the ancestral family home, to check out the new 'baby'. There was no way for me to know what to expect, as I had never attended this kind of ceremony before. I knew that my own ceremony would not be conventional, but I wasn't going to complain about having my very own party.

Entering the courtyard at Lagos Street I was taken aback by the sight of the canopy, tables and chairs, and decorations. They had gone all out for me, in spite of having met me only a week previously. There were people who had known me for twenty years back in England who hadn't thrown a party in my honour. The mosquitoes had already declared their undying love for me across my arms and neck, but this was something else. *I could get used to this*, I thought, smelling the aroma of cooked food escaping from one of the ground-floor rooms, which was acting as the event kitchen.

This was so humbling, and I felt more than slightly nervous about what was to come and what would be expected of me. Sweat beads flowed down my face, but it wasn't clear whether this was due to the intense heat or the thought of having to present myself in front of this small crowd. They were my family, but at the same time they were largely complete strangers, and this would be the first impression they got of this much-talked-about relation who had been found. Would I be warmly received by the wider family or seen as a disappointing way to pass the time? I guessed I would soon find out.

The ceremonial host of the event was my cousin, Chief Iyeke Osula, dressed in a white floor-length robe with coral beads around his neck and wrists to denote his status as chief and prince. 'Ceremonial' would be a fitting word for his role, as the true masterminds behind the occasion were Uncles Ephraim, Blessing and Ayo as the elders of our immediate lineage. My aunties Esohe and Grace also contributed, as did Nauna and Marcellin, who was dressed resplendently, like a queen. Uncle Blessing's wife, Auntie Nohinoke, 'Auntie OK' for short, was overseeing proceedings behind the scenes, making sure everything ran like clockwork. She spoke about my mother with great affection and was a fierce lioness, committed to giving me the best possible homecoming in my mother's memory, as if I were her own child.

Family members began to flood in and take their seats under the canopy. Dressed in anything from native wear to smart casual, a selection of elders and a sprinkling of young people had made an effort to be there. Uncle Ephraim formally welcomed all the guests, taking his position at the front in a manner that made me sure he had done so countless times before. Scanning the compound, I was curious that there were so many elders, and with the business introduction up front I suspected my celebration was a hook for a larger fish. With such a large family it would be difficult to get everyone gathered together, and even so this was a select delegation rather than even a quarter of the potential relatives. It wasn't that I was unimportant; rather there seemed to be something political about the occasion, with my return being the catalyst and opportunity – a catalyst for renewed unity to rekindle family alliances that had begun to dwindle.

Like a skilful politician, Uncle Ephraim urged the elders present to rally around the newly appointed Chief Osula in his opening address.

Even though my Uncle Biola, Grandpa's eldest son, had died many years ago, the title had only formally passed down to his son over the past year. This party was perfectly timed, like hitting two birds with one stone.

If I didn't initially believe that those gathered were my relatives, I sure did after they spoke. They loved to give speeches, taking the floor boldly when given the opportunity. Talking and storytelling seemed to be in the Osula family DNA, and they did both in abundance. It was very formal for a party and felt more like a ceremony, which of course it was. Rather than relax me, this 'party' caused my tongue to tie as I waited for the inevitable invite to take the floor.

I was wholeheartedly received into the family as people spoke glowingly of Priscilla, or rather Omosede. There had been knowledge of my existence, if not my exact location. I was constructing a mosaic of my mother via the fragments of their memories, which created a swell of pride towards the woman who had given me life. Before I had time to process all this information, Uncle Ephraim motioned to me to stand up and respond.

Lanky, bespectacled and awkward in dark jeans and brown shirt, with my newly gifted prince beads on my right wrist, I stood and took a deep breath. I had never felt so much like a foreign tourist in my life as I effectively stood as the 'white man' in the canopy, about to speak publicly for the first time.

'I'm very grateful for you all,' I said, 'especially for your patience as I learn to speak my native tongue for the first time. It may be at a snail's pace, but I'm trying my utmost to learn quickly. Part of the reason I'm here, the obvious reason, is to learn as much about who I am and where I come from as possible. And I'm delighted with and extremely proud of everything I have learned up to now, including being part of a royal family, such as we are So I'd like to say a few thank yous... I think I'll do it chronologically.

'First of all, our sister (cousin) Emmy and big sister Auntie Nauna, in their absence. It was through them and technology that I was able to trace the family. Big thanks to Uncle Ephraim, Uncle Blessing, Uncle Ayo and my new mummy Auntie Esohe. And then Auntie Marcellin, who was the very first person to meet me, in London, and told me what a special family I'm a part of. That was a very special day. And to everybody I've met on this journey so far, please forgive me; I'm new. I'm very grateful for your coming out to welcome me and give me my new name. It's really good to have a Bini name now, to complete the circle. It feels like I'm being dedicated as a baby. So it's very, very special. You're all witnessing a new birth.

'Obviously, I'm very sad because unfortunately, my mother is not here. But I want to honour her in all that I do. I'm honouring her in finally coming home. It was always her wish that I would find my way home, and I believe it was her prayer before she died. Even my middle name, Ekundayo, means "sorrow turning to joy". I think it's very fitting for this occasion in this chapter of my life. Though I wasn't able to fulfil my life-long ambition of meeting my mother, I feel like I've met her in all of you. Thank you for my new name, Osagbo. God is indeed great. Thank you.'

Just before I spoke, they had given me my new name: Osakpolor, meaning 'God is great', and I had just butchered its pronunciation. The name had circulated and been signed off, then delivered within this assembly by Uncle Ephraim. It was stated that it had been chosen by my uncle Ayo, who henceforth became 'Daddy Ayo' to me as a placeholder and surrogate father figure in the family. He was an upstanding and disciplined man, so I couldn't argue with this choice of role model. At the same time, Auntie Esohe had been asked to stand up, and it was declared by the host that she was now my new 'mother', as the immediate junior sister of Priscilla. I was the proud son of two new parents, owner of a new name and officially inducted into the Osula family. All that was needed was another elaborate story, which came right on cue.

Uncle Blessing, short and slightly rotund with a light complexion like Great-Grandpa Idugboe his father, took centre stage. What he lacked in height he more than made up for in presence, and his booming voice was ideal for oratory. He was comedian, dinner host and historian rolled into one and was about to bring me up to speed on the family's origins.

'Now, I will begin the story of your royal ancestry. This Osula family is a royal family… it begins with Princess Aghauyubini.'

Princess Aghauyubini? I had heard this name before. I remembered it had popped up in the book I had been binge-reading. The fact we were a royal family was not news to me; it was *how* we were royal that was the revelation.

'The firstborn child of Oba Osewede was Aghauyubini, which means "I will yet go back to Benin". He had a special love for this daughter; she could get away with anything and had a lot of influence. Whatever she wanted she got, which gave her a lot of power. So at the death of her father, there was contention for the throne. She had brothers but was very influential with the chiefs and the hierarchy, who supported her to claim the throne. She was about to it and they had agreed to crown her. The process of coronation actually started. But on the seventh day of coronations, just as they were to crown her, she started bleeding. Because of her bleeding, everything could no longer be touched. If she touched anything it would be spoiled and become unclean, according to tradition. Because of this, she gave the throne to her full-blooded brother, who became Oba Adolor. She asked her brother to send a title for her son, Obasuyi (not the eldest but the one from her chosen marriage, the man she loved), so her brother brought 'Osula', a hereditary royal title for all the descendants of Prince Obasuyi, the first Osula and son of Princess Aghauyubini.'

The name Adolor stuck out to me, a strong name I thought as I archived it in my mind alongside potential names for a son someday. Equally gifted at storytelling, Auntie OK made a poignant observation after her husband's tale ended: 'The Osula family is peculiar in that the women play a major role in this family from the beginning. I feel it would be fitting that whatever name Osakpolor answers to, he compounds it with Osula so that Omosede's name is not lost.'

This was not only a lovely sentiment but made a lot of sense to me. Nigerian culture is generally patriarchal and children bear their father's name, though in this case we owed the foundation of our royal blood and ancestry to a woman. It was poetic that I had inherited this legacy from my own mother, a woman. The logic was ironclad and the motion was accepted by all present. From this day forward I would be known within the family as Antony Osakpolor Aris-Osula. I wasn't held up over a cliff like baby Simba in *The Lion King*, but I was a full member of the pride. It didn't matter that it was my mother's last name or that I had been born illegitimate. It had been decreed and would be sustained. Indeed, there would have been no other way, as Auntie OK was one fierce lady. She possessed a heart of gold, but if you dared cross her you would feel the bite of this lioness's teeth. Thanks be to God she was firmly in my corner!

The parallels of having strong, fiercely independent princesses in my bloodline, ancient and modern, were not lost on me. Much of Aghauyubini was in my mother it seems. A fuller picture of my mother's life in Nigeria was emerging, closing major gaps and giving me a stronger insight. It still hurt that she couldn't tell me her story in person and never would in this life. In my imagination such a homecoming had always been about a tearful, face-to-face reunion. In a way it was still all about her, as Priscilla Omosede Osula was everywhere I went in this town. Scarcely a moment passed by without a family member, or even a family friend, seeing her face in mine, often while putting a hand against their forehead to indicate the origins of this particular trademark feature of mine. Whether I resembled my father would not be so easily discoverable in this city, and it remained a mystery, with no one able to enlighten me.

After the ceremony I relaxed on my mattress, which was like a make-shift sofa. Auntie Esohe was staying with me there and made sure I had constant company. From the time I had landed in Benin, Auntie Esohe had been gathering any photographs of my mother she could get her hands on to present to me. Imagine meeting your parent for the first time on a piece of faded photographic paper that's older than you. As grateful as I was, any glimpse of her was bittersweet. With her smile and piercing brown eyes, which creased into prominent cheekbones, her beauty seeped through the ageing chemicals and paper.

As a self-taught professional photographer, it felt like a poetic way to engage with my mother. I only wished I could capture her with my own lens. She looked just like me, or rather I looked just like her. I wasn't from another planet after all, as my face had found its match. Even more so my daughter Eva, who could have passed as a clone of her late grandmother. Poring over my mother's childhood photos proved this again and again, as they shared the exact same profile and expression. As I combed through photo after photo in the pile, it struck me that I was older than my mother had been in the most recent photo in my possession.

Auntie Esohe observed me as I scanned through the pile, taking in every detail. Laughter filled the air as she relived her memories with Egbon. Even now, the title was still used in reference to her late sister, as the eldest daughter in the family this was a position of status and respect, even within an anecdote. 'Ah, Egbon… she would be in the shower singing in da morning when we were waiting to prepare for school,' she said. 'We'd be banging on de door and she would pretend not to hear us. Or the times we'd come into the kitchen when she was cooking, asking for food, and she'd say "Ah, am I your maid?"' My mother no doubt took advantage of her elder privilege status, especially with regard to bathroom usage.

Auntie Esohe broke through the laughter with a deep intake of breath and a sigh, indicating a change in tone. 'You see, your mother was the eldest daughter in the compound. She took care of us, her junior siblings, along with Mamma Bini, your great-grandma. As first girl she had a lot of responsibility, and it was hard as she grew older. When she was eighteen, she went looking for her mother in Lagos.'

It turned out Egbon and I had something besides our foreheads in common. Neither of us had been raised by our mother in infancy and we had both possessed a primal drive to find the one who had given birth to us.

'Ah, your grandpa, my father, loved his children too much, o! He didn't want to be apart from any of them. Even if he wasn't with the mother, he would send for the child to live in his compound so they were all raised together.'

Wouldn't it have been easier just to have children with one mother? I thought to myself, realising I wouldn't have been around to have that thought if he had done so. 'What if a mother didn't want to separate from her child?' I asked.

'Well, son, your grandpa was a powerful man.' The implication was obvious: he got what he wanted, the cards being stacked in his favour in terms of money, status and power. Although I wasn't satisfied with this revelation, I wasn't going to stand in judgement of my grandfather, a man I had never met. There were too many variables involved, such as culture, context, and the nature of the relationships.

Grandpa was married, just not to my grandmother, technically making her a mistress and their daughter one of the many 'outside' children. Fortunately, this was not taboo in the family and my grandfather, to his credit, at least treated all of his children equally, as well as nieces, nephews and any child of the wider family he took under his wing. Of my grandfather's many children, all bar one – his eldest son, the late Chief Abieyuwan – were 'outside' children, his mother being the sole official Mrs Chief Osula. My mother was the third sibling of seven at the time, and the first daughter. Taking into account natural tensions with her stepmother and the burden of being first daughter, I can understand her desire to break free. She knew her mother was back in Lagos, having declined to be one of several women living in the family compound in Benin.

'Your mother went to stay in Lagos with your grandma. Your grandpa, heeeyyyy, he was not happy about it, but your mother was very headstrong. Stubborn. She clashed with your grandma, too, as she was already grown when she arrived there. Next we heard, she'd left that place to live in England. When she returned, we heard she'd left a child behind. By the time your grandpa heard and looked for her, she'd already tragically passed.'

I sat there drinking in this new information, not knowing exactly how to process it, but I knew that Auntie Esohe was a reliable narrator. No one on the Osula side seemed to know much about my mother's life post-Benin. It became obvious that she was fiercely private and driven to mark out her own life free from the pressures of a large family. The years she spent in Lagos and the childhood city she returned to in adulthood were shrouded in mystery. That mystery included how she met my father and how he had become a simple crossed-out entry on my birth certificate. Apparently, Grandpa's heart broke when Omosede left home, but I got the feeling it must have broken my grandmother's heart first. Not seeing her daughter grow up must have taken its emotional toll.

Having this context allowed me to see things from my mother's point of view, realising that I likely understood her more than anyone else on the planet. I shared that deep drive to discover my roots and carve out an identity for myself. Travelling all the way to England alone spoke of the lengths she had gone to in pursuit of a new life. I wondered if, even in her wildest dreams, she imagined a scenario where I would come looking for her; like a private investigator placing the details of her life on a timeline, along with every photo and interview I obtained from those who knew her. There was still so much unknown information and mystery, but things were moving in the right direction.

As week three in Nigeria began, it felt as though business was wrapping up in the great Kingdom of Benin. I'd had the reunion party, done the tour and met numerous people with the last name Osula. Mission accomplished, and it was almost time to return home. Any unanswered questions would not and could not be found in Benin. I knew exactly where I needed to go next... Lagos was calling.

Uncle Ephraim had arranged for me to stay with his nephew, my elder cousin Emmanuel, in Lagos. Auntie Esohe was asked to accompany me on this trip as my guide and companion. I was advised by my uncle to manage my expectations after telling him of my quest to find my grand-mother. He was well into his seventies, and as his elder brother was more than ten years his senior, he knew she would easily be in her eighties if she were alive. Living to the ripe old age of eighty was a rarity in Nigeria, so this was a pragmatic assumption, as was the likelihood that she would most likely have moved house. Thirty years was a long time, after all. This sowed a seed of doubt in my mind, as the logic was sound. It was just as well I wasn't fuelled by logic, but by some of my late mother's stubborn-ness and a healthy dose of crazy faith. There was no way I had gone all that way and not visited the last known address of my mother. Besides, I was beyond curious about the 'businesswoman' grandmother my mother claimed would have been too busy to have me back with her in Nigeria.

With bags packed, I gratefully embraced Auntie Marcellin and Uncle Ephraim and said a final goodbye to Lagos Street. I had already completed my goodbye tour of the rest of the family, which, bearing in mind its size, was no short task. Uncle Ayo gave me fatherly instruction and encouraged me to bring my family 'home' as soon as I was able. I promised to return imminently, and not out of duty or politeness but from the bottom of my heart.

I got into the car for the traffic-ridden drive to the airport with Auntie Esohe beside me, convinced that this was not an ending but a beginning. I was convinced that my days in Lagos would lead to some kind of dis-covery, such was my optimism. Fortunately, Auntie Esohe shared this outlook rather than the pessimistic outlook of those back in Benin. She was a strong source of encouragement and I knew she would have marched into a mountain of fire with me, such was her loyalty and giving nature. I wished I could take her back to England to live with us, not just having her accompany me on this flight. The kids would have loved her and she them, giving them a slice of what life in a Nigerian family was like. I inwardly vowed that if I ever made it to Hollywood I would take her to live with us. The thought never crossed my mind that Auntie Esohe might not want to leave her beloved Nigeria, the only country she had ever known, and her humungous family network.

From what I had heard about Grandpa, Auntie Esohe was very much her father's daughter with regard to being generous to a fault and a people person. Despite having been a high-flying playboy in his youth, Alfred Osula was legendarily benevolent. Generations of Osulas had been raised by his hand, from siblings to wider family members, and he had been gravely serious about his responsibilities as the head of the family. He directly funded foreign tuition for his brothers, Ephraim and Victor, who studied in England during the 1950s, when such privileges were expensive and opportunities was rare.

The late Alfred Basigie Osula was more than a Bini chief and royal family member. He was a well-known socialite who trailblazed across a number of fields in colonial and postcolonial Nigeria. As the first Nigerian manager of the nation's premier newspaper, the *Daily Times*, in the early 1950s, he broke a glass ceiling that gave him access to opportunity, wealth and a lifestyle of dreams. I saw many black-and-white photographs of him with important-looking white people who were clearly part of British high society. He often hosted such visits due to his role at the *Daily Times*, a sister publication of the British *Daily Mirror* newspaper, which belonged to British owners and was headed up by Cecil King. This led to constant travel back and forth for Grandpa to establish business connections and report to the owners. Having a finger in many pies became a way of life for him. He ran bars and hotels in high-flying Lagos and then in Benin, oversaw Miss Nigeria contests and even headed up the Nigerian Football Federation in 1963.

These revelations were fascinating for me, the biggest being that my grandfather had been a media professional, and a pioneering one at that. I have always felt a tug towards working in media, so the fact that Grandpa had run the biggest newspaper brand in Nigeria floored me. It was in my blood, it seemed, and it meant that I shared something pro-found with this man I would never know but whose footsteps I had unconsciously followed. I never received the benefits of being his firstborn grandson, and I had no idea how close I had come to obtaining this privilege.

I was told an inconvenient truth by Auntie Grace one afternoon in Benin. Apparently, Grandpa not only knew about me but had found me after showing up at my door in England. This cast a new light on everything. The details were too sketchy to outline anything with any certainty, though there were fragments of plausibility in this anecdote. I had discovered a smoking gun years earlier that lent the story credence. The legal case I knew about that had resulted in Mr and Mrs Aris becoming my legal guardians, with me as their ward of court, had come about due to this visit. Somehow my grandfather had traced their location and asked for me to be released into his care, which they declined. To them he was a stranger, as he would have been to me in spite of sharing blood and history through my mother. As a child I had found a document with the name 'Chief Osula' labelled on it in print. I remember asking Mum about it and being chastised for being nosey. As a teenager I glimpsed it again, and now regret not investigating it thoroughly.

My heart felt heavy on hearing this. I had mixed feelings, as on the one hand my adoptive parents had fought for me, but on the other that fight had allegedly been against my biological grandparent. They had effectively cut me off from my heritage, culture and any connection to my late mother. Being the black sheep with identity issues could have been avoided and my path could have been a more conventional one. But what would it have been like for a three- to four-year-old to be ripped from the only home he had ever known? I had a mum and dad; they just weren't of the same blood. This man from Nigeria shared my blood but was a stranger to me. The situation, if you'll excuse the pun, was far from black and white. Both parties had fought for me, which nullified all childhood insecurities of being unwanted, but only one side had won. Someone's heart was always going to be broken as a result of this legal outcome. How was I supposed to feel about this bombshell? It hadn't been possible for me to pick a side then, and it wasn't right for me to stand in judgement all these years later. I had to believe that they had all had my best interests at heart and felt they were on the side of right.

One thing is for sure; life would have been completely different growing up with Grandpa. I can't possibly say that it would have been better or worse – just different. My grandfather was a man of means, but he was in poor health by the latter half of the 1980s and died by the time I was ten years old. What would have happened to me then? In such a large family I'm sure someone would have given me a home and a bed. The location and nature of that arrangement is where it would have become interesting, as many orphaned members of large families end up as a houseboy or girl to an uncle or auntie – given home and shelter but having to work hard for their supper. And they had to forget about getting an expensive education or having opportunities handed to them.

The dice had been rolled and I was satisfied with where it had landed when contemplating the various alternatives. I couldn't afford to look back and wonder what could or should have been. That ship had long sailed. A new voyage was ahead of me and I was determined to find land. I had a fresh mission in Lagos, and as the wheels hit the tarmac I was already through the fatigue and planning my next moves. The dice had been rolled again and I would have to wait and see where it would land.

CHAPTER FOURTEEN

Prince of Benin

B enin was great, but as a city boy Lagos had instantly seeped into my blood and imagination. The hustle and bustle was infectious and had really captivated my heart. It's a city that feels unpredictable, with the pendulum constantly swinging between excitement and danger. I was on the last leg of my three-week pilgrimage to my 'mother's land' by this point and the strain of missing my family in England was felt strongly. Only three more days to go until I would be reunited with them, I reminded myself, and I only had one final piece of unfinished business to settle.

'So you're sure that this is the right address?' Auntie Esohe said while thumbing through the decades-old blue letter with its faded ink.

'This is the only address I have, so we'll see,' came my anxious reply. This letter was all I had for navigation, but the taxi driver seemed as confused as we were. I thought my auntie knew Lagos like the back of her hand, having spent her formative years growing up there, so I was puzzled. I wondered if this area of the city, 'Shomolu', even existed as we drove around what could have been described as 'downtown Lagos' for a long time. The scenery wasn't as glamorous as that of Victoria Island, but it was clearly older and in some ways had more character and energy, even as we were viewing it through a car window.

As if by magic, my auntie excitedly indicated to the driver that she knew where we were headed, having made out a missing piece of information from the faded ink address. 'Ah… o-kaaaay! Driver abeg, turn left here and then sharp right, o!' came the excited instructions from Auntie Esohe once she had solved the riddle.

I had learned to keep as quiet as possible in public, especially during taxi rides, so they didn't overcharge me, or worse, hold me for ransom. A foreigner like me could fetch a decent amount of money, and taxi driving was hardly a lucrative business.

Auntie assured me that we would find the house and all would be well. At this point I started to prepare myself for the likely outcome that after thirty years my grandmother was either long deceased or at best had relocated with no forwarding address. This was more than a long shot, but I had to roll the dice. Besides praying that we didn't crash as I sat in the back of the taxi without a seatbelt, I tried to encourage myself. I had come all this way and made connections that I could only have dreamed about beforehand. Finding Grandpa's side of the family should have been enough to embolden me for whatever was yet to be discovered. That reunion would have seemed impossible a mere three months previously, so being optimistic wasn't necessarily wishful thinking. Finding Grandma would have been the cherry on top of a life-changing cake, but was I being too greedy?

The taxi pulled up in an area of the city that was vastly different from the part my cousins Julian and Emmanuel lived in. This was more like the African cities I had seen on TV, which were slightly rundown and overcrowded. Growing up on a council estate I knew the difference between uptown and downtown wherever I was in the world, as some things always remained the same.

As we exited the taxi, I was grateful to have arrived in one piece, all things considered. In front of us stood a large maisonette with its own courtyard and gutter system at the front. There were similar houses to the left and right, but no connecting house directly next door. Parked vehicles lined the street, packed up like tinned sardines, and we were only just about able to get in and out ourselves. This was Yoruba town; you could hear it in the loud voices that filled the atmosphere and see it in the broad gestures of the people interacting with each other. If I closed my eyes I could have been standing in Peckham High Street, a district of south London, so familiar were the sounds and smells.

Though I didn't understand Yoruba, I could somehow recognise it when I heard it. Fortunately, I had my very own interpreter with me, like the robot C-3PO in *Star Wars*, who spoke millions of languages. Auntie Esohe didn't speak millions, but she was multilingual, speaking a few Nigerian languages and most importantly being fluent in Yoruba. Without her this expedition could not have happened, and I was grateful that she was my secret weapon for success.

As we stepped towards the front gate, we were met by a teenage boy in a vest and slippers, who I gathered was the house help or security guard. Auntie Esohe instructed him to summon the madam of the house to come out to the courtyard. The plan was to ask whoever lived at the address if they knew anything about the mother of a Priscilla Osula, and if so whether they knew where she had relocated to. My grandmother's name did not appear on the letter, and none of my family members on the Osula side knew it. This made an already difficult task even more complicated, as we had to rely on the tight-knit African tradition of living closely with one's neighbours and knowing everybody's business. Older women seemed to be the best at keeping unofficial records of the comings and goings of their neighbours and who was related to whom. If the owner of this property were an elderly woman, it wasn't beyond the realms of possibility that she would be able to assist us with some valuable information, or at least put us on the right track. After all, Auntie Esohe was a walking encyclopaedia of local knowledge and family history, and she wasn't even that old. Best-case scenario I would get some sort of lead and hopefully be able to follow it up before I left the country in a few days' time.

'Don't worry. It's going to be fine,' came the confident statement from my auntie, who intuitively sensed my growing anxiety and impatience. 'See, I told you,' she said as the young boy walked back towards us with a tall, white-haired woman close behind him.

This must be the madam, I thought to myself, hoping to get the conversation over and done with quickly.

'We'll ask the lady and then take it from there. It will be fine, dear,' came Auntie Esohe's reassurance.

I remained open-minded as she met this elderly lady halfway, customarily bending her knee to her elder as they began to talk.

Surfing on my phone, feeling frustrated and bored, I wondered what was taking so long as I occasionally glanced over to check their progress. As I only spoke English it didn't make sense for me to get involved, so I detached myself as soon as they started speaking in the native tongue. There was something impressive about this elderly woman. She was solid and strong despite her advancing years, standing tall in a floor-length native gown with a crown of shortly cropped white hair. Back and forth they went, each gesturing towards where I stood. My auntie must have been telling her my story and appealing to her for help. My story was so familiar to me that I often forgot the effect it had on people and how sad it made them. This exchange was beginning to take far longer than I had envisioned and I hoped that my auntie wasn't telling the long version of my story or we would be there all night.

With one final gesture towards me, Auntie Esohe broke out of Yoruba abruptly to make a matter-of-fact announcement in English with her eyes fixed on mine. 'This is your grandma.'

Beg your pardon? came the unspoken response to this major revelation. *Let's back up here,* I thought to myself, confused and stunned. Before I had time to process this news, the elderly madam had run over to embrace me. She fell to her knees and wailed.

I looked over at Auntie Esohe with a glance that communicated, *Is this for real?* which was met with a smile and gentle nod of the head, a single tear streaming down her cheek.

And just like that, I had met my grandmother. *So, this is my mother's mother!* I inwardly processed the fact that the plan had worked, and so quickly. Nothing could have prepared me for this; no manual, workshop or talk on how to meet your grandmother. I didn't even know whether she spoke English, which meant that understanding me might be problematic without Auntie Esohe's help.

'Ah, Tony, Tony, Tony… my son,' said Grandma, answering my silent question. She clearly could, just like many of my relatives, though she did not feel compelled to in her own country, on her own doorstep.

The second thought that ran through my mind was that she knew my name. She knew all about me, even though this was the first time she had met her grandson in thirty years.

As we helped her back up onto her feet, Grandma pulled me closer for a long embrace, shouting for joy and praising God for this moment. She had quite a firm grip for an elderly woman, almost winding me with her hug. I, on the other hand, remained speechless, watching the whole thing play out like an out-of-body observer taking notes.

As I glanced towards the house, a smartly dressed young man in office wear headed towards us. He was shorter than me and looked as if he was in his early to mid-twenties. I had no idea who this was, but he ran up to embrace me. I just went with it. After coming up for air, he introduced himself as Akindele, my cousin. His mother and my mother were sisters. This information suddenly made the spontaneous hug much more comfortable. Akindele had been at the house by chance, being a good grandson and visiting his grandmother. Before this moment he had been her only grandson. Now she had two standing in front of her.

Auntie Esohe and I were excitedly invited into the house, where the reunion party could continue in private and on sofas. As we walked through the main door we were came to a corridor, and on the left was the family room. It contained two comfortable sofas, a dining table and a TV, with family photographs everywhere. I couldn't help but notice that I was not in any of them, and neither was my mother. I spotted that Akindele had siblings, two sisters, and glimpsed his parents in a family photograph. So that was what my auntie looked like.

This was the house of Madam Grace Ayoola Oteyelu, and I, along with Auntie Esohe, was an esteemed guest of honour on this unexpected day. Grandma engaged me in conversation as best she could, speaking English quite well, but much more slowly and laboriously than her native tongue. We were both just chuffed to be speaking to each other at all. Auntie Esohe interjected to clarify things and narrate from time to time, helping the conversation flow and bringing everyone up to speed. My grandmother remarked on how much Auntie Esohe resembled her father, Grandma's ex-lover Chief Osula, and said she remembered her as a child. It turned out this was not the first time they had met, and she knew some of my mother's other siblings, too, including Uncle Ayo. I learned that as the family had lived in Lagos for many years before relocating to Benin, there had been various interactions years earlier that I was unaware of.

Grandma motioned to my face as she exclaimed, 'Osula, o!' referencing the resemblance and how I was unmistakably descended from Alfred Osula. She laughed as she remembered him. 'Ah, that rascal Osula, o!' stating with pride how she had retained her independence and refused to be one of his 'wives' in Benin. My grandmother, a proud feminist in 1950s Nigeria? Wow, it was no wonder my mother made the decisions she did; it was clearly in her blood. She had descended from an independent and strong woman who would be controlled by nothing and nobody. My mother had lived inside this woman's womb. The closest I would ever get to meeting Priscilla was through this encounter with the woman sitting in front of me. My own and my mother's origins began in large part with this dear lady.

Before I had a chance to ponder any deeper insights, the door was flung open. A sudden whirlwind came rushing into the family room, a petite lady contained within it. As I looked up, I just about caught sight of a short, bespectacled lady with red-tinged, braided hair and large hooped earrings as she hurled herself towards me. The next thing I felt was a tight hug, gripping me close to her ample bosom. I quickly deduced that, like Akindele before her, this was another member of the family tree, as my T-shirt became soaked with salt water around the area where her head was resting on my chest.

This was my introduction to Auntie Omotunde, otherwise known as Daisy, the youngest of my mother's sisters. Auntie Daisy was beside herself with emotion, and once she'd caught her breath and loosened her grip, she spoke to me in English. 'Oh, Antony my darling. I am your Auntie Omotunde, but you can call me Daisy.' This was a relief, as the name Omotunde was a bit of a mouthful. She looked as though she had just seen a ghost, but rather than feeling scared she was elated that a lost part of the family's past had revisited them. An ordinary day had, by a strange twist of fate, become the most eventful day ever for this unsuspecting household.

Daisy was a lively, fast-talking, street-smart lady. I instantly felt at ease in her company, as her warmth and energy were contagious. With her thick-rimmed glasses and red-dyed hair, she was more contemporary and fashion-conscious than any of the relatives of the older generation I had met thus far. I could imagine being taken out and spoiled by this auntie, who would likely compete to be my favourite of them all. As the youngest of Grandma's daughters, I figured she was roughly the same age as Claire.

Taking over from Auntie Esohe, she was the perfect narrator to tell my mother's backstory from their family's perspective. 'Antony, your mum was a very independent woman. When she came to live with us, she was already grown and had her own mind. We loved having our big sister home.'

I had already learned that my mother was the eldest of four daughters, followed by Aunties Abiodun, Iyabo and our narrator Omotunde. 'Grandma is a very strong woman, so she and your mum clashed. Your grandma still saw her as her child, but your mum was not having any of it,' Daisy said with a chuckle, looking over at her mother.

Grandma oscillated between laughter and deep sadness, as if the memories had come crashing back to her, having been long buried.

'By the time she was pregnant with you, she had already decided to travel to England. Our uncle helped her travel. She loved it there, and she would send photos of you... She was so happy and loved you very much.'

Hearing this touched my heart while simultaneously ripping it apart. Auntie Daisy had her own grief, too. She clearly lamented the fact that they hadn't grown up together and that their time had been short-lived. The few years my mother lived with them had made an impact, though. My two aunties from either side of my mother's gene pool sat trading stories about Omosede and how she had liked fine jewellery and spent hours in the bathroom pretending not to hear her siblings' protests. It was wonderful too see all three women laughing and reminiscing, bringing their daughter and sister back to life. Akindele and I listened intently, both outsiders to this shared experience, but keen learners.

Auntie Esohe volunteered the fact that I had brought photographs of my family with me. As the photos were passed around, it was my turn to fill in the gaps. They were in awe of the wedding photographs, remarking on how beautiful the bride and groom were. It dawned on me that they should have been there, and that this was but one of many significant absences over far too many years.

Grandma had no more time for tears as she raced through, until she stopped suddenly, fixated on one particular photo. 'Ah, dis is Omosede reborn,' she boldly exclaimed.

As I suspected, it was Eva who had caught her great-grandmother's eye. The delight and sheer joy on her face as she grasped the picture and kissed it was worth the entire trip to Nigeria alone. I had not considered the impact of losing a child, and then at the same time losing a grandchild. She had known that I was alive but not my whereabouts, and had simply prayed that God would bring me home.

Well, it had taken twenty-nine years but her prayer had been answered. Even better than that, I had come directly to her door like a special delivery. I was the gift that kept on giving, as not only did she have me but also a granddaughter-in-law, great-granddaughters and another unborn great-grandchild. Her Omosede was a grandmother, her Tony a father. At eighty-three years old, a grand age in Nigeria given its low life expectancy, she deduced that it was only God who had allowed her to live long enough to see this day. I was inclined to agree with her.

The time grew late, and Auntie Esohe and I had to travel back to our cousin's home on Victoria Island, which was a fair distance away. We promised to continue the reunion the next day, when they would be our guests at our cousin's home in Ikoyi. Grandma naturally didn't want me to leave, having only just got me back. Perhaps she was fearful that once I had left and she went to sleep, she would awake to find that our visit had been nothing but a dream. I couldn't blame her, as I was pinching myself, too. On a practical level it simply wasn't safe for us to be out any later, so we went on our way. Sleep was good that night, as I had accomplished another major goal and it felt amazing. However, it would take a long time to put my mind back together after having it blown into so many pieces.

Yet another auntie, Iyabo, travelled across town on hearing the news that her lost nephew was in town. But when she accompanied Auntie Daisy and Grandma when they came to see us, the sight of her confused me. Having studied the photographic evidence, I had decided upon studying the photographic evidence that my mother looked like her father's side, hands down. Yet looking at Auntie Iyabo, who had no blood ties to the Osulas whatsoever, was exactly like looking at my mum in many ways. She had the same smooth, dark-chocolate skin and structured cheekbones, and was as introverted as her sister and mother were loud. She spoke even less English but reached out to me with her embracing eyes and smile. The set was not quite complete, as Auntie Abiodun and Uncle Akindele Senior lived in another city, Ibadan, which was several hours' drive away. But this would offer the perfect excuse to return, as well as to meet my other cousins, Akindele's sisters. There would be plenty more family to discover over time, as I had only just scratched the surface.

I was beyond grateful for everything the Osula family had done for me in Nigeria, but I was also glad that I hadn't listened to them about finding Grandma. That weathered, torn, faded blue paper had led me to the treasure of an extended family and more branches of my family tree. I couldn't help but wonder if my mother, Wynne Aris, had understood the value of this piece of paper and purposefully preserved it for me to 'accidentally' find someday. After all, her photographs and old letters had never been locked away or placed anywhere a child could not have successfully reached and rummaged through. I figured she had kept information to be passed down like a precious heirloom the same way she had kept jewellery in her box. I could only imagine that she would have been happy for me, having come so far. Mum and Dad had done a lot for me, and I would never have wanted to erase them from my history. The hard truth was that they had been dead for seventeen and ten years, respectively, which felt like enough time to quash any feelings of disloyalty. Why would they have denied me the opportunity to reconnect with living family, heal old wounds and get some closure? I had to believe that I would have had their blessing.

✳ ✳ ✳

My last day in Nigeria had arrived and my feelings were mixed. The fact that I was going to miss this place was an understatement. Ten years earlier I'd had my first taste of West African life in Ghana; now I was standing in the city where I had likely been conceived. This made sense, as when my mother hadn't been pregnant when she left Benin, but she had been by the time she left Lagos for the UK. Either way, Africa felt like home. How far I had travelled in a decade. If it hadn't been for Jahlene and the children I would have stayed, either a bit longer or indefinitely. I had my people there and a lot of catching up to do.

Hugging Grandma goodbye was borderline traumatic, as expected. How could she be sure that she would ever see me again? She couldn't possibly have known the tenacity of her firstborn grandson and his determination to see things through. I promised to bring the whole family next time and placed great value on my word. We had only had two days together, but it was two days longer than either of us expected to have. If Grandma could have kept me in Nigeria, I have no doubt she would have.

She almost got her wish, as getting to the airport in time was a gargantuan mission. Between the legendary traffic of Lagos and the many hoops and obstacles at Murtala Muhammed Airport, I was surprised I didn't miss my flight. I'm amazed anybody ever makes their flight at all!

My elder cousin Emmanuel, referred to as Uncle Emmanuel out of respect, had driven me to the airport, accompanied by Auntie Esohe and Auntie Daisy. Uncle Emmanuel was a pastor and regional overseer of all Lagos churches in the Redeemed Church of God, the nation's biggest denomination. The world really is a small place, as he and Auntie Daisy were already acquainted. He had been her pastor for a few years but neither had ever made the connection that they had a relation in common. Uncle Emmanuel had practically grown up with my mother in the famed Lagos Street, Benin. As the son of my grandpa's younger sister, he had idolised his favourite uncle, seeing him as a paternal figure, as so many in the family had. The way Uncle Emmanuel took care of me that day was, I believe, in direct correlation to the debt he felt he owed his uncle, mentor and father figure. If he could just get his uncle's grandson out of Lagos and onto a plane without incident he could consider the debt paid in full!

After saying a few words, he was content to leave me in the capable hands of my aunties, the Lagos bodyguards. No one was going to mess with me on their watch. It was like having two surrogate mums for the price of one. I was the son neither had ever had. Likewise, I had never had an 'auntie' before, and just as I started getting used to having one I found myself saying goodbye to two.

I would have tried to sneak them into my luggage, but at this airport they went through your case by hand to see what you had to trade with before letting you check in. Everyone at the airport was on the hustle, and it was grating. You couldn't ask for directions without the helpful person expecting payment, and at each station you were asked, 'Money for water, sah?' It's a lot more intimidating when you are asked the same question by an airport security guard holding an assault rifle. Lagos was a tough place full of alpha males and females, and street hustler types. The airport was no different.

Auntie Daisy taught me, 'You have to shine your eye in Lagos.'

I took her advice, keeping my eyes sharp and my wits about me at all times.

The very worst place to have an emotional meltdown would have been in the departure lounge of this airport. But the floodgates opened and the tears escaped down my face without authorisation, ignoring the memo about where we were at the time. *Please let's not do this here*, I said to myself, but it was too late. All attempts to look Lagos-boy street tough had evaporated into thin air. There was no way of controlling the surprising tsunami of emotion that hit me at that moment.

Both aunties were also crying and telling me it was OK, though I knew this was more than the sadness of departure. I suspected it was the release of all that pent-up pain and frustration over my great losses, and my grief finally finding a release valve. Sorrow had finally found its joy; the true meaning of Ekundayo.

With the three of us huddled together, sobbing our hearts out, we must have looked an interesting picture. Neither auntie wanted to see me board the plane, but the window of opportunity was about to close. One had spent plenty of time with me, the other was only just beginning to get to know me. As they waved goodbye, my walk towards the departure gate brought the situation to an end.

From that moment on I was alone again and had to toughen up for the next round of airport staff on the lookout for a mark. My eye could not be shone if it were red and puffy with tears. I would not allow this momentary harassment to spoil what had been the most life-changing trip ever. This same Nigeria that so many people had told me not to visit or to treat as if I were going to a war zone had been the making of me. I had fallen in love with this country and felt a deep connection with the soil that few people could understand. The blood of at least three powerful tribes, Edo, Yoruba and Itsekiri, ran through my veins, and I was descended from royalty via two of them. I may well have been a 'coconut', but I was also a prince, and that legacy could never be taken away from me.

Neither could the fact that I had been born the son of Princess Priscilla Omosede Osula. Every time I look in the mirror now, or catch a glimpse of my daughter, I see my mother. The void is no longer dark and elusive, but has a face that emerges. Maybe my mother was more involved in this homecoming than anybody could have thought. A firm believer in Christ, with a faith that apparently deepened during her last few months of life in Lagos before she died, it's possible that she, as one of the cloud of witnesses, left me some of the breadcrumbs that led me home.

As I tried to get some sleep on my night flight to Amsterdam, a peace came over me that I had never felt before. It was as if I were being tucked into bed by someone with a soothing voice; not the stewardess, but my mother, softly saying, 'Well done, son. You came home!'

CHAPTER FIFTEEN

Star Driver

Hollywood magic has been in my life for as long as I can remember. My earliest memories of film involve sitting at my mother's feet gazing up at the TV to watch American greats such Fred Astaire, Ginger Rogers, Judy Garland, Burt Lancaster and Sidney Poitier. On the British side of the pond, my mother used to watch classic films from British film studio Rank, with the famous gold-painted man hitting the golden gong at the start of every film. This programmed me to expect British accents and black and white featuring actors such as suave, erudite David Niven and physical comedian Norman Wisdom.

Those early preschool years with Mum, and the days when she let me skip school with the slightest ailment (which was really about our mutual desire to be in each other's company), were defined by watching really old movies. This transported us into an era or world that was totally foreign to the one we presently inhabited, which was typical of my mother. She was a natural escapist, and inhabiting a fantasy world came easily to her – the matinee binges were no exception. I vividly remember watching the bold, bright Technicolor-saturated movies of the 1940s that looked almost like cartoons they were so colourful. The most famous of the classics was *The Wizard of Oz*, with its bombastic reds and yellows. There was something magical about the way cinema transported us, and watching these movies felt like peering out through a window or portal into another reality.

Dad loved movies even more than Mum. My mother got swept up in them, whereas my dad was intellectually engaged. Dad was the nocturnal film-watcher, in that he was never around during the day due to his job, so the kinds of movies he watched, and that I would stay up for at least half of, were the more contemporary and impacting ones, such as *The French Connection* and *The Godfather*. Mum mainly watched films for the actors and the glamour, whereas Dad was much more into the storyline and the vision of the film, often talking to me about the background and meaning of it, and its context in real life.

I remember watching the Dustin Hoffman classic *Little Big Man* at around eight years old. Around twenty years old by that time, it had Hoffman portraying a soldier in the old West. Having been taken in by a Native American tribe after a battle, he learned their ways and became one with them, only to see them massacred by the brutal American army he had formerly been a part of. It was one of those 1970s classics that was pessimistic and dour but had something to say, and my father used it to teach me about people being the same; about how cruel and unjust the world could be. Perhaps it triggered memories of his time in the Air Force, travelling to poor parts of the world across the seas. As young as I was, I got it. Dad had a way of talking up to me rather than down, which stimulated my inquisitive mind and innate maturity. I remember crying at parts of the film and being shocked at how inhumane people could be to each other.

On the lighter side of the spectrum, Dad often took me to see new movie releases at most of the great cinemas in London's West End, including the Empire Leicester Square and the Odeon – flagship movie theatres which, until recently, housed premieres for the biggest film releases on the planet, with every big Hollywood name walking the red carpet outside them at some point in their career. We didn't do the premieres, of course, but the magic of going into these grand cinemas was still in the air as we sat in our seats looking up at the huge curtains, soon to reveal an even larger screen. The taste of toffee popcorn will for ever be associated with the memory of 1980s movies such as *Dirty Rotten Scoundrels*, *Turner & Hooch*, *Back to the Future Part II* and *Part III*, *Indiana Jones and the Last Crusade*, *The Adventures of Baron Munchausen* and many more. Sometimes Dad would take me to see what would have been a mindless kids' movie to him and endure it for my benefit, though he never let on that he was suffering through the ordeal. Maybe he secretly enjoyed those films, too.

In my home, watching movies was like a religious experience. In the absence of church they were the nearest I ever got to religious ritual during my childhood, and I never, ever needed to be dragged along kicking and screaming. No, in movies I found worlds that made sense, with an escapism that inspired me and triggered my young, fertile mind to create its own fantasy worlds that would turn minutes into hours and days, with enough imagination to power Disney for years.

Speaking of the Mouse... As a child with a gift for drawing, it was my dream to become a cartoonist for Walt Disney Studios. My creative mind had been captivated by its epic, groundbreaking movies such as *Fantasia*, which was still a step beyond most animated productions decades after its release. Countless hours were spent creating my own characters, getting ready to debut them in their own animated features and cartoons when the time was right; a whole encyclopaedia of characters and tales sitting in a sketchbook in my room, waiting for their time in the sun. Except that time never came, and instead of the sun their unfortunate destiny lay in a much darker place: the bin.

You see, the same young fertile mind, rich in the soil of imagination, was also plagued with self-doubt and pangs of creative frustration and angst, no matter how much affirmation I received, especially from my father. I strove for absolute perfection, even as a child. Instead of brushing off my mistakes and inability to recreate what I saw in my mind on the page, I would screw up the paper and throw it away. One day I went to the extreme of consigning my entire portfolio of the best cartoon creations the world never knew straight into the belly of the bin.

I believe it was at this point that the constant dichotomy of lover of entertainment and frustrated creative was truly born, and this cloud would follow me like a looming shadow for many years to come. It reared its ugly head whenever I had a breakthrough of creativity, waiting to self-sabotage and bringing my potential crashing back down to earth.

Although I believed that I was somehow destined to be a creator and curator of art, I settled with merely tasting. Like a moth to a flame, I frequently found a way of being around the thing I truly loved while resisting taking part for fear of betraying a higher calling. If only I had realised that this desire and latent talent was as much a part of my chemistry and DNA as the melanin in my skin. The truth is, the flare for the dramatic and creative never left me. Years of memorable sermons, my success on air in media and the ease with which I was able to spin an entertaining yarn were testament to the natural performer trapped inside. Through my work in radio and my freelance TV and magazine projects, I was able to get very close to the flame of entertainment. If I had been a frustrated actor and stand-up comedian in the pulpit, I was a front-row pundit by the football pitch in my media work, hollering and whooping at the glimpse of greatness.

A perfect example came as I witnessed the meteoric rise of actress and singer Jennifer Hudson. This twenty-first-century Aretha Franklin burst onto the scene as a contestant on the hit show *American Idol*. What made it interesting was that, in spite of her ridiculously high level of singing talent, she was not appreciated by the show's kingmaker judge, Simon Cowell. I often measured my ability to spot a future star in the making on the show according to Cowell's judgements, but in the case of Ms Hudson he was having the most blatant of off days. Jennifer had a voice that literally made my spine tingle and the hairs on my body stand to attention.

Like every good Phoenix-rising-from-the-ashes story, being booted out of a talent show was not the end for Jennifer. In fact, it was the beginning of a sharp uptick in her career. That oversight was corrected when the director of the 2002 film version of *Chicago*, Bill Condon, brought the classic musical *Dreamgirls* to the silver screen, recasting the original Jennifer Holiday as the spurned diva Effie White, played by Jennifer Hudson.

I sat in awe at the cinema watching *Dreamgirls* during its pre-release BAFTA screening at the close of 2006. It was a prestigious, exclusive event that Ms Hudson attended in person and it proved to be a seminal moment for me. Jennifer was seated close enough to wave at, and at the close of the movie, after the Q&A, I saw my opportunity to fly towards one of the hottest flames in town. If I could just get to her and arrange an interview to hear more about this phenomenal success and how she was handling it, especially as, like me, she was a person of deep faith and spirituality. At this point in time she was a star on the rise, but not at the level where security guards were posted miles out in front of her.

With athlete-like speed, I was able to get her attention and make contact. 'Excuse me, Jennifer. I'm Antony from Premier Christian Radio. I'd love to talk to you about your faith and this exciting journey,' I sputtered.

'Premier *Christian* Radio… Sure, that sounds fun. I'd love to,' came her reply. Emphasising the 'Christian' part of the title let me know we shared common ground. Just as I was about to seal the deal, a hand came out of nowhere, soon followed by the body of a mature white lady with 'gatekeeper' written all over her. This was a high-ranking PR person, and she scrutinised me with razor-sharp precision to determine whether or not I should be sharing the same air as her high-profile client.

Once I had explained my interest in arranging an interview with Jennifer, the PR agent asked for my business card, but fortunately I had left the office without one. I say 'fortunately' because I know how the game works; if she had taken my contact information it would have got 'lost' when she realised my station didn't have millions of listeners. It was a niche religious broadcaster with a faithful audience, particularly among the black, churchgoing community, which listened en masse. The PR agent had no choice in front of Hudson, who had already said yes, and reluctantly gave me her business card instead. I promptly followed up the next day, securing the biggest interview of my career up to that point.

I have been privileged to interview many celebrities in the business and some of my favourite artists, too, but this one was a game-changer. This interview with Jennifer Hudson preceded my going to drama school and the pursuit of a dream to graduate from being a fan of acting to becoming an actor, and more broadly to someone who was creative. What was significant about this meeting with Jennifer was that she was a Christian on the cusp of greatness and recognition in the biggest entertainment capital on the planet: Hollywood. Furthermore, she had just received a nomination from the Academy Awards for her role as Effie White. And I was sitting right across from her in the same way Oprah Winfrey had been a couple of weeks previously. She was hungry, young and black, just like myself, and a person of faith in an industry that often ridiculed and spurned people like us. It defied my expectations to see how universally embraced she was.

The interview took place at an opulent hotel. Every outlet was talking about Jennifer by this point. This was no surprise really, as her on-screen performance had been spell-blinding and deserved every wave of applause she got. I asked her how she was dealing with this success, as much for myself as out of interest in her, because I couldn't help but constantly parallel our lives. She was living out her dreams, whereas I was journaling hers and suppressing my own. She was a great interviewee; open, honest and raw in a way that only happens at the start of a career before the polished slickness sets in, along with a jadedness that comes from the press jumping on your words and weaponising them. She was frank and honest when it came to talking about her faith. Her words flowed like a river, with constant shoutouts to the Lord and how He had guided her path. It was great material for the station, but even better fodder for my soul. It was in this hotel room that the thought of recapturing my childhood dream to perform was slowly reignited. It felt intoxicating being in Hudson's whirlwind, even just for a minute. She was the closest I had come to someone on the cusp of a game-changing moment.

Just weeks after our chat she was standing on the Oscars podium clutching that little golden man in her hands, making history as a black actress winning Best Supporting Actress aged just twenty-five. She was only the third to have the honour, right behind Whoopi Goldberg in 1991 for *Ghost* and Hattie McDaniel back in 1939 for *Gone with the Wind*. Hattie McDaniel wasn't even allowed to sit at the same table as the other white nominees at that time. Jennifer had achieved something I dreamed of achieving as a little boy on a council estate, staying up late to watch this magical show full of glitz, glamour and people I recognised from the movies. I had never met anyone who had experienced the luxury of holding that little gold man in their hands, but now I knew it was possible.

Jennifer wasn't the first person I had met who was a bona fide Hollywood star, though. No, that honour went to someone a lot closer to home. Funnily enough, this actor also hailed from a big Broadway-musical-turned-movie sensation, namely *Mamma Mia!* The actor in question, young male lead Dominic Cooper, had been sensational in the movie *The Devil's Double*, playing Saddam Hussein's maniacal son and his doppelgänger in a heightened true story, and he and I had gone to school together. Dominic was in the year above, but I knew him on first-name terms. I vividly remember him being the star of our school productions and knowing was earmarked for acting greatness even then. He was the standard we were measured by at school, and as easy as it would have been to resent his obvious talent, he was actually the nicest guy imaginable – humble and approachable with it. Although I haven't seen him in years, I am genuinely proud every time I see him on screen, either in movies or being interviewed on TV.

Was it possible that another star could come from the womb of south-east London? More to the point, if the answer was yes, was there a chance it could be me? At the very least I was emboldened to give it a shot, and once I had decided to be out on the pitch rather than observing, I gave myself to the journey one hundred per cent. It was tough for Jahlene to keep up with the constantly evolving new me; like living with a Russian doll as it revealed its multiple layers. What had always been inside me creatively never completely left – it just found other outlets to leak out of and manifest, laying low until the time came for me to embrace it and unleash it onto the world. That may sound overdramatic, but that's what it felt like: a tidal wave of energy that had been repressed for more than a decade.

Outside of ministry, Jahlene had never seen me so energised by anything, or so rabidly hungry and ambitious. It scared her a little, as her default mode is comfort-oriented and low-maintenance. It freaked her out that I was showing growing signs of discontent with our life and impatience with the status quo. Perhaps she was concerned that she might be on that list of things I was outgrowing in my journey of rebirth. I never asked her, but I could see in her eyes that she found the whole thing overwhelming. Either in my confidence or through sheer arrogance I knew she would remain by my side every step of the way. If she could stick with me through homelessness and empty pockets, surely she would be with me on the brink of major Hollywood acclaim!

After acting school and meetings with Hollywood coaches, I needed an opportunity to be seen and get out there. All the training in the world could never get me actually doing the thing I loved. I was burning money like nobody's business, as acting classes weren't cheap, and I had suspected the teachers were never going to tell me I was ready to go out there and take no prisoners. It wouldn't have served their business model. By early 2010 I had moved on to the stand-up comedy classes inspired by the the success of the Susan Batson experience.

That acting class had provided the catalyst for the search for my mother and finding my family, so that alone made the cost worthwhile. It had also stirred up a lot of things inside of me, like an inner whirlwind at a time when life was about to get much more complicated. My two small girls would soon be joined by a little brother.

In late January, months after my first voyage to Nigeria, Baby Aris-Osula decided to arrive. Rain was pouring down heavily as my father-in-law drove us to the hospital. It was the fastest turnaround yet, as we were in and out the same day. Things moved so quickly that I forgot to look down at our baby right away to confirm what we had!

Prince Adolor Raphael Basigie Omobowale Aris-Osula was born on a Monday at 12.32 p.m. weighing seven pounds. He looked strikingly like me in the few infant photos I had of myself as a child. He had my eyes, chubby face and high forehead. Adolor was caramel brown and was exactly the same weight as Tiani at birth. My assumption had been that I was more of a 'girl dad', but when I held him for the first time I felt instant love and joy about being his dad. We finally had a son, and he had come at a time when I felt whole enough to model the type of man I would want my son to become one day. The look on the girls' faces when we brought him home for the first time was priceless.

His arrival was a blessing; a welcome addition to the family I loved. But Adolor's birth also added a growing sense of anxiety. How was I going to provide for three children when I was already struggling with two? I had to be a better husband, father and man. No more hiding away; my dreams needed to kick into reality pretty soon. I needed an agent, but how could I get an agent without a showcase? At the time my school wasn't providing them. I could have joined one of the many casting platforms out there, where you pay to display your monologue or scene in the hope that some top industry brass will be in the audience. Confidence wasn't my strong point, in all honesty, and coping with feeling under pressure was a problem for me. Fear of rejection was even worse, so parking myself in front of industry-leading decision-makers was a paralysing prospect.

Cue the intervention of my friend, fellow Christian and stand-up co-median Jason Kavan. Jason was a veteran of the Edinburgh Fringe circuit; the Mecca of Scotland for all comedians, actors and performers showcasing their material on the biggest annual fringe circuit on the planet. Many a career has been launched in this Scottish city, known to be a hotbed of talent and a barometer of what would be the next big thing in show business this side of the pond.

Jason hadn't broken through to the big leagues, but he was constantly on the cusp. He grew stronger and his reputation increased each time he took his act to Edinburgh, and he capitalised on this when he returned to London and performed on the brutal late-night stand-up comedy circuit. He was edgy and a risk-taker on stage. He wasn't afraid of being a bit blue or simultaneously bringing up his faith or religion, though never in a preachy way. By no means was Kavan a preacher. In fact, some members of the God Squad wouldn't be comfortable with his material or with the idea of him doing stand-up comedy at all. I was in awe of him for getting up there, baring his soul as part of the Herculean challenge of making people laugh, which he did more often than not. Not only was he in stand-up comedy but he was also a struggling actor, so I asked him how he found his agent. All I needed to know was how to go from undiscovered to hot right now. Or at least warm enough to be put on someone's books.

'I'll put you on to my agent, Chloe…' were the magic words that came out of Jason's mouth.

I couldn't tell you the rest, as I was hypnotised by these ones, which I believed were going to be game-changing. Chloe ran screen-acting classes as well as representing actors as a professional agent. Besides being a nice little sideline earner, the classes were an opportunity for her to spot talent and approach anyone she considered to be commercially viable. The golden rule, I was told by Jason with the seriousness of someone initiating a person into a secret society, was *not* to approach Chloe about being represented by her. That was the ultimate no-no, like telling people about Fight Club. She must come to you when something catches her eye, he intimated. Great. So how did I make that happen? This acting business seemed to be a never-ending maze of time-consuming uncertainty, twists and turns, but the deeper down the rabbit hole I went, the more I wanted it.

As if she had read my mind and granted my wish, she pulled me to one side at the end of the first session and uttered the words I had been longing to hear: 'Tony, you're quite good. Who represents you at the moment?'

Chloe was an intimidating figure, small in stature with mousy hair and piercing eyes that scanned your internal organs as closely as your acting chops. She was pleasant but absolutely no-nonsense, and her accolades as an agent spoke for themselves. She had tasted Hollywood as an actress herself, so she was able to share from both sides of the table and I think that made her even more ruthless and surgical in class when she scrutinised our performance. Such were her put-downs and hard-to-please critiques that if and when you put a smile on her face and got her excited, you felt as though you had invented fire or out-performed Brando in the euphoria of that moment. If Chloe rated you highly after an 'audition' performance it was hard-earned. This was a big deal because she had no qualms in telling you if you were rubbish.

Suddenly, the acting showcases didn't seem so terrifying after all. Too late – I was in boot camp and I couldn't get out! I was the lucky recipient of a gold star on a few occasions, but more often it was a middling report and a few unfortunate times a straight-up 'What the f*** was that?!' As a highly sensitive person, driven by people's feedback, this was torture for me. Not only did Chloe analyse your performance like a dentist would a tooth, but she also asked the class to chime in and they didn't hesitate to point out what had sucked about your audition. But if I wanted to enter this business for realsies I would need some serious toughening up.

Chloe had a right-hand man, her partner Bryan. He was super laid-back, tall, almost model-like, and wore a baseball cap. A fellow agent, he applied the balm after Chloe had finished with you, gently putting you out of your misery like a sick dog.

I learned a lot from these classes and from Chloe's brutal honesty. Unlike the artistic community I had experienced at Caravanserai, they were about the cold business of acting, giving me the other side of the coin.

There was a chance to attend another course with Chloe; a showcase of sorts, which consisted of several weeks of intensive classes and feedback, with producers and directors invited to attend at the end. Chloe would partner you with another actor and you would have to work with them outside the class, using as much of your free time as possible to craft your scene and master it for this great opportunity at the end of the rainbow.

For various reasons this didn't going too well and I hit rock bottom. With a couple of weeks to go until the showcase, the scene needed nothing short of a miracle to bring it together for a positive outcome. At this point, as if by magic, I landed the lead role in a major international commercial. Boom! During my first few weeks on Chloe's books she had lined me up with a couple of auditions.

'Could you do a take without your glasses, maybe?' the casting director had suggested. He was part of the team at Nina Gold, a legend in the business known for casting major shows such as *Game of Thrones* and various high-profile movies. This was a big deal.

'Sure, of course,' I replied, nervously taking off my glasses with the eagerness of one desperate to avoid anything that would upset the casting team and forfeit my being put through to the next round.

I was auditioning for the role of an African truck driver and had to speak in a convincing Nigerian accent and adopt the swagger of a Nigerian blue-collar worker who had just finished a shift driving his truck. The truck in question would be carrying the premier alcoholic beverage of West Africa, Nigeria's own legacy brand, Star Beer. This television commercial (TVC) would coincide with the fiftieth anniversary of Nigeria's independence and would be the most expensive commercial in African history, with no expense spared to commemorate this milestone. No big deal, then.

I must have lined up with every black actor in Britain for the first round of auditions. All I could see was a sea of black male bodies covering every square inch of the building. What was the point of being here? The odds were not in my favour. Trying to distract myself from this self-doubt, I overheard some of my fellow auditionees talking to each other like veterans, sharing stories of film sets they had just been on or a play they had just wrapped up. That hardly helped, as I was as green as the Incredible Hulk and felt like a fraud sitting there waiting to be called into the audition room.

I guess I fit the very generic bill when it came to what they were looking for: a black male with broadly West African features. As an educational exercise, I got to see with my own eyes the desperation that black actors have when it comes to finding work in the UK. There simply isn't enough to go around, no matter how good an actor you are. A TV commercial that would be filmed in a foreign country and wouldn't even be seen in the UK had practically every black male actor in town auditioning, with familiar faces among them that would surprise you.

As I heard my name called out, like being summoned into the doctor's office, I walked into the audition room. A fresh wave of nerves rushed over me.

* * *

I later received the unexpected news from Chloe that I had been successful. Filming would begin in Nigeria at the exact time I was supposed to be performing the showcase. It was a high-profile, high-paying gig, and like any good agent, she told me to forget about the showcase and get on the plane.

Getting the Star Beer commercial was a dream come true. Two and a half years into taking the acting plunge, I had landed my first professional job. Slight reservations about promoting an alcohol brand aside, this was a big deal. As a non-drinker, the prospect of free beer for life didn't excite me that much, but the fact that it was one of Nigeria's biggest and oldest brands did. As the lead actor, my face would be seen by a potential audience of close to a hundred million in Nigeria alone. I would be at the forefront of one of the nation's favourite brands and I had only reconnected with that nation eight months earlier. As I imagined myself driving that truck through the various decades of Nigeria's past, I was simultaneously escorting myself to national stardom. It just wasn't *my* nation. There was no way in my mind that I could be a part of such a major project and it not lead to the floodgates of opportunity opening. *Hollywood, here I come… Just taking a detour through Nigeria first.*

As I boarded the British Airways flight for what would be a two-week shoot, I felt like a kid on Christmas Eve. I was used to walking straight past the first-class section, but not this time. I had my 'golden ticket'. First-class return ticket in hand, I experienced the difference with all my senses. As I was ushered past the magic curtain and escorted into the spacious cubicle, I smiled. There was no neighbour to engage in forced polite conversation or navigate past on the way to the toilet. I was on my own island, complete with a reclining chair that transformed into a bed and had a menu on the table. *A menu?* Just when I thought this ride couldn't get any better! There was so much more choice than the chicken or beef that would have been on offer beyond the curtain in economy. It spoilt every plane trip for me going forward!

Jahlene would love this, I mused as I flicked through the channels on my TV screen. *Not to worry. Once I take over Hollywood we'll be flying this way all the time,* I confidently reasoned as I reclined my seat. One big job and I was already living the high life and getting adjusted to it.

There was one problem staring back at me as I looked into the roomier-than-usual toilet mirror. The previous day I had been rushing around in preparation and there had been no time to get a shave at the barber's down the road. My beard trimmer was broken and it would have been cheaper to go to the barber's than buy a new one, and quicker, too. As a black man, the hair follicles cause the hair on my face to grow out then burrow back into the skin again if not cut correctly. If you cut too close, the hair pushes back, causing a painful flare-up. The worst thing you can do, according to the barber, is use a wet shaver, as it cuts too close.

It wasn't that I hadn't known this as I put the wet blade to my foam-covered face the day before. I just thought for some reason I could get away with it. Time had run out the morning before, so it was this or have a very rough, unkempt, gap-filled beard. 'See, it isn't that bad,' I'd said to myself, feeling my face, which felt like a baby's bottom it was so smooth. I had looked handsome; clean-shaven and smooth. Now I wondered who this man staring back at me with the spotty face that looked as if it had just been kissed by a thorny bush could be. An army of reddish bumps had started to congregate, taunting me.

'Oh no!' I mouthed to myself in disbelief, immediately realising what I had done. It turned out the professional barber had been right. *How can I turn up at Lagos airport looking like this?* I could hardly fade into the background when I was the lead actor. Dread came over me during the flight as I contemplated the prospect of being replaced by a local actor. I pushed such scary thoughts to the back of my mind and tried to enjoy myself. After all, I had no idea when I would be flying first class again, so I ensured that I got Star Beer's full money's worth.

Upon arrival at Murtala Muhammed Airport, a place that had become familiar, I was greeted by Munir – a long curly-haired, chain-smoking Moroccan producer. He was short and handsome in a rugged, don't-care way. I had corresponded with him via email, but this was our first meeting in the flesh. He seemed pleasant and accommodating, but clearly had no time to waste, having already placed the schedule into my hand as the driver loaded my baggage. I was bamboozled by all the information as I tried to adjust to Munir's pace. Along with most of the production team, he had already been there a few days, and I could see the stress dripping off him with the sweat from the intense heat. My job was relatively easy in comparison. All I had to do was show up, do my thing and hopefully get to cool down in my trailer between takes.

As I took in the sights and sounds of Lagos, reuniting with the motherland, it hit me that no one had mentioned my face. Maybe I had exaggerated how noticeable it was in my head, or maybe it had miraculously disappeared during the flight. *So far so good,* I thought as we drove straight to one of the filming locations, where they had started second-unit filming.

As we exited the vehicle, I took a deep breath to prepare me for the start of what was to be an exciting but intense schedule of filming across Nigeria within a two-week window. All the core crew members were there from the art design, lighting and camera departments.

Our director, the only other British national on the largely South African and German crew, came over to inspect his actor. He slightly resembled Damon Albarn from 1990s Britpop group Blur, though he was taller, and slightly more composed and conventional-looking. Looking me up and down with a slightly incredulous expression, he asked, 'What's wrong with your face?'

I was busted. It clearly was as bad as I'd thought. 'Oh… this? Had a bit of a flare-up. Shouldn't last too long.'

This was the best reply I had to offer. I already knew by this point that I hadn't been the director's first choice for the role. It had come down to a choice between me and a broader, more rugged-looking guy back in England. I guess he felt the other guy was more the truck-driver type, but the top brass had felt differently. My mind imagined my rival for this role sitting by the phone being told to board a plane straight away as the gig had now passed to him.

I braced myself for the reply at the end of a long silence, with the director's hard-to-read eyes still fixed on me. He motioned to an assistant, who came over and started examining my face. Before long there was a small crowd gazing at the spotty-faced actor from England. So this was how the Elephant Man must have felt!

'Well, I hope it clears up in a few days,' came the long-awaited reply.

I could relax. The gig was still mine. I just had to figure out a way to undo the damage done by that nasty wet shave. This would not be the last show-business lesson I had to learn on this trip, but it was easily one of the most embarrassing.

When asked whether you can perform a particular skill, accent or activity for an acting job, it is very easy and tempting to say yes, even if it's slightly short of the truth. Sometimes agents even encourage this, then tell you to learn whatever it is quickly before the job begins. Then you have to squeeze in some skydiving lessons, acquire a black belt in karate and polish those tap-dancing moves by the time the camera starts rolling. Though I did have a provisional driving licence and could technically move a car from A to B, I had never driven a large commercial truck before. In fact, I hadn't even passed my driving test.

The morning after 'razor-gate', I was summoned to attend a make-shift truck-driving boot camp. In reality, this was simply a plot of land around a building with a huge truck parked on the grounds. Old and weathered, it had clearly seen better days and been worked hard. My instructor for the day came out of the vehicle, all string vest and flip-flop-wearing enthusiasm. He was probably being paid well to be there, and for what he likely thought would be a straightforward job. Everything about this truck intimidated me, and I immediately regretted giving any indication that I could handle this beast. My job was to drive around Nigeria delivering crates of Star Beer. I just hadn't realised I would be expected to do it for real.

As I took the wheel of the truck and placed my foot on the accelerator, the sheer power of the engine vibrated through my core. A tiny bit of pressure on the pedal flung the instructor and me into orbit. Agitated, he urged me to slow down and ease off, but my foot was either stuck or frozen as we headed towards the sole building on the grounds at full speed. My heart raced. Everything was happening at lightning speed.

My instructor was flailing his arms and yelling, but then he somehow managed to remove my foot from the accelerator and commandeer the steering wheel just in time. We stopped metres away from the rundown building. This was undoubtedly the closest I had come to a near-death experience.

Members of production came racing over to the truck, checking for damage and making sure I wasn't traumatised. Even if I was, I certainly wasn't going to show it. As they say, the show must go on, and I was still alive.

It should come as no surprise that I wasn't allowed behind the wheel of a moving vehicle for the duration of the shoot. Outside of mid-shots and close-ups, the driver wasn't always me. They couldn't take the risk or get insurance to have me behind the wheel, so I inadvertently created work for a local guy after all. My long-distance 'double' was at least twenty years older and looked nothing like me, but at least he could drive. So I swallowed my pride and gave thanks once again that I hadn't been given the heave-ho.

The days running up to the actual shoot were spent having costume fittings, which were overseen by the delightful Nigerian double act of Benita and Mary. These two young fashionistas were roughly my age, friendly, infectiously upbeat and, importantly, non-political. On any set or gathering of human beings there will be politics. In this case there were two distinct camps under the umbrella of production. The 'Alpha' crew was the main production company from Europe, commissioned for the project and running the show. The 'Beta' crew was the local Nigerian pro-duction house taking care of local logistics and subservient to the senior team. Tensions and misunderstandings frequently flared up due to culture clashes and different work philosophies. There were no villains or heroes on either side, just tired, overworked individuals. I often found myself caught in the middle.

I was looked after by the main crew, but I also felt a kinship to the local crew. Bonding with the Nigerian contingent was important to me, especially as some felt I had robbed the opportunity from a local Nigerian actor to lead in this prestigious commercial. It made sense to show them

I was one of them and not an aloof foreigner. Anytime I could eat and socialise with them I did, but I also tried not to alienate myself from the largely white main crew. Even as the lead actor on a shoot thousands of miles from home I was juggling loyalties and playing bridge-builder across the divide.

Benita and Mary were a breath of fresh air. They made this back and forth between camps so much easier and were natural morale-boosters, their neutrality offering a light-hearted refuge from production issues and heated exchanges. Benita was short, curvy and toffee-coloured, with a long, reddish weave in pigtails and a flare for bright colours and vintage make-up. She was cheery and enjoyed her job as stylist, which required her to continuously flit between camps. Being a smart cookie, she knew far more than she let on and remained professional at all times, knowing how hard it was to get such a high-profile job in Nigeria. Her assistant Mary was tall and dark-skinned and was adorned with bronze-tinged, shoulder-length locks. She had an athletic build and a smile that could grace the cover of a magazine. Super-efficient and dedicated, she had a natural gift for coordination and checking that I was OK. Together, they made things fun and took my mind off missing my wife and children on the days when it was really bad. It was like having two sisters on set cracking jokes and easing the moment-to-moment tension in the atmosphere.

They started me off with small incidental shots while my face cleared up. I was given a wonder cream called Damatol for my razor bumps by one of the Nigerian crew's fixers. It did the job but felt like fire lathered on my face with every application, and it stung for a long time. But a man had to do what a man had to do – they could only shoot me from a distance for so long.

We travelled up and down a lot during that first week. The places we stayed were reasonable but nothing to boast about, and not the finest the country had to offer by any stretch. No one on the main crew had seen the best of what Nigeria had to offer, as evidenced by the stream of put-downs and complaints. This was disheartening. Nigeria had its problems, but it also had its unique beauty. If I could have left stayed with one of my many relatives in Lagos each night and taken a member of the crew with me, they would have been gobsmacked. We were staying in rural areas and impoverished or old locations that weren't considered tourist attractions, so what did people expect?

Professionalism was high and the level of skilful improvisation on display when problems arose was remarkable, but this was not a holiday. A holiday would have included friends, or better still family, whereas I was essentially on my own. However well people got along, almost of the banter and bonds would end when production wrapped. Late nights, early mornings and endless travelling began to grate on everyone.

When we were told by senior producers that we would be staying in Lagos and upgraded to the luxurious five-star Eko Hotel towards the end of the shoot, morale skyrocketed. This was the Lagos the crew needed to experience and be won over by. They would love this city the way I did, and I would of course resist the temptation to say, 'I told you so.'

The Eko Hotel Lagos was a grand, high-end oasis that felt like a too-good-to-be-true mirage in the desert. It was a well-timed treat to inject us all with positive vibes. With its large, spacious foyer filled with ornate African architecture and its decor mixed with modern, continental design, this place was a dream.

I looked around as we checked in, feeling woefully under-dressed, and spotted the first set of white people on this trip outside of our production team. Predictably, they had the swagger of affluence that attracts attention anywhere, but even more so in this city. You could look like the Elephant Man or have a face full of bumps, but if you wore expensive jewellery and flashed some change you would inevitably attract an entourage of beautiful women. The sight of a sole middle-aged white man with two or three native women on each arm turned my stomach. This kind of scenario was not uncommon here, and I shuddered at the thought of what went on behind closed doors. It felt like lifting up a beautiful exotic stone only to see maggots and cockroaches swarm out. What appeared beautiful had a rotten underbelly if you took the time to notice.

This was arguably the most expensive hotel I had ever stayed in, and it was intimidating. Entering my large hotel room alone compounded how much I missed my wife, who was thousands of miles away. I was surrounded by beauty and the fruit of wealth, but I felt hollow and lonely. It was like having a major win but no one to share it with. This was a small taste of what the life of a professional performer must be like, with endless travel and hotel rooms. On stage it was lights, camera, action. Afterwards it was tour buses and empty rooms at the bottom of the mountain. It's hardly surprising that so many turn to drugs and alcohol, though neither have ever remotely appealed to me.

The first thing I did, of course, was inspect the bathroom. It was clean, but something else caught my eye. The large mirror confirmed that the face bumps were still firmly entrenched, though not as angry or raw as they had been days before, at least.

'Put some more make-up on his face. And Antonio, soften the lens for the close-up, please!' came the instruction from our director, who looked tired and dishevelled.

My face wasn't entirely razor-bump free, but like with the stunt-driver situation it was providing employment for the full-time make-up artist, who gave sole attention to my spots. Antonio, our genius Italian cinematographer, rose to the challenge of not allowing my predicament to ruin the look of the footage. All curly-haired, intense seriousness, he was making an arthouse movie at all times rather than a run-of-the-mill beer commercial. Fortunately, it was being shot with an old-school film look rather than with unforgivably sharp digital effects. This screamed old Hollywood with the soft-lens look. My cinema-loving parents would have been so proud.

I felt like a piece of poultry cooking on a barbecue grill under the heat of the big lighting rigs. I felt ridiculous as I sweated away in the driver's seat of the truck I was faux-driving, but I had arrived. My khaki, standard-issue Star driver uniform transported me back to 1960, the year of Independence. This sweaty driver was officially a time traveller, driving around a Nigeria from nineteen years before he was even born.

Benita and Mary were on board to make sure I continued to look good in the clothes they had laboriously sourced and maintained to be camera-ready at all times. Every outfit I wore through each decade of driving the truck had to look period-accurate and appealing to the eye, even if it only appeared on screen for seconds. My favourite outfit was a green military shirt, complete with side hair parting. All I needed was a pair of aviator sunglasses and I would have looked as if I had stepped off the set of TV show *M.A.S.H.* with my American army look.

No expense seemed to have been spared on the sets, either, ranging from crowded street scenes to nightclub interiors. There were support artists galore dressed in whatever period-appropriate attire was required for the shoot that day. Ladies with miniskirts and beehives, gentlemen with afros and sideburns; it was retro magic. One day a troupe of ladies adorned with red beads and fabrics congregated on the street to do a traditional dance. There must have been at least thirty, and it felt like an old Hollywood musical. As I observed the intricate detail and the effort made in terms of art direction by the South African husband and wife team for what would amount to seconds on screen, I was in awe. Everything that had been shot over several long, arduous days and nights would be edited into a one- or two-second clip. The faces of hundreds of eager background artists assembled from across the town would not even be shown in the final product, yet they endured the blazing sun and the long hours. If they weren't complaining I had no right to, as however imperfect my face was, at least it would get some screen time.

Port Harcourt, Ibadan, Epe, the old stadium at Surulere – you name it, we filmed there over the two-week period. It was important that a major commercial toasting Nigeria's big celebratory year was filmed in the actual country rather than in neighbouring South Africa which was common place in the industry. It would have been a slap in the face to film elsewhere, even if it would have been easier for production.

I was the face of one of Nigeria's biggest brands of the moment, this 'oyinbo' (culturally white) boy from London. Once the finished commercial was released in Africa, those I spoke to observed that it showed my face more than the beverage itself. That was fine by me, as it announced me to my mother's land in the most spectacular fashion imaginable. I would for ever be associated with this huge moment in Nigerian history and culture.

The commercial was promoted as a monumental occasion with a press conference to boot, but my invite must have been lost in the post, as I only heard about it from digging around online, eventually seeing the final product on YouTube. Titled 'Sunset to Sunrise', it played more like a short film than a conventional commercial, shot beautifully by Antonio with epic wide- sweeping shots and a grainy celluloid texture. They had even used legendary musician Victor Uwaifo's classic song 'Joromi' as I drove around, beaming with national pride. As an Edo man like myself, I liked to think that they made that choice on purpose as an affectionate salute. A national homecoming for this long-lost Edo prince of Nigeria. After watching it ten times, I decided I loved it and was beyond thrilled.

It hadn't initially dawned on me that my face showed no trace of blemishes anywhere in the final product. Whether this was due to the skill of the camera operator or make-up artist, I was beyond grateful. In many ways I saw this as my debut venture into film, such was the way it was produced. Project it onto a cinema-sized screen, play it on a loop and nobody would know the difference. I wasn't just the driver for Star Beer; I was the 'Star Driver'. This was my moment, and I was going to ride this thing all the way to the stratosphere.

CHAPTER SIXTEEN

Star Dust

'Rain, rain, go away, come again another day.'

Back in rainy England I found it incredibly hard to adjust back to an everyday routine after a taste of the limelight. Just a few days previously I had been staying at a luxury hotel, had my own Winnebago trailer and was being given the star treatment. There is no subtle way of putting it; life back home felt flat.. The contrast was massive and my morale was low.

With the addition of Adolor our family home was a really pleasant environment, but the smell of dirty nappies and taking care of his business wasn't. Sitting at my desk in the office was no better. It was merely an upgrade from the smell of baby business to the smell of stale coffee. The white plastic-coated work desk with the black plastic desktop computer blinking in front of me was stifling my mood. My colleagues Dave and Martin teased me endlessly about being the face of Nigerian beer, especially as I didn't drink. It amused them that my stardom was restricted to an overseas territory that definitely wasn't Hollywood. They'd say, 'Here, Tone… do you have any Nigerian beer lying around by any chance?' or, 'Excuse me, are you the face of Nigerian beer?' and ask for my autograph. They weren't being malicious; they were just bored in the office and having a boisterous joke.

Whatever region my commercial had aired in, it was a big deal to me, and was my first professional credit. With a population of nearly two hundred million in Nigeria alone, someone would surely see this face. Chloe and Bryan realised they had a workable commodity in their hands after all. However much I may have disappointed in class, I was making a strong impression out in the field. For a time I was a golden boy on their books, as my booking-to-pencil ratio was decent. A pencil meant that the casting for the role had come down to the final two. Castings often brought out every actor under the sun, so this was pretty impressive. My work colleagues and even my fellow actors at the agency could mock all they wanted, but I had earned a stripe and it would only be a matter of time before I gained more.

Jahlene had witnessed my transformation from strait-laced and serious Ned Flanders to confident and bold Idris Elba wannabe overnight. Finding my biological family had changed everything, and this was the next step in my evolution following my creative renaissance a year previously. She felt as if she was married to another man, or perhaps a number of different men. I didn't even recognise myself in the mirror most of the time, so rapid was the transformation. It wasn't that I was fake; more that I had been hidden within a cocoon that was my public outer shell – the me I felt needed to be accepted by those I chose to be among.

My body didn't even look the same after shedding three stone. Rather than having man boobs, my chest was flat and lean. I had lost my large, prized derriere in the meantime, but that was a small price to pay to see my toes rather than a mound of flab as I looked down. The energy coursing through my body as a result was incredible, like electricity powering my cells. But as I zipped around, faster than ever, it never occurred to me that I was leaving my best friend behind. I was taking my new body out, having adventures in actor land, while she was at home changing nappies and running after toddlers.

Jahlene was a creature of comfort and resisted change, whereas I was fed up with the status quo and pushed boundaries wherever I could. For too long I had done the sensible thing as I watched others jump off the cliff and land squarely on the ground of success. I felt God was giving me a second chance to take a call to adventure after I had either misread the first memo or understood it too narrowly. Preaching was part of the deal, but perhaps my pulpit was broader than the church and the canvas bigger than singing to the choir. There was a voice bubbling up inside me, and maybe acting was the vessel.

However, the question was: at what cost? My marriage? We were undoubtedly growing apart at a steady pace. I had shot out of the starting blocks, and as I sprinted ahead, looking over my shoulder, I could see Jahlene virtually standing still. We weren't competing against each other, but neither were we in sync. As a result, we had ended up in different lanes going at different speeds. I was drunk with the taste of new wine, intoxicated with its new possibilities. 'Planet Me' was my new home, and it had a population of one. I was enjoying my stay there immensely.

I tried to justify it to myself. What was my wife's problem anyway? She wouldn't be complaining when we arrived in Hollywood, living next door to the stars. This season of change was as much for my family as it was for me, I told myself with conviction. Sometimes I told Jahlene this, too – often during an argument when I was about to stay out late for the third night in a row. There were no misdemeanours, I was just attending events and workshops in the hope that the right connection would lead to the big league. She didn't care about that. She cared about the screaming baby depriving her of sleep and being exhausted by three little people. More than that, she cared about me and the fact that I was becoming a lodger in our home. Her needs were simple and hadn't changed much since she was eighteen, when we first met. Back then she hadn't cared that I had no money, and she cared even less now that I wasn't yet a famous actor. She embraced me for who I was at this time as much as she had back then. But as touching as this sentiment was, it wasn't enough, because I wasn't content with being me and was constantly reaching for more.

Over the next few years there were some false starts and almost break-throughs, but no prize. The marriage was strained but held together by ever-thinning superglue. We loved each other, even if we failed to connect with each other half the time. I became more extroverted while Jahlene retreated deeper into herself.

Baby Adolor helped distract us from the growing gulf most of the time, as did raising the girls. Having a son motivated me to be a better man. This meant being a better provider and role model; a man rather than a boy playing grown-ups, which is how I often felt inside. Part of being a man in my eyes was being a success, and as I was in my thirties I felt the pressure of a ticking clock to deliver the goods. It was time to live up to the promise Susan Batson had recognised in me years before. She might have been wrong, or maybe she was just being kind, but I was already running after this train. At least in my head I was, as there was always a conflict of interest with competing activities at church, where I was the youth minister, and behind a camera as a freelance photographer. Too many balls were up in the air, even for a master juggler, which I was not.

Smaller roles in commercials came up, and these were enough to keep my foot in the door and the dream alive. It wasn't the movie business, but it was on screen. I studied the film industry like a birdwatcher studied birds or a trainspotter a train.

When the Walt Disney Company announced in 2012 that it had bought Lucasfilm and *Star Wars* from George Lucas, my jaw hit the floor. As a huge *Star Wars* fan since childhood this was amazing news, especially as part of the deal meant shooting brand-new films in the saga. As a hungry actor this was even greater news, especially as production filming would take place a mere few miles outside London. This became my next mission. I joked with Chloe that when they began casting for the first film, she had better send me along to audition.

So when casting began sometime in late 2013 or early 2014, I was constantly waiting for the phone to ring. The phone rang and sometimes it was Chloe, but zero times was it about Star Wars. She must have thought I had been joking in that earlier conversation. I found out that some of the actors on her books did get 'the call' for the movie. *What the…?* And to add salt to the wound, casting was at Nina Gold. The same Nina Gold that had cast me for the Star Beer commercial four years previously. It took me a while to realise that the worlds of commercials, film and television rarely collided. My time driving a truck in Lagos didn't qualify me to wield a lightsaber or shoot a blaster in an imperial space station. But like Han Solo, I wouldn't be told the odds. Nothing was going to stop me fulfilling my destiny to be in this movie, just like Luke Skywalker before me.

Actors and 'support artists' (SAs for short) are not only different tribes in the industry but different species, too. You couldn't have a career as both, and one didn't lead to the other in any way, shape or form. A serious actor wouldn't want to be seen dead moonlighting as an SA on a film or TV set… unless, of course, that set was in a galaxy far, far away. Everyone and their grandma wanted to be on the *Star Wars* set. It was the holy grail of the entertainment industry, and word got out that the production team was on the lookout for enthusiastic SAs.

After some CSI-level investigation work, I found out which agency was to supply them and applied, as there was no way on earth, or indeed on any other planet, that I was going to miss out on this. There was no need to tell my agents about this, contractually or otherwise; besides they would probably either have tried to dissuade me from doing it or laughed in my face. I had the last laugh, though, because after a number of rounds of calls for SAs to populate the biggest film in the world at that time, I was eventually selected. To say that it was a dream come true would be putting it mildly. It could only have got better if I had a single line of dialogue to say or, better still, got to act.

Emotions overwhelmed me because *Star Wars*, as for millions of other people, was the first movie I ever saw and loved, and it held a special place in my heart. This single film franchise represented why I had wanted to be involved with movies – either in them or reviewing them – in the first place.

Harrison Ford may have played Indiana Jones, as well as other iconic roles, but to me he would always be Han Solo, so the fact that he was returning to the part was awesome. I would have been at the front of the cinema at a midnight screening for this film, no matter what. Imagine how I felt upon discovering that I would actually be *in* the movie. Blink and you'll miss it, but I was in it just the same. I didn't care. I would be a part of movie history and *I* knew I was there, whether I was seen or not.

At the costume fitting over at Pinewood Studios I discovered I would be part of the Resistance. I also discovered that production was taking no chances with leaks and wasn't messing about security-wise. This was easily the most cloak-and-dagger movie production anywhere in the world, and with director J. J. Abrams at the helm this came as a surprise to no one. He had a reputation for being the most secretive filmmaker in the business, and this would be next-level. I saw things in the costume department that the world wouldn't see for nearly two years.

The excitement around this project was at fever pitch. The night before the first day of filming felt like the eve of every holiday at once. Even the prospect of getting up at 3 a.m. for the next few weeks would be a small price to pay. So much of this experience was like being in a secret society which you were not allowed to talk about it. There is only so much I can say about this magical moment without Mickey Mouse showing up outside my house with a baseball bat. What I think I can say is that I got a wink and smile from a certain smuggler returning not only to the universe but to the set after a well-documented hiatus. Getting to see Harrison Ford, the late Carrie Fisher and even having a between-scenes chat on the grass with C-3PO himself, Anthony Daniels, was the stuff of legends. My favourite character is Chewbacca, so seeing the late Peter Mayhew remove that iconic mask after a take was a moment I never thought I would see in my lifetime.

As a Resistance trooper, my job at the base was to secure the unit against enemy forces. My real job was to stop grinning like an idiot by the time the cameras started rolling. Before I took my position on set, I was paraded in front of the bigwigs for inspection by costume designer Michael Kaplan himself. I had J. J. Abrams and uber-producer Kathleen Kennedy to thank, as they had picked me out from the line-up, had someone place a blaster rifle in my hand and made the decision to have my blast helmet shield up. When there's a remote chance of being spotted on screen, you want to ensure that your face is at least partially visible. I was just grateful that I wasn't a stormtrooper.

Hollywood stardom this wasn't, but I didn't care. How many people get to take their marching orders from Princess Leia while looking badass with a prop gun the size of their forearm? The Force was strong with me, and it would be only a matter of time before I got my big break with a part showing my face and my mouth moving on the screen.

* * *

That break came less than a month after my first round of support artist filming dates in the galaxy not too close by. I had auditioned for a minor role in a new movie about notorious East End gangsters the Krays. The project would be directed by Brian Helgeland, who either wrote or directed classic films such as *L.A Confidential, A Knight's Tale* and *Payback.* These movies starred big-name actors such as Russell Crowe, the late Heath Ledger and pre-meltdown Mel Gibson. This was legit Hollywood, so it would be my first venture into the world of movies.

Auditioning for the role was the first time I had experienced the projects director being in the room, offering feedback. There was a good feeling in the air, though I had learned not to read anything into what happens in the room in an attempt to predict the outcome. A bad audition had previously led to a callback, and even me getting the gig, while great chemistry in the audition on other occasions had led to deafening silence.

Building your hopes up in the world of showbiz is a recipe for heartbreak, so you have to take it all with a pinch of salt.

'Congratulations, Tony. You got the part,' came the elated voice of Chloe on the phone, interrupting another mundane day at the office.

It was happening, and to make this news even better it turned out I would be featuring in a scene opposite the movie's lead, Tom Hardy, who was playing Ronnie Kray. *Academy Award nominee* Tom Hardy, may I add; he who had been in some of the most critically acclaimed and commercially successful films in the last ten years and was considered by some as this generation's Marlon Brando. Could this really be happening to me?

My breakthrough role was that of a Lagos immigration officer standing in the way of Ronnie Kray's African dream. Kray had flown to Nigeria to create a utopia with his ill-gotten gains, and I was the obstacle squaring up to him. An obstacle that, for a little bit of paper crossing palms, might just move out of the way to let him pass unhindered. This was Lagos, after all, where anything could happen. In truth it was Ilford, at a disused hospital dressed up as the 1960s airport. Dressed in a short-sleeved beige officer's shirt, complete with gun holster and large black officer's hat, I looked like a man of authority not to be trifled with. Time travel was becoming a habit for me, as I was back in the 1960s and playing a Lagos native yet again.

Wherever I was, there was no mistaking that I was on a film set, with all the rigs, crew members and the sense that time was money. Film sets have their pecking order, and as an actor you are far higher up the food chain than a support artist. I had been treated very well in the galaxy across town – in fact I had never enjoyed on-set catering as much in my life, even though, truth be told, I and others were at the bottom of the food chain. This was just part of the job, and in that kind of system everyone had a defined role. Just a few weeks later I had been upgraded to actor status and boosted up the food chain, with my own trailer dresser and sofa to relax on. During a long stressful day, it's the little things that put a smile on your face.

But while I was smiling, enjoying the ride, I could feel the gritted teeth and burning eyes of some of the support artists assembled together for the shoot, looking over at me, wondering who I was and who I thought I was. Part of me wanted to go over and tell them I had been one of them not too long ago, but I couldn't let this get to me. After weeks of hanging around in the background, I had to get focused and prepare to actually say and do something in front of the camera.

Hardy was as delightful as I had imagined. He dismantled that saying about not meeting your heroes, humbly introducing himself to me as 'Tom', when all I could think of was that he was an acting legend. He wasn't that much older than me, but what he had achieved in the business was extraordinary and something to aspire to. One of the greatest actors of a generation was extending his hand to me by way of introduction. My inner self told my outer self to play it cool and not embarrass us. *If only Giles, Susan and Charlotte could see me now*, I thought, inwardly pinching myself.

That was the last time I saw or spoke to Hardy for the rest of the day's shoot, as when he emerged from his trailer he was Ronnie Kray; not an actor playing the notorious East End gangster, but the very unpleasant embodiment standing before us all. Before a take, during a take, after a take it was all Ronnie Kray. Feeling like an amateur footballer promoted to the World Cup and playing beside Ronaldo, I was compelled to up my game. There was no time for imposter syndrome here. They must have seen something in me for my military-issue-boot-wearing self to be stood there.

That day I was a loud, rambunctious, calculating immigration officer played in a broadly comedic way. Director feedback was affirming, praising my choices and only once asking me to take it down a little. I even got the thumbs-up and shouts of 'You were great' from the crowd of SAs dressed in colourful 1960s garb, which was better than scowls and dagger eyes. I had to resist the thoughts in my head that were telling me I was a fraud who had snuck onto the set, and instead embrace the notion that I

deserved to be there. This was it; the moment when everything came together and I would be shot into space like a shooting star. 'From Star Beer
to stardom' had a poetic ring to it, and I was ready to shine bright. The
year 2014 would be the one when everyone would learn the name Antony
Aris-Osula.

'Hi, Tony. Listen… bad news, I'm afraid. You got cut from the scene,'
came the short and sweet stab to the heart from Chloe on my mobile.
'Sorry. You'll still be invited to the production screening,' came the follow-up consolation.

Someone hadn't just stuck a pin in my prized balloon; a hundred balloons had been blown up with dynamite at once.

'Oh… Thanks for letting me know. At least I had the experience, eh?'
I said, feebly trying to convince myself that had just come out of my
mouth was true. Just like that, my Hollywood takeover had come crashing
down before it even started, and in one short phone call. *That's showbiz,* I
heard in my head, recalling the interviews of A-list stars recounting the
times they had been cut from a movie that was destined to be their breakthrough role. If it could happen to them, it could happen to me. This
should have been encouraging, but I was still gutted. I would have to tell
all the people I'd mentioned it to that I wasn't going to be in this new
movie after all.

I sat there at the production screening shortly before the film's wide
release with the deluded hope that my scene would magically pop up on
screen and that the phone call had been an elaborate joke. The start of
the end credits definitively confirmed that this was not the case. *Great
movie. Just a shame that it was missing the presence of the next Denzel Washington
or Idris Elba,* I silently joked in an attempt to cheer myself up. One thing
was for certain. Breakout role or not, I wasn't prepared to give up my
dream without a fight.

Auditions came and went, but none led to the dizzying heights of landing a movie role. Had I peaked too soon? Every actor has a 'type' and

mine was pretty much set in concrete. I was always the 'African Guy', never the bride; being called in time and again for parts that wouldn't be seen in my own country. You had to have thick skin to be in this business, able to eat disappointment and rejection for breakfast.

For me, disappointment was breakfast, lunch and dinner for the longest season. I was in a career wilderness, with the acting gig grinding to a halt and the radio job without a ladder to climb. Flying out to the one place on the globe where my face was recognisable, Nigeria, also proved unfruitful. I had met with the head of the actors' union out there in a bid to explore any opportunities in the country. Segun Arinze, an actor himself and a household name in the country, was related to Auntie Daisy's friend. Nigeria is the capital of 'who you know' hook-ups and this was true in every aspect of life, not just within the entertainment industry. Nollywood may not have been Hollywood, but I figured it would be better than 'No-wood'. This four hundred-million-dollar industry was nothing to scoff at, even if the content wasn't top notch, and any slice of that pie was worth a bite.

My discussions with directors and producers all concluded with the same phrase, as if they were reading from a karaoke screen: 'You need to be on the ground to work in this industry.' Translation: 'You need to live in Nigeria.' That would mean leaving my family for an indefinite time to make my mark and place a flag in the ground. Star Beer had given me a head start, as everyone in Nigeria had seen this commercial by now and it had become a cult classic. As a calling card, starring in the biggest commercial in Nigerian history wasn't too bad. I had a decision to make.

Predictably, Jahlene wasn't exactly thrilled with the prospect of my leaving her and the children for an indefinite time overseas. Nigeria was no short distance away by any stretch. She didn't have to tell me that she would stand by my final decision, as she believed in me and didn't want to stand in the way of my opportunity. She also trusted me. Lagos was a place where anything could happen for a price. Buying friends and beautiful company would be easy, only to find that you were suddenly no longer James Bond but a Bond villain. Womanising and fathering children outside marriage was a part of my family heritage that I had no desire to emulate. Whatever path lay in front of me I dared not move without having the peace that came with that still, small voice. From the age of thirteen I had followed the same voice that whispered in my spirit. Listening to the Holy Spirit was my trusted compass. He had always guided me home safely and in peace. Peace was the litmus test. No peace, no deal.

No matter what options Lagos and Nollywood had to offer, I knew there and then that none of them would lead to peace. A slightly different dream seemed much better than no dream, but at what price? I could justify and sell the plan to my wife convincingly enough, but not to my Holy Spirit compass. I knew that being absent from home, where I belonged, would be a big mistake. Taking my family with me wasn't an option, either. All the expense and uprooting would have been a logistical nightmare; a gamble that wasn't worth the risk. England was home. We may not have had much or owned our own property, but this was where we belonged. Jahlene had sacrificed a lot for me and our family over the years. Maybe it was time for me to return the favour and do what was right for us all.

Pursuing my dreams had been steering the ship all this time, sometimes into choppy waters, and though we never hit an iceberg we rarely found the shore. I had dropped the ball at home, with my three children getting used to my cameo appearances in the house. *What good is world fame if I'm a stranger in my own family?* I asked myself. All the accolades and awards in the world couldn't compensate for that. If becoming famous meant being loved and appreciated, then didn't I already have that? My family were my number one fans, and their love for me was unconditional – whether I was projected onto a super-large screen or washing dirty dishes.

It wasn't that I had to abandon the dream altogether; rather I had to recognise that it had become an idol for me and that I needed to realign my priorities. God, family and then whatever came after that in a distant third place. My name wasn't lit up in neon lights and my star did not ascend, but I was content with being a rock. Rocks are not glamorous, but they hold things together and can be built upon. It dawned on me that my job as father and husband was to be the foundation my children could stand upon to reach for the stars.

So I took off Dorothy's ruby slippers, slipped on my running shoes and joined my wife on the race track. This time we would run together, keeping a gentle, steady pace, with neither of us outrunning the other. It felt so good to have my running partner back, and I looked forward to seeing where this race would take us – together.

.

CHAPTER SEVENTEEN

I Am

'How on earth could I be forty? I mean, I could count and it was 2019 in the month of June, but this number had always been far on the horizon. It had long been looming, waiting to happen, but right now? It felt like a tax return showing up six months early, handed to me on a sunny beach during my summer vacation.

I had spent so much time getting worked up about reaching this new age that when it came I wondered what all the fuss about. Officially a grown-up, I suddenly had more in common with the incompetent cartoon comedy dads, like Peter Griffin in *Family Guy* and Homer in *The Simpsons*, than the trendy young dudes. The best punishment I could give my teenage daughter Tiani would be to ask her to accompany me in public, every step taken in fear of the prospect of being seen with her dad. Love you too, sweetheart. I had always thought I was a cool dad! Nevertheless, I had reached this milestone and was determined to not only own it but to wear it with flamboyant style. If forty was truly the new thirty, then I would look twenty-five.

I also looked a million dollars in pearl-white blazer and trousers, a gold satin waistcoat and a sleek gold tie. I could have made the cover of my very own album, such was the effort. Walking down the staircase into a dimly lit basement function hall looking like Idris Elba on his wedding day or having earned his angel wings, I was part of an equally impressive ensemble. Four other angels in shiny white flanked me around a large, three-tier white cake with a black trim, splashes of gold icing and gold candles in the shape of a four and a zero on the top. Someone had clearly forgotten to light the candles pressing into this delicious-looking cake, but it didn't matter, as between the bright white outfits and sparkling smiley teeth there was enough light to illuminate the entire room. The Aris-Osula clan was turned out and showing up in regal fashion.

You could have been mistaken for thinking you were in attendance at a wedding or renewing-of-vows ceremony, as Jahlene looked stunning in her single-shoulder knee-length dress and flawless make-up. I had punched above my weight in landing this woman, and I wasn't ashamed to say it.

The two of us had never looked better, perhaps even topping the way we had looked fifteen years earlier on our wedding day. Not that we looked shabby back in the day, but over time we had grown into our skin, radiating an acquired confidence as we matured. 'Ageing like fine wine' would be a more sophisticated way of saying 'black don't crack'. Jahlene still looked twenty-five.

Tia and Eva looked all grown up in their white dresses and afro puffs; one in petite white shoes and the other in crisp designer trainers. The choice in footwear pretty much summed up my very different girls: Eva's pristine style versus Tia's street-cred chic. Adolor mirrored my look with his mini-me white shirt and trousers, sans waistcoat and blazer, with a satin gold tie. At nine years old, even my youngest child was growing up fast, I thought as I watched him mingle with guests, checking in with them to see if they needed anything.

We all looked like Hollywood, more than prepared for this rare family photo moment. The backdrop was an orange brick wall with two over-sized inflated foil balloons forming the number forty at opposite ends of the cake table. As the light hit the shiny gold metallic surface of the balloons, a warm golden aura backlit us like a setting sun. The night was magical and I was going to party like it was 1999… twenty years ago! Gosh, I was getting old.

The most important people in my life who were able to be there that night were present. The very closest of those who couldn't, due to their passing, were represented via framed photographs next to the three-tiered cake on the main table. A photo of Mummy Wynne holding me in her arms as a toddler sat opposite a photo of my dad in a suit, proudly standing by my eighteen-year-old side as I graduated from sixth-form college. The third and final photograph was my favourite picture of Priscilla, which I had been given during my trip to Nigeria. It was important to me that they were present in some sense; that they were all remembered and honoured as the foundation stones of my life. It hurt that they were absent, and I had to force myself not to stare at the photographs or linger too long lest a volcano of emotion erupted at a moment's notice.

The flash of cameras and smartphones contributed to the flood of light emanating from the scene. Within moments, the DJ, Fitz, spun the black birthday party staple – Stevie Wonder's 'Happy Birthday' – on the decks so that it blared loudly from the speakers. To give the moment some extra 'oomph', my master of ceremonies, close friend and birthday twin Joel Barrett, called up one of the guests to sing along. Stella Betton, a professional singer and one of the few people who had followed my all-white dress code, took the microphone and commanded me and my family to stand as she serenaded us. We also had to do an unrehearsed public dance to the music, which, although awkward, was worth it for the look on Tiani's teenage-angst-ridden face. At any other time I would have felt just as awkward and reluctant as she did, but I had already decided to go for it that night, as it would come around once and once only. If I couldn't be silly and let my hair down at my own big bash, when could I? As I danced in a circle, holding the hand of my wife on one side and the closest of my three self-conscious children on the other, I was the happiest man in the room.

What a journey this last decade has been, I thought to myself, my thirties passing in the rear-view mirror as I stepped into this new season of my life. Thirty had been a mixed bag for me. It had ended with a spectacular experience that took me across the globe, but it had begun under a dark cloud of turmoil and depression. That milestone year I thought I'd lost myself as a consequence of living for everybody but myself. As I hit this big birthday ten years later, I genuinely felt renewed, reinvigorated and reborn. In spite of the initial countdown to the flashing number, I felt a rejuvenation and excitement inside that I hadn't felt since I left my teens.

Perhaps this corresponded with my reply to a new call to adventure after taking some time out to become more stable and secure for my family. Six months earlier I had quit my job – the radio job I had been hanging on to for dear life since I was twenty-five. Having a secure job wasn't a bad thing, especially when I was an auditioning actor and sometimes had to get away at a moment's notice. The problem was that security is rarely the ingredient for personal growth. Faith was the required magical ingredient for this journey, as leaving the comfort zone of the known to head into the unknown provided the electric shock pads that this flatlining heart needed to beat again. It needed a sudden and violent jolt of electricity to remind it that it was alive and that the divine calling was still on the table. God hadn't changed His mind. I still had a message to share and people to help and inspire.

When I had my midlife crisis back in 2009, I didn't know who I was. On the cusp of forty in 2019 I had been through my adolescent wilderness' with its temptations, isolations and visions of my Maker. Like Jacob from the Bible, who wrestled with the Angel of the Lord for his blessing, I was determined to fight for my identity; not with others, but with the one who made me. I needed to be blessed with a higher purpose and a sense that I was in the world to contribute meaningfully to it somehow. It didn't matter if anyone knew my name or whether it appeared on billboards. I was fighting for my birthright and wouldn't be leaving this world without it.

Wearing so many masks over so many years had taken its toll, and it was time to present the real me to the world. Don't ask me how, but I learned during this wilderness time in the lead-up to my fortieth that I had dodged a serious bullet when those doors of opportunity closed. When you don't know who you truly are, fame and success are a dangerous combination. Nothing happens before its time and I needed to develop character. Rather than going through the motions of family, I needed to *be* family – especially a loving father and husband. This was no consolation prize, but the very foundation of everything that would be built in my life.

A powerful sense of direction had come over me between 2017 and 2018, filling me a crazy vision akin to that of Noah from the Noah's Ark story in the Bible; the one with the big boat, the flood and the rainbow. I wouldn't be building an ark, but I would be building a ministry and walking on water in the direction of a 'voice'. That voice had interrupted my life in a big way just before Christmas 2018. Fittingly, it was the confirming prophetic word of a renowned Christian prophet from America but based in the UK, with the same name as a famous Hollywood actress, who launched me into this new era of my life with confidence. Dr Sharon Stone told me God had said that this was my time to 'walk on water', and, sink or swim, walking on water was exactly what I was about to do.

* * *

In the autumn of 2017, after years of being a behind-the-scenes-guy at Premier Christian Radio, my status had begun to change. Peter Kerridge, a tall white man from Newcastle in his early sixties, with eagle eyes that scanned across the office, was looking for new on-air talent. He had been CEO for many years and knew who I was, even if he was unaware of what lay dormant inside me. We had shared a few pleasant exchanges, but he was an all-business kind of guy, focused on building up the station. I'd had sporadic on-air experience over the years, interviewing celebrities and packaging film reviews and entertainment features, but had never been a live presenter at the desk. Due to a mixture of my not pushing the door enough and no one coming knocking, I had been an undiscovered asset sitting right under the station's nose all this time. Taking over Hollywood had been my focus, to be honest, and radio had not been on my radar. Maybe it should have been, because it turned out I was pretty good on-air, and I found myself on a training course for potential presenters.

You always need a destiny-helper in life, and at Premier this was Charmaine Noble-McLean. A light-skinned black woman with a broad, infectious smile and a large curly afro crown, Charmaine was director of content at the station and my former line manager. Even more significant than that, she was the person who had hired me all those years ago. We had bonded over many things over the years, including our die-hard love of *Coming to America*. It was her belief in me that led to my last-minute inclusion on this training list.

That belief was not misplaced, as by the conclusion of the three-month training I had passed. What I lacked in technical aptitude, fumbling my way through faders and buttons, I more than made up for in personality and energy. "I just never know what's going to come out of your mouth next," Peter would say with a laugh.

Truth is, neither did I. I was told that I was unpredictable and had an anarchic wit that offered something unique at the station. The rough edges could be sanded down – that was what the training had been for – and it was only a matter of time before my name was added to the presenter cover shift list. I was then pulled into the studio to watch and learn from the master presenters. For one thing, it was a much-needed break from the confines of my desk and from staring at the green audio wave forms that made me feel as if I were in *The Matrix*. Like Mr Anderson before he became Neo, I was desperate to break free from the desk job, and now I'd had a taste of this new role I wanted more.

I eventually became a regular on-air voice at Premier Christian Radio, starting my first weekly music show on its DAB sister station, Premier Praise, at the start of 2018. At the same time, my once co-worker who had been promoted to programme controller and manager, Dave, confided in me that he was moving on. We had seen many colleagues come and go over the years, especially in our small production department, but Dave was and still is a truly amazing broadcaster. Unlike me, radio was in his blood, and he ate, breathed and slept it; truly born to be on air. When he told me he was leaving to go to a mainstream station I was delighted for him… after feeling a bit sorry for myself. The same age as me, he was one of the few people left at Premier that I could relate to.

It was more than that, though. His departure served as a reminder of life outside the Premier comfort zone that I was too scared to explore and not quite ready to walk into. I was afraid to step out of the familiar and take a leap of faith. We often joked about our situation being like that of the main characters in *The Shawshank Redemption*, desperate to get out of prison but terrified at the same time. During the office send-off on his leaving day, I wasn't sure whether the sudden tear streaming down my cheek was for him or for me. Either way, it struck a chord inside me and the impromptu tear felt like water breaking through a dam.

'You're listening to Praise. I'm your host, Antony Aris-Osula, and that was Matt Redman with "Ten Thousand Reasons",' came the words, enthusiastically spoken into the microphone, that were being recorded for my forthcoming show that Saturday. The show was an eclectic mix of contemporary Christian worship music with a sprinkle of gospel and old-school hymns thrown in for good measure, framed around my chatty, fun persona. Sometimes I took up too much time and overran my links, forgetting that the real star of the show was the music. Audiences across the nation had me for three hours on a Saturday night whether they liked it or not. I enjoyed the opportunity and the chance to sink my teeth into something.

But everything changed when my appetite vanished. You can't bite into thin air, and everything dissipated for me regarding radio the moment I heard that familiar internal voice say, 'Time's up.' I knew it was the Holy Spirit. Like a parent entering your bedroom to announce 'Bed time!' while you're playing with your toys, a sigh came from within me, as I had felt as though I was just getting started. The instruction was unshakeable and crystal clear in its clarity and urgency, however. The same internal voice had told me a year earlier that I would get a regular, nationwide on-air gig. At that time this was like a junior dishwasher at a restaurant being told that he or she would be promoted up the ranks to chef with a click of the fingers. It wasn't impossible, but it was highly unlikely.

One thing about spending time in the proverbial wilderness is that you latch on to whatever company you find there, bonding tightly with every step. My time with God had trained my ears to hear Him speak and to discern His prompting. Like any good parent, He knew what was best. By this point I had been a radio presenter for almost a year and had grown immensely. This previously closed door was wide open, except that rather than leading me to higher opportunities within the station it led me out onto the street.

The timing was weird. Nobody understood my decision to leave; not even me. Why go now when the going was just getting good? The new programme controller Bernard and I had clicked, and he had come up with all sorts of tantalising plans for my radio career. But it was too late. The door had opened and it was time for me to obediently step through. It became clear that this opportunity had become a boat, and a boat was exactly what I needed to step out of in order for the faith to kick in.

I sat in Studio One, the prized main studio that was the benchmark of arrival as a presenter at our station, and looked around. Drinking in all the details – the mixing board, monitors and desk – I felt satisfied that after all those years of working in radio I had actually become a presenter. Nostalgia filled my heart, as this was the last time I would prerecord a link and switch off the studio lights after hours as Premier Praise's Saturday night host. When I got home that evening, I sat down to write my resignation letter.

If I was ever going to get off this boat it had to be before I hit the shore of forty. All my excuses for resisting progress were relegated to the bench as I stepped out in purpose. It's hard to say goodbye, especially after fifteen years, and Christmastime is not the best season emotionally or financially, but it had to be done. What was the point in starting a whole new year in a place I had already mentally left? The best gift I had given that year was my commitment, and the best one I had received was a new vision for the future. For the first time, my identity, desire and spirituality were in sync, converging organically into a singular moment. There was no audience to please this time, no duty to perform, just simple submission to a life of truth and purpose.

This purpose was storytelling; allowing the stories to flow through me and find expression. Storytelling had always been in my veins. No Osula could be found without a story coming out of his or her mouth, and we were pretty good at it, too. I never realised my first assignment would be to start with my own story to-date, having first lived through the highs and lows of it. The realisation that all roads had been leading up to this point hit me across the head like a baseball bat. The fact that the number forty in biblical metaphor represented a time of trial and passing, a time of testing, wasn't lost on me. This move would be like a graduation party.

Jahlene was thrilled for me, for us, as she had known all along that there would be a moment when everything came together. I often mistook her introversion for lack of observation and insight, just because she didn't always speak it out the way I did. A typical extrovert assumption! I was totally wrong and as she found her feet, first as a special needs school assistant, then in promotional work, she repaid me for my error by supporting the family financially while I was out of a job. She saw that I had become stagnant, like Ethan Hunt in *Mission: Impossible*, rejecting a mission in order to sit on the sofa watching Netflix instead. She knew I needed to heed the call to adventure this time, as our story was about to get really interesting. There was unfinished business and the epic conclusion of our life story remained unwritten. It wasn't going to write itself, so we made the leap.

Would we move to Hollywood, next-door neighbours to the stars? Pastor that megachurch and be Oprah-level life gurus? For the first time in our lives, we simply didn't care. We would go wherever we felt God was leading us; we just wanted to walk on water and let Him do the rest. Whether we floated or sank would be revealed in the doing, and we were determined to be doers. Faith was no longer just a belief system for us but a way of life, and we wanted to live it to the full.

* * *

As I stood in the rustic basement of the Mekan Turkish restaurant in Cat-ford, I felt overwhelmed. My fortieth birthday had arrived, and I was sur-rounded by friends and family from all walks of life; a beautiful mix of people I had collected over the years, all of whom had contributed some-thing to the life of the man who was standing before them in a white suit. Gazing out into the hall I saw various tribes representing different seg-ments of my life: Emmanuel Church members, Bible college peers, ex-Premier colleagues, even friends from the Ferrier Estate. Various circles had come together from a number of my different life stages. It felt more like a goodbye send-off than a birthday party; like the season finale of a sitcom.

Walking around the room, I took photos, did some dad-dancing and stole moments of conversation here and there with people I hadn't seen in a long time, like Wayne. Wayne was a busy north London pastor, as well as a husband and father of two girls, so I rarely saw him outside of big occasions like this. I had him to thank for taking me out that night in January 2000 when I first glimpsed Jahlene. I don't think I ever told him that, as I knew he would flash that Cheshire cat grin of his that said 'I TOLD YOU SO!' in bold letters without ever moving his lips.

He was a good friend and a brother at heart, whether we always saw eye to eye or not. We slipped outside for some fresh air and a chat, made up of perfunctory small talk that really said in its subtext, 'I love you, man.' He had turned forty around two years previously, so he welcomed me to the club. We reminisced about the time when, as Bible school students we had clandestinely ventured out to a very different kind of club. We couldn't believe how time had flown. It was almost twenty years since we had seen in not just a new year, but a new century together. From wingman to best man, Wayne had certainly seen my journey up close, and in his own way he let me know that he was proud of me. At least, that's what I took from the cheeky grin and hug that was typical Mr Brown. He soon had to leave, as he had to preach early the next morning at his church. As I saw him walk off to his car, I wondered how he had become so respectable. How had either of us become husbands, fathers and men who grew up?

Of all the photographs taken that night, the greatest of them all was completely spontaneous. I was talking to Claire and my mother's sister, Auntie Adenike, when the photographer spotted an opportunity for a captured moment. Claire was the sister who had always been in my corner and Adenike was one of the warmest women I knew, and had flown in from Dublin especially to be there. As far as I'm aware, no one from the Aris family had ever met anyone from the Osula family or anyone related to my mother. This was a rare and special moment, and as if by instinct, the photographer had us in his cross hairs, ready to take the shot.

As our picture was taken in front of the gold-sequined backdrop I had picked up earlier from the fabric shop in Lewisham, I couldn't believe I had done it. I had finally bridged the gap; not just in my psyche, but by uniting the two families that had contributed to who I was: one by blood, the other by nurture; one through circumstance, the other through the continuation of a family saga. Without either family this story wouldn't have existed, white or black. Being flanked by these two special women wasn't just a lovely photo opportunity, but a powerful, unplanned and symbolic gesture.

As I danced the night away to Earth, Wind and Fire, the Jacksons and Stevie Wonder – effectively the soundtrack of my childhood – I felt closure as a chapter of my life found its resolution. I would have my happy ending after all, neither solely 'Aris' nor 'Osula'. It was clear that I was both, and that is what I chose to be. As I slipped and slid to the music on the increasingly sticky floor, narrowly avoiding an accident, I gave God thanks for my life and the journey that still lay ahead. He had been good to me, and I vowed to praise Him for the rest of my days.

On the invitation flyer I had called my party 'A Night to Remember', a reference to the pop group Shalamar, without knowing just how prophetic it would turn out to be. I glimpsed over at my family: Jahlene dancing the night away, having earned some carefree time, and the children at a table, either eating what was left of the party food or transfixed by their smartphones. My tribe, my people, my future. *Well, that was the first forty years. Here's to the next!* I toasted myself in my thoughts.

The last song, Earth, Wind & Fire's classic 'And Love Goes On', filled the air, and the words couldn't have been more appropriate as I felt the love in the room. I was far from perfect, but I had certainly moved some distance away from the confused young chameleon, desperate to belong and find his tribe. The 'be' in 'belong' finally made sense to me now, and I didn't have to strive for my identity any more. I simply had to walk it. I was a coconut prince by choice, in an ironic, emblematic way. The very term 'coconut', previously used to wound me, had been redefined and embraced, in that there was more to me than met the eye and I couldn't be reduced to a stereotype based on my outer shell.

I love being black, but no one gets to tell me how that works for me or to prescribe what I should be. Even though I discovered that I had been born into African royalty, my identity as 'prince' speaks more of my acceptance of my worth and value outside the validation of others. I feel I have come a really long way. I am no longer trying to be something I'm not, seeking belonging or acceptance. I began this long journey looking for my mother, and instead I found myself, 'Antony Aris-Osula', and I simply 'am'.

TOP ROW

1. My biological mother, Priscilla Omosede Osula outside the family home

2. Myself in traditional attire outside same family home decades later in 2009

3. My grandfather, Chief Alfred Basigie Osula as a young Lagos socialite

MIDDLE ROW

4. On a trip to a village in Benin with my Uncles, Auntie and cousin Chief Osula

5. Me and my maternal grandmother, Madam Ayola Oteyelu in Lagos

6. On-air presenting on Premier Christian Radio broadcast across the UK

BOTTOM ROW

7. Behind the scenes filming of the Star Beer commercial in Lagos 2010, dressed in 1970s set scene costume

8. Me with recording artist and actress Jennifer Hudson during the DreamGirls London press junket in 2007 shortly before winning her Academy Award for Best Supporting Actress

9. My family; Jahlene, Tiani, Eva and Adolor celebrating with me at my 40th birthday in London flanked by photographs of my three parents in their absence

EPILOGUE

Magic BlackBox

What on earth is going on here? I think to myself, slightly spooked. As I look down to where my right hand should be, it's disappeared into a seemingly bottomless black hole in a black box on our dining table. This box had formerly been the home of a brand-new smartphone, lovingly taken out by yours truly moments earlier. As great as the phone is, it can't compete with this weird phenomenon in the mesmerising stakes.

As I reach down, I touch the end of something. It feels like bread… the thick-crust baguette kind. My guess proves to be spot on as I lift it up and out of the box, and I'm aghast that it fitted into this tiny space. Before long I'm going back in to see what else I can get from this lucky dip. I call out to the family, and first to get here is Adolor, simultaneously confused and in awe as I hand him a pint of milk. His face turns from bewilderment to excitement as the endless stream of groceries exits the box and spills out onto the table. We have truly stepped into the twilight zone.

Soon Jahlene catches wind of what's going on and joins the fray, her hair a nest of thick blonde curls atop a face wearing a smile like the cat that got the cream. She catches the shopping as I throw it out of the box and is soon assisted by Eva, all stripey top and dungarees, and already towering over her mother at just twelve years old. I notice her eyeing up the ice-cream tub as she places it down in a slightly territorial manner, reserving it for later.

As we excitedly play pass the parcel with this endless supply of Tesco shopping items, I spot a face laughing, head shaking, from the corner of my eye. It's Tiani, standing there in her pink hoodie, holding her smartphone horizontally to capture this strange scene on video. She is amusing herself as we are caught in the moment of this magical, too-good-to-be-true, shopping extravaganza.

'Aaaand, *cut*! That was great, guys. Let's do another one just like that...' came the voice from across the room, its owner sporting a baseball cap and PPE mask while looking at a handheld monitor. This was Alex, the director, standing next to a cameraman who was pointing his camera our way, ready to reset the scene.

The scene in question captured this fanciful tale of the magical black box filled with Tesco shopping that was spilling out onto our dining room table. Except it wasn't our dining room table. The black box had a hole in the bottom that sat atop another hole in the table that enabled a hand to reach up and pass me the food as if by magic. The magic of show business, that is. This was our real home, but for the moment it was also a live set, complete with props and faux décor, for a major TV commercial.

Tesco is the biggest supermarket brand across the UK, and its telecom subsidiary, Tesco Mobile, was fronting a campaign to help low-income families with their shopping and phone bills during a difficult time. This was the summer of 2020, in the middle of a worldwide pandemic, the Covid-19 virus, which has affected millions and changed the world as we know it. We were one of these struggling families at this point, as neither of us was able to work during the lockdown due to the nature of our freelancing. This advert turned out to be a lifesaving job and an answer to prayer. Questions of how we were going to eat had genuinely plagued our minds, so we found it very apt that we were filming a commercial about supernatural food provision. God truly has a sense of humour.

As well as this being shot during the pandemic – the first gig for all the crew after an easing of the lockdown – it was also a period of international tension. Protests and riots blazed across the major cities of various nations. The catalyst for these was an incident that had sent a shock wave across the world: the murder of an unarmed black man, George Floyd, in Minneapolis by police officer Derek Chauvin, over a twenty-dollar bill. We had been here before, but this time it was different. The officer kneeling on George's neck for nine minutes as he begged for breath had left us all breathless. Age-old wounds between black and white had been reopened and there was blood everywhere. The world responded in many ways, but the universal question was did 'black lives matter?'

Politics aside, this was a watershed moment, and it prompted further responses, such as a rush to represent black people across all platforms, including in business, culture and media, as a sign of support and perhaps also in compensation. Suddenly, there was a realisation that black folk, at least here in Britain, ate and drank, purchased goods and were visible. Were we cast in this commercial due to this awakening? Who knows? Tesco has a track record for championing minorities in its promotions, and has even been criticised for its stance on fair representation. Some lovely people commented that they would never shop there again on the YouTube page for our commercial.

Whatever the case, we were not the only black family on UK televisions commercial-wise, so our casting wasn't inevitable. They must have seen something in us, black or otherwise; something that would speak to a nation of millions over several months. We auditioned, they loved us and the rest was history. And not just for me, Tony the thespian, but the whole Aris-Osula clan: Jahlene, Tiani, Eva and Adolor. The entire family band was present and accounted for.

The jubilation in our home was tangible, and the fact that production would be using our actual home to shoot felt symbolic. We felt that God had told us even before the pandemic that our house was like Noah's Ark, protecting us from a coming calamity and preparing us for a new future together.

It wasn't lost on us that it was the ten-year anniversary of the filming of my first acting gig, the Star Beer commercial in Nigeria. That time I had been alone overseas, filming an African household brand for an advert that would only be seen across Africa. Now I was with my tribe, filming an ad for a British household brand that would be beamed across my home nation. What a difference ten years had made. Everyone we knew would see us, and we even had strangers approach us on the street or waving from a distance; black, white and other.

To be able to share the spotlight with my family was an amazing gift that brought a tear to my eye. At a difficult time globally, being able to represent a loving family – a black family, front and centre, being normal (in spite of the magical scenario) and joyful – felt important. We weren't changing the world, but maybe we were shifting perceptions or at least contributing to a sea change by reflecting it. It showed a husband and dad obsessed with his new phone, a mum excited that she wouldn't have to go shopping for days and children fantasising about who would get to eat that tub of ice cream, all played out to an infectious soundtrack crammed into a thirty-second clip. If it had felt as though the Star Beer commercial was announcing me to Africa, it certainly felt as if this Tesco one was showcasing the Aris-Osula clan to the UK, and maybe even the world. An ordinary family born out of extraordinary circumstances was living up to the name Ekundayo by bringing joy out of sorrow.

* * *

Eva was directed by Alex to close the refrigerator door, all skipping and smiling, and the last shot of the commercial was filmed from the refrigerator's point of view. This felt like an open door for us all. If only Dad and Mummy Wynne could have seen this moment, and not forgetting my biological mother, Priscilla. I wonder how she would have felt to see her grown-up son, the 'coconut prince', and her descendants displayed for all to see in a land she had believed was filled with promise. Out of the shell of the coconut, a family had come forth and been revealed. African, Jamaican, British and oh, so much more. Who knows what adventures lie in wait? We look forward to facing them together.

Acknowledgements

It is only fitting that I start by giving personal thanks to my Lord and Saviour Jesus Christ, in true Oscar-podium fashion. Except I genuinely mean it – badum-tss. On a serious note, my life would not have held together without God's love and guidance, and His cosmic hand over me.

To Jahlene – the second-most-important love to me after God. Don't worry, you're the first human, and you're competing with a deity, lol. Jay, you have been with me since for ever, through my highest highs and lowest lows, and you've loved me unconditionally and been loyally by my side through every fight. We've practically grown up together, and I wouldn't have wanted any other playmate. You truly are the Bonnie to my Clyde – minus the shootout pact, of course. Thank you for being my best friend and saying yes all those years ago. We've got so many exciting adventures ahead. I love you.

To Tiani, Eva and Adolor: I love you guys, too. You have shown me what it means to love three little people so much it feels like my heart could burst through my chest. Dramatic, I know, but it's true. Before I even found my roots, you were the tree that bore fruit in my life, making it richer. My proudest days were the ones when you each arrived, and then each day since, watching you grow. You are my most precious legacy and I'm privileged to be your dad.

To my beautiful departed and beloved parents, my precious human trinity. Wynne and Albert Aris, Mum and Dad, it's been decades now since I last saw you, but you are always in my heart and mind. This story wouldn't exist without you both, and I hope I've made you proud in the retelling. I'd rather still have you in my life, but it wasn't up to me. I'll always be grateful for the home and the love you gave me. I love and miss you both. Priscilla Omosede Osula, my birth mother, I never got to know you, but I know you in my heart, in my very blood. Words cannot express how painful your absence has been throughout my life, but that was out of your hands. I owe you my existence, and this journey is a tribute to you; the honour you didn't get to receive in your short life. I will always honour and make you proud. Love you, Mum. May you all rest in eternal peace.

To Claire, my big sister: thank you for always being there for me and helping me feel that the connections to our family past were not lost. To my sister and brothers, Anne, Lindsey, Martin and Terry: I've tried to be as respectful of our shared past as possible and to honour our departed parents. They are true heroes at the heart of this story, and I will honour them as long as I live. The Aris family was much more than blood.

To my delightful grandmother, Madam Ayoola Otuyelu, my birth mother's mother: you are the closest person I have, connected to her, and I'm overjoyed that I have been reunited with you. You are a strong woman full of grace and character, and I am beyond proud to be your grandson. Love you, Grandma. I love and appreciate all of my many uncles and aunts, immediate and great. There are too many to mention by name, but all hold a special and dear place in my heart. You were the amazing prize at the end of my quest, and I'm grateful that I found each one of you.

To Jacinta Gordon: from the very earliest versions of this book, you have read and given brilliant feedback that encouraged me to press on and to stop shying away from the uncomfortable bits. It hurt sometimes, but you were right and I am grateful. It takes a writer to push a writer, right?

To my good friend Joel Kneedler: bless you for the early input, where you, as a decades-long publishing professional gave me the affirmation I needed to see that this project was worth the blood, sweat and tears, lovingly nudging me towards the finish line. Thank you.

To Angie Le Mar, my beloved big 'sister': thanks for all the wisdom and friendship shared over the years, and over coffee at our local Costa. Speaking of 'shares', we could have been rich if we'd invested in some there, considering the number of times we've drunk coffee as we unpacked the meaning of life, the universe and everything in between. Love you dearly, and I'm grateful that you are my friend as well as a comedy legend par excellence.

To Deborah Paul: it's been a long time since we crossed paths, but I will never forget your prophetic word for me the evening we met at a church in Notting Hill. You saw me writing this book in the Spirit and releasing it to the world while I was already dragging my feet about writing it without your knowledge. A true prophet doesn't merely predict the future but brings it out in people, empowering them. Thanks for showing me the power in my pen.

To my wonderful editors, Joy and Rachel: I didn't envy you the task of wading through this magnum opus, but you exceeded my expectations, and kudos to you both for turning my ramblings into coherent sentences. You've both helped me turn my dream into a living reality, and for that I am truly grateful. Thank you.

Finally, to all the coconuts out there: this is a manifesto to rip up the script handed to you – outside black, outside white – whatever the label, you are so much more complicated than the box people put you in. It's taken much of my life so far to be at peace with the way I am, even after finding my roots and the answers to most of my many questions. I hope my journey has inspired you to know that just being who you are, with all your idiosyncrasies, makes you the most fascinating person you will ever know. Get to know who you are and then share yourself generously with the world. We might be in urgent need of you! Thank you in advance for giving all that you have to offer.

ANTONY ARIS-OSULA

Actor, writer, and presenter, he has worked in broadcasting for many years as a radio producer and presenter. As an entertainment correspondent, he interviewed many prolific people from the worlds of entertainment such as Academy Award winners Cuba Gooding Jr and Jennifer Hudson, actors David Oyelowo and Stephen Baldwin to name a few as well as inspirational speakers such as Bishop Noel Jones and the late Dr. Myles Munroe. As an actor, he's featured in national and international commercial campaigns for major brands such as Tesco, Heineken, and Amazon and hopes to soon make his directorial debut with his own future projects.

An avid storyteller, Antony also loves to listen to other people's stories helping them find meaning and direction with their real-life experiences as a personal coach and mentor. He believes not only in the power of story and storytelling but feels that it is a key part of understanding your identity and place in the world. As a public speaker, ordained minister and U.N. affiliated Peace Ambassador he communicates across various platforms impacting people with this message encouraging people to inspire others and leave a mark on this world.

PLEASE LEAVE A REVIEW

scan this code →
or go to :
amazon.com/review/create-review?
&asin=B096FXLGSQ

> THANK YOU for reading this book. I enjoyed writing it and sharing it with you the reader.
>
> I'd LOVE for you to keep in touch with what I'm doing and the future stories I'm writing. You can follow me online at the social media handles on the right and check out my author page on Amazon.
>
> Speaking of which, it would really help me out if you enjoyed this book (or not) to leave an honest review by scanning the QRcode on this page which takes you to a review page.

STAY IN TOUCH...

🐦 **antonyarisosula**

📷 **arisosula**

f **antonyarisosula**

www.amazon.com/~/e/B096HJJ5PX

also available as eBook & Audiobook

Also...

Please check out my YouTube channel with my family ItstheArisOsulas for the best family vlog entertainment...

Printed in Great Britain
by Amazon